Anglican Theology
and
Pastoral
Care

Anglican Theology
and
Pastoral
Care

James E. Griffiss, Editor

MOREHOUSE-BARLOW
WILTON, CT

Morehouse Barlow Co., Inc.
78 Danbury Road
Wilton, Connecticut 06897

ISBN 0-8192-1364-6

Library of Congress Catalog Card Number 84-62463

Printed in the United States of America

Contents

Introduction

Some people would argue that there is no such thing as Anglican theology because Anglicans have frequently drawn from many different theological traditions and have reflected in their theology virtually every point of view possible for a Christian (or even a non-Christian, it would sometimes appear) to maintain. To a considerable degree such a judgment is true: there certainly is no one Anglican theology. However, there does seem to be an Anglican context, or in the broadest sense, a tradition within which Anglicans engage in theology. It is a tradition which has been shaped by many factors in our common history: the Book of Common Prayer, a sacramental spirituality, the regular reading of Holy Scripture, and, more recently, what Anglicans in the United States and elsewhere have been learning from their ecumenical involvement with other Christian communities. The present collection of essays draws upon that tradition as a way of understanding pastoral care, and the several authors have developed a common theme which would seem to suggest that there is a sense in which we can speak not only of Anglican theology, but also of an Anglican way of understanding pastoral care. The common theme in these essays is an understanding of the Church as a sacramental community of people who are being formed and nurtured by God's care in Christ and the Spirit and who are thereby enabled to care for others.

The Anglican tradition has always laid great emphasis upon pastoral care as the first responsibility of the parish priest and of the bishop in the diocese. While there have been many times when that responsibility was neglected, the concern has appeared over and over again in our history as that which gives primary focus to our sense of theology, liturgy, seminary education, and mission. It was the ideal of the Church of England in the Caroline period; it provided the impetus for the establishment of the episcopate in the United States; and it was, under the influence of the Oxford Movement and missionary expansion in this country and elsewhere, the most significant characteristic of Anglicanism in the 19th century. And still today, the Episcopal Church in the Book of Common Prayer and other formularies continues to hold before clergy and lay people the ideal that the first responsibility of the Church is pastoral care.

Unfortunately, however, for many people such an ideal has become nostalgic, one that was desirable in a more stable world but scarcely possible in our more complex and industrialized society. The Church as the shepherd of souls has become an archaic image for many clergy and lay people. And yet the need for pastoral care is greater than ever precisely because of those conditions which have made it seem archaic. The loneliness, isolation, and fragmentation produced in our society by our greater complexity have caused people to turn to many other places for the pastoral care which the Church no longer seems able or willing to provide.

The purpose of these essays, and the common theme of all of them, is to recover for the Episcopal Church its theological responsibility for pastoral care and to explore the ways in which it can be exercised in the Church today. Each of the writers has attempted to fulfill that purpose from his or her perspective. William Petersen, in the first chapter, begins his discussion of the history of pastoral care in Anglicanism by turning to Chaucer, who set forth the ideal of the good parish priest as a governing image for many later Anglican pastors, and he shows how that image has affected our common life through the many changes and controversies of Anglican history. Kenneth Leech writes out of his experience in the Church of England, yet also as one with a profound knowledge of the American situation. He discusses spiritual direction as one of the ways in which pastoral care is carried out, and he shows what might be called the particular Anglican style for the care of souls. At the same time, however, he argues that spiritual direction may be very dangerous for the Church if it leads to a privitized notion of pastoral care and neglects the social dimension.

Ruth Barnhouse, a practicing psychiatrist as well as a priest, suggests that many clergy have uncritically taken over models for pastoral care from current psychiatric practice. The danger in doing so, she argues, is that they may not recognize that the models have assumptions which are incompatible with Christian faith, especially in their neglect of a person's value system. Her conclusion is that while Christians can certainly use secular psychiatric models they must be constantly alert to what, as Christians, they believe about God, the world, and our humanity. My essay explores some of the several models of pastoral care in order to locate them within the larger context of the scriptural and theological tradition. I have argued that pastoral care is first and foremost a theological activity, grounded in what Christian people believe about God and his care for us. I conclude that only in the community of the Church can individuals be pastors and that pastoral care is not a private or specialized activity for which only certain people are qualified.

Louis Weil has discussed the local congregation as the immediate framework for pastoral care, with the Sunday Eucharist as the focus for an extensive and interwoven pattern of ministry. In order that the eucharistic community may know what it is doing and what it must do, he stresses the importance of catechesis—the formation of Christian people in faith and practice. O. C. Edwards further develops the notion of catechesis by discussing the role of preaching in the formation of a Christian community. Analyzing many current studies on pastoral care and preaching, he concludes that the first purpose of the sermon is to build up a worshipping and sacramental community which can care for itself and others.

Finally, Richard Grein has analyzed the pastoral role of the bishop as that has developed in the history of Anglicanism and even more as it has become a major focus for bishops in the present day. He sees the bishop's first responsibility as pastor to be defined by his relationship to the gathered community, and he sets forth a model by means of which bishops today may exercise their pastoral ministry for both clergy and laity.

There is a serious lacuna in this collection of essays: all of the contributors are ordained and, with two exceptions, immediately involved in theological education. One of the points made over and over again in the essays is that pastoral care is not limited to the ordained ministry, and so we ought to have had an essay from a lay person who engages in pastoral care. To do so, however, would only have been a token. The ministry of lay people is a dimension of pastoral care which is very new to the Episcopal Church; to explore it would have required more than one chapter. Perhaps this volume, because it is so clerical, will lead to another collection which will explore in greater depth how lay people are beginning to see their ministry of pastoral care.

Finally, it is to be hoped that this collection of essays from an Anglican perspective will be helpful to the larger Christian community. First, it should be helpful to others in understanding our concept of pastoral care as a primary responsibility of the Church and so help them understand why we act the way we do and why we think certain aspects of Christian faith and polity so important. Second, all of the contributors hope that our reflections on pastoral care may help other Christian communities to rediscover in their own traditions how and why Christian people ought to care for one another so that the Church may witness to the unity of all human beings in the one who is the great shepherd of the sheep, Jesus Christ.

James E. Griffiss
The Presentation of Our Lord: 1985

1

On the Pattern and in the Power:
A Historical Essay of
Anglican Pastoral Care

William H. Petersen

Any consideration of pastoral care must perforce have in view the entire Christian community, perhaps even more! For Anglican theology tends to view the Incarnation as that reaffirmation of all creation by a cosmic Divinity which impels us, in turn, to regard nothing less than the entire human community as the object of redemption. A historical discourse on the principles and practice of pastoral care, however, comes quickly and inevitably to focus primarily on the clergy—bishops, priests, and deacons—as bearers of special responsibilities in the life and mission of the Christian community in the world.

The history of Anglican pastoral care begins long before the sixteenth-century reformation of the Church of England; a most effective articulation of the principles and practice of pastoral care among English-speaking Christians is, for instance, to be found as early as the Venerable Bede's eighth-century *History of the English Church and People*. That prodigious work points us at least a century further back, to the highly influential ideals and extensive pastoral advice of Pope St. Gregory the Great, to whom the entire Western Church in its many subsequent forms is everlastingly indebted. Yet even then we would not have indicated all that needs to be said about roots unless the apostolic ideal that informed the development of Gregory's *Regula Pastoralis* were acknowledged.

We should, however, be close to bedrock by taking note of that postresurrectional dialogue at the conclusion of the Johannine Gospel, when the Apostle submits to some rigorous examination about his readiness for ministry:

> He said to him the third time, "Simon, son of John, do you love me?" Peter was grieved because he said to him the third time, "Do you love me?" And he said to him, "Lord, you know everything; you know that I love you." Jesus said to him, "Feed my sheep."[1]

Feed my sheep! There precisely is the pastoral imperative, not only to the Apostle but to all who come to have a part in pastoral care. It is on this dominical pattern and in the power promised to faithful practitioners that the history of Anglican pastoral care is rooted and grounded. But, typically of Anglicanism, this claim is to be taken in an inclusive rather than an exclusive sense; that is, we deny to no other ecclesial tradition such a grounding and rooting, but at the same time we wish the courtesy of dominical and apostolic origins to be acknowledged by others in respect of our own principles and practice of pastoral care.

With that statement, however, the discussion is thrown directly back into the tangled thicket of the sixteenth-century reformations (there were several) in the Church of England, for the dominical and apostolic character of the extant principles and practice of pastoral care were precisely (and sometimes literally) the burning issues of contention in that tumultuous setting. And yet, in the very fires of that century, the inherited tools—the forms and manner of pastoral care—were forged again and reshaped to the requirements of a new era in the life and mission of *ecclesia anglicana*.

It was an achievement of sorts for the typical practitioner of pastoral care—the parish priest—in sixteenth-century England simply to have survived for any length of time in one cure. Since religion directly affects our basic values, the heat of the forge of religious controversy is in itself dangerous enough. Add to that the fact that first one party, then another, and yet a third or fourth wields—now one, now the other—the hammer and tongs meant to shape the tool and then temper it to quite different designs.

At the outset of *The Anglican Spiritual Tradition,* the retired Bishop of Ripon and noted ecclesiastical historian John H. R. Moorman presents a very moving portrait of a fictitious, but not unlikely, priest who served in one parochial cure during the successive reigns of Henry VIII, Edward VI, Mary I, and well into Elizabeth's time. Moorman's serious-minded and atypically well-educated parson, James Whyte, exhibits a sincerely consistent character throughout a series of situations calculated to be radically inconsistent. From the conservative but nonpapal orthodoxy of Henry's time, to the swift succession of two very different prayer books in the brief reign of Edward, to the convulsive attempt to return to the "old religion" in Mary's five regnal years, to the more-apparent-than-real "settlement" of the Church "as by law established" in the long reign of Elizabeth, "his concern was with his parish and his people. All he wanted to do was to build them up as faithful members. . . ."[2]

How often through all these events must priests and parishioners have uttered some form of the Psalmist's cry, "When the foundations are being destroyed, what can the righteous do?"[3] And yet it is precisely to the point at issue whether the foundations were being destroyed or rediscovered in the process. It is the answer to this question that will best exhibit the history of Anglican pastoral care for critical scrutiny.

It may be well, nevertheless, to distance ourselves slightly from the many controverted points of reform in the sixteenth century. Little has been—little can be—resolved by polemical reference among conflicting Christian traditions to the complex situation of that period. If one were to be intellectually and morally consistent from a present point of view, then one would have had to change sides many times during the sixteenth century.

It is, perhaps, best to go a bit further back in English history, to a time when all Europe was keenly aware that a reformation of the Church "in head and members" was necessary. My contention is that Anglican pastoral care from the time of the sixteenth-century reformations of the Church of England has been directly shaped and indelibly stamped with an ideal of the good parish priest, the character of which was profoundly and effectively articulated nearly two centuries prior. And though this characterization refers only to the priest as pastor, we may by extrapolation understand that ideal, *mutatis mutandis*, to include the episcopate and diaconate as they were subsequently reformed and retained among Anglicans.

The ideal to which I refer—even in its own time a reforming one—was put forth by no less than Geoffrey Chaucer (*ca.* 1340-1400), in *The Canterbury Tales*. I quote in full a portion of Chaucer's "Prologue." Among that wonderfully diverse company of pilgrims wending their way on April holiday to St. Thomas Becket's shrine at Canterbury:

A good man was ther of religioun,	
And was a poore Persoun of a town,*	*parish priest
But riche he was of holy thought and werk.	
He was also a lerned man, a clerk,*	*scholar
That Christes gospel trewely wolde preche;	
His parrishens* devoutly wolde he teche.	*parishioners
Benigne he was, and wonder diligent,	
And in adversitie ful pacient*	*patient
And swich* he was preved* ofte sithes.*	*such *proved *many times
Ful loth were him to cursen for his tithes,*	*excommunicate for non-payment of tithes
But rather wolde he yeven,* out of doute,	*give
Unto his poore parisshens aboute	
Of his offring and eek* of his substaunce:	*also
He coude in litel thing have suffisaunce.*	*enough
Wid was his parissh, and houses fer asonder,	
But he ne lafte* nat for rain ne thonder,	*neglected
In siknesse nor in meschief,* to visite	*trouble
The ferreste in his parish, much and lite,*	*rich and poor
Upon his feet, and in his hand a staf.	
This noble ensample to his sheep he yaf*	*gave
That first he wroughte,* and afterward he taughte.	*acted
Out of the Gospel* he tho wordes caughte,	*cf. Matthew 6:19-20
And this figure* he hadded eek* therto:	*metaphor *added also
That if gold ruste, what shal iren* do?	*iron
And if a preest be foul, on whom we truste,	
No wonder is a lewed* man to ruste.	*ignorant, simple
And shame it is, if a preest take keep,	
A shiten* shepherd and a clene sheep.	*(exactly what's said!)
Wel oughte a preest ensample for to yive*	*give
By his clennesse how that his sheep sholde live.	
He sette nat has benefice to hire*	*didn't hire a substitue priest at lower pay
And leet his sheep encombred in the mire	
And ran to London, unto Sainte Poules*	*St. Paul's Cathedral

To seeken him a chaunterye* for soules,	*become a "mass priest"
Or with a bretherhede to be withholde,*	*become a guild chaplain
But dwelte at hoom* and kept wel his folde,	*home
So that the wolfe ne made it nat miscarye:	
He was a shepherd and nought a mercenarye.	
And though he holy were and vertuous,	
He was to sinful men nought despitous,	
Ne of his speeche daungerous* ne digne*	*severe *haughty
But in his teaching discreet and benigne,	
To drawen folk to hevene by fairnesse	
By good ensample—this was his bisinesse.	
But it were any persone* obstinat,	*if anyone were
What so he were, of heigh or lowe estat,	
Him wolde he snibben* sharply for the nones:*	*rebuke *on that occasion
A bettre preest I trowe ther nowher noon* is.	*none
He waited* after no pompe and reverence,	*hankered
Ne maked him a spiced* conscience,	*over-fastidious
But Cristes lore* and his apostles twelve	*wisdom and practice
He taughte, but first he folwed* it himselve.[4]	*followed

Insofar as literature holds a mirror up to reality so we can more clearly see it for what it is, then here we have before us not only much direct and implied criticism of a pastorally deficient and overclericalized Church but positively, the lay-poet's Christian vision of true clerical virtue and a statement of the authentic character of pastoral care manifested in the parish priest. This fourteenth-century articulation of an ideal of pastoral care may serve as a kind of litmus test for Anglican *pastoralia* as it developed in the literature and practice of the Church of England after the intervening turbulence of the sixteenth century. To this, I believe, must be added a *caveat,* namely, that to speak of the sixteenth-century reformation of the Church of England as if it were completed by the time of the Elizabethan Settlement (and its justification in John Jewel's *Apologia* or Richard Hooker's *Laws of Ecclesiastical Polity*) is at best misleading.

Reformation differs from revolution in that the latter seeks to start *de novo,* whereas reformation assumes there is something worth renewing rather than discarding. Therefore, *if* reformation of the Church involves (but means more than) the manner in which European nations dealt with the long tradition of papal claims to ultimate pastoral jurisdiction and feudal overlordship of Western Christendom; *if* reformation of the Church involves the consideration of modified behavior in the way Christians relate to one another, how they speak of what they believe, how they worship, the manner of the Church's organization for ministry, the drive and direction of mission, and the relation of the Church to general society or culture; *if* reformation involves all these things, *then* it may truly be said that the reformation in England was not confined to the sixteenth century but continued at least through the seventeenth century and perhaps even later. In fact, with some justification one can claim that *reforming* rather than *reformation* may be an essential part of Anglican ethos. It is to the tracing and criticism of this claim in the history of Anglican pastoral care that this discussion must now turn.

In an essay of this brevity a number of problems of periodization, scope, and selectivity arise. With respect to the first, three generally useful periods for consideration of our subject can be set forth. They roughly correspond to the seventeenth, eighteenth, and nineteenth centuries. By scholarly consensus we can discern an initial "classical" era from the accession to Great Britain's throne of James I (1603) and the adoption of the Canons of 1604 (dealing largely with the duties and behavior of clerics) through the "Glorious Revolution" (glorious because bloodless) of 1688—a watershed in the cultural life of England and, indeed, of English-speaking Christianity. There follows almost exactly a century until, across the Channel, the French Revolution and, across the Atlantic, the constitutional beginning of the Episcopal Church in the United States (both in 1789). This period can be pastorally characterized in bipolar terms as defending the establishment or devising new experiments. The third period—an expanded nineteenth century—runs from the 1789 revolutionary and ideological challenge to traditional Christianity through the final cataclysm of Christendom as marked by, and represented in, the implications of the Great War of 1914 to 1918.

By sheer weight of chronology in such a periodization and with regard to the scope of this essay, the sources and exhibitions of Anglican *pastoralia* lie principally within the Church of England. It will, nevertheless, be necessary to give some attention to development or modification of pastoral care as the Episcopal Church represents a transplantation of Anglicanism onto American soil.

With respect to selectivity and in congruence with the previous statement of Chaucer's pastoral ideal, the historical exhibition of principles and practice of pastoral care will be largely confined to presbyterial types, though some attention will be paid to episcopal or diaconal examples as pertinent times, places, or persons warrant.

The conclusion of the present essay will attempt to indicate my reasons for carrying the story only as far as the early twentieth century. Suffice it to say here that, though it may not have been perceived *in medias res,* the world that is the object of redemption —and, therefore, the societies that provide the very field for pastoral care—sustained vast and radical transformations between and subsequent to the global wars of the twentieth century. Those transformations were of such proportions as to raise serious questions about whether or how far our Anglican heritage of pastoral care is applicable in a world on the verge of the twenty-first century.

I. Classical Anglican Pastoralia
1603-1688

This seminal period may be divided very neatly into three parts by virtue of the crisis in the Church of England occasioned by the outbreak of the Civil War in 1641. That strife culminated in the beheading of Charles I in 1649, the suppression of episcopacy and the *Book of Common Prayer,* and the Lord Protectorship of Oliver Cromwell during the Commonwealth/Interregnum. The nearly three decades from 1660 to the end of the era witnessed an initial restoration of the monarchy and episcopacy, a new Act of Uniformity to which was attached the imposition of the 1662 *Book of Common Prayer,* and a series of parliamentary acts intended to hinder or suppress dissent (Nonconformity).

Thus, in what follows, we have first to explore the dimensions of the "classical" pastoral style before the Civil War. Second, some appropriate indication will be given of its survival and modification as an underground alternative to the Church of England in the Commonwealth period—a legal establishment that had replaced episcopacy with presbyterian polity, the Articles of Religion with the Westminster Confession, and the *Book of Common Prayer* with the Directory of Public Worship. Following the Commonwealth/Interregnum a certain modification of Anglican pastoral style can be discerned, and a brief examination of that change will provide our transition to the next major period, for more than the politics of toleration or the lack of it were at work by the late seventeenth century to effect modification of pastoral style.

We may begin, then, with two typical presbyterial exemplars of pastoral care—the city preacher and the country parson. In the former case I refer to John Donne (1571/2-1631), Dean of St. Paul's Cathedral in London; in the latter case, to George Herbert (1593-1633), Rector of Bemerton near Salisbury.

John Donne as a literary figure is largely the recovery of our own century and, if known at all, is generally remembered as the author of the lines, "Any mans *death* diminishes *me,* because I am involved in *Mankind;* And therefore never send to know for whom the *bell* tolls; It tolls for *thee.*"[5] If Donne is remembered beyond this, it is for his poetry, variously erotic or religious or —how Anglican!—both. It is less well remembered that John Donne was one of the greatest and most popular preachers of his day, whether his homiletical efforts were directed to the learned congregations of court and cathedral or the mass gatherings attendant on sermons delivered in the open-air pulpit of nearby Paul's Cross.

It is Donne as preacher and mediator of pastoral care that I want to discuss in the present context. The following passage from a Christmas sermon, preached on the text "Lord now lettest thou thy servant depart in peace, according to thy word: For mine eyes have seen thy salvation" (Luke 2:29-30), may lend itself to scrutiny in light of our subject. The biblical scene, of course, is the presentation of Jesus to Simeon (whose words are quoted) in the Temple:

> At the time of this presentation there were to be offered a pair of turtles [turtledoves]. . . . Thus was our Savior presented to God. . . . How was the joy of Noah at the return of the dove into the ark multiplied upon Simeon at the bringing of this Dove into the temple? At how cheap a price was Christ tumbled up and down in this world? It does almost take off our pious scorn of the low price at which Judas sold him, to consider that his Father sold him to the world for nothing; and then when he had him again, by this new title of primogeniture and presentation, he sold him to the world again, if not for a turtle[dove] or for a pigeon, yet at most for five shekels, which at most is but ten shillings.

> And yet you have had him cheaper than that today in the Sacrament.

Whom has Christ cost five shekels there? As Christ was presented to
God in the temple so is he presented to God in the Sacrament; not
sucking, but bleeding. And God gives him back again to you. And at
what price? Upon this exchange: take his first born, Christ Jesus, and
give him yours. Who is yours? The heart is the first part of the body
that lives; give him that. And then, as it is in nature it shall be in grace
too, the last part that dies; for it shall never die.

"If a man eat the bread that cometh down from heaven, he shall not
die," says Christ. If a man in exchange of his heart receive Christ Jesus
himself, he can no more die than Christ Jesus himself can die. That
which Aeschines said to Socrates admits a fair accommodation here.
He saw everybody give Socrates some present, and he said, "Because
I have nothing else to give, I will give you myself." "Do so," says
Socrates, "and I will give you back again to yourself better than when
I received you." If you have truly given yourself to him in the Sacrament,
God has given you yourself back so much mended as that you have
received yourself and him too; yourself in holy liberty to walk in the
world in a calling, and himself in giving a blessing upon all the works
of your calling and imprinting in you a holy desire to do all those works
to his glory.

And so having thus far made this profit of these circumstances in the
action itself applicable to us as receivers of the Sacrament, that as the
child Jesus was first presented to God in the temple, so for your children
(the children of your bodies, and the children of your minds, and the
children of your hands, all your actions and intentions), that you direct
them first upon God, and God in the temple, that is, God manifested
in the Church, before you assign them or determine them upon any
other worldly course, and then, that as God returned Christ as all other
children, at a certain price, so God delivers man upon certain, and upon
the same conditions.

He comes not into the world, nor he comes not to the Sacrament as
to a lottery, where perchance he may draw salvation but it is ten to
one he misses, but upon these few and easy conditions: believe and love,
he may be sure. And then also, that the sacrifice, pigeons or turtles,
was indifferent, so it were offered to God, for any honest calling is
acceptable to God if God's glory be intended in it.[6]

This, of course, is but a brief passage in a much longer sermon,
but it is remarkable in several ways. First of all, Donne is perfectly
orthodox in consideration of the following doctrines: God, Christ,
Humanity, Salvation, the Sacraments, and the Church. If, in
reading the above passage, one were not aware of that orthodoxy,
then it is a credit to the preacher's pastoral abilities that his
doctrine is lively and not a dry-as-dust repetition of theological

formulations. Second, there is a rootedness in Scripture and a constant allusion to it. Third, the illustration is diverse but calculated by one means or another directly to address the condition of the hearers. For, on the one hand, Donne throughout employs the language of the marketplace to invite the majority of his listeners into the text and the scene it presents. By this means he relates the graceful and justifying word of God to them. But, on the other hand, his more cultured hearers are not left disappointed at common metaphors—not likely, indeed, with the classical example drawn from the life of Socrates! In this, among other things, we may see a fulfillment of the expectation announced in Chaucer's pastoral ideal: "He was a learned man, a clerk."

Finally, there is broached in this passage a controversial but very pressing point of theology, or so it was in Donne's time. To whom is salvation offered? To all or only to the predestined elect? The answer affects more than the doctrine of salvation, for it impinges also on ecclesiology, our understanding of the Church. John Donne, as practitioner of pastoral care to the people committed to his charge, sets forth the typical Anglican approach. Though implied in the sermon, his point is stated more directly in two of his *Holy Sonnets*. To the soteriological aspect of the question we find a terse response in the first segment of "La Corona":

> 'Tis time that heart and voice be lifted high,
> *Salvation to all that will is nigh.*' (emphasis added)

It is, however, in the following sonnet that Donne most persuasively sets forth his answer to the ecclesiological aspect of the question and, in so doing, gives a positive statement of the Anglican penchant for comprehension or inclusivity:

> Show me deare Christ, thy Spouse, so bright and clear.
> What! is it She, which on the other shore
> Goes richly painted? or which rob'd and tore
> Laments and mournes in Germany and here?
> Sleepes she a thousand, then peepes up one yeare?
> Is she selfe truth and errs? now new, now outwore?
> Doth she, and did she, and shall she evermore
> On one, on seaven, or on no hill appeare?
> Dwells she with us, or like adventuring knights
> First travaile we to seeke and then make Love?
> Betray kind husband thy spouse to our sights,

And let myne amorous soule court thy mild Dove,
Who is most trew, and pleasing to thee, then
When she'is embrac'd and open to most men.[8]

In terms of the continual seventeenth-century ecclesiological polemics among Christians, Donne has here set forth the most typical Anglican position with its implied pastoral bent—but the point of the final couplet tells at least as heavily against the exclusivist Puritan strain in the Church of England as it does against the Continental situation.

With respect to Chaucer's pastoral ideal, we can hardly accuse Donne of having run off to St. Paul's "to seeken him a chaunterye for soules" (such things having been eliminated in the reform); nor do we have in Donne, as one of the chief ornaments of the Anglican pulpit in his own or any time, "a shiten shepherd and a clene sheep." The quality of Donne's personal faith lay always at the base of his exercise of pastoral care. This is nowhere better attested in his own writings, nor indeed in our remembrance of them, than in his poem "Wilt thou forgive that sin, where I begun," which we sing as a hymn.[9] There is here in him and for us that essential quality of a lively sense of need for continual repentance informed by an utter reliance on God's merciful grace as impelling us to confession, assuring us of pardon, and drawing us into sanctification.

It may be asserted, in response to this rather lengthy exhibition of John Donne, that he was exceptional. This must instantly be admitted in two senses. By far the vast majority of the practitioners of pastoral care in this classical period (or any other) of Anglicanism were parish clergy and not cathedral deans. Also, most clergy of the Church of England were not city (which until the nineteenth century meant London alone) preachers but country parsons. Some test, then, of the claims made thus far may be essayed in regard to Chaucer's ideal of pastoral care in examination of George Herbert as an exemplar in this formative period of the parish priest.

The chief source for any such test would be Herbert's own *A Priest to the Temple, or The Country Parson: His Character, and Rule of Holy Life.* This work is nothing short of a classic of Anglican pastoralia. It enjoys the added authority for its contents of being attested in the life of the author in that parochial setting. The work is, nevertheless, the statement of an ideal that may be applied in practice. As Herbert says in his preface:

> Being desirous (through the Mercy of God) to please him, . . . and
> considering with myself, That the way to please him, is to feed my Flock
> diligently and faithfully, since our Savior hath made that the argument
> of a Pastor's love [cf. John 21:15-17], I have resolved to set down the
> Form and Character of a true Pastor, that I may have a Mark to aim
> at: which also I will set as high as I can, since he shoots higher that
> threatens the Moon, than he that aims at a Tree.[10]

He goes on to accomplish his task in thirty-seven chapters (each
a long paragraph) and two (by our standards) fulsome prayers,
the one to be prayed before, the other after, preaching. A cursory
sampler of the subject headings will impress the reader with
Herbert's comprehensiveness.[11] For any who pursue the matter
further, it will appear as a treatise form of discourse on those
subjects directly met or implied in Chaucer's statement of the ideal
parish priest. The same character may be seen initially in Herbert's
overall remarks on "The Parson's Life," where he is described as

> exceeding exact in his Life, being holy, just, prudent, temperate, bold,
> grave in all his ways . . . The Parson is very strict in keeping his word,
> though it be to his own hindrance, as knowing that if he be not so,
> he will quickly be discovered, and disregarded: neither will they believe
> him in the pulpit, whom they cannot trust in his Conversation.[12]

We can perhaps best see a development on the character of the
country parson as a practitioner of pastoral care in Herbert's "The
Parson in Mirth":

> The Country Parson is generally sad, because he knows nothing but
> the Cross of Christ, his mind being defixed on it with those nails
> wherewith his Master was: or if he have any leisure to look from thence,
> he meets continually with two most sad spectacles, Sin, and Misery;
> God dishonored everyday, and man afflicted. Nevertheless, he sometimes
> refresheth himself, as knowing that nature will not bear everlasting
> droopings, and that pleasantness of disposition is a great key to do good;
> not only because all men shun the company of perpetual severity, but
> also for that when they are in company, instructions seasoned with
> pleasantness, both enter sooner, and root deeper. Wherefore he
> condescends to human frailties both in himself and others; and
> intermingles some mirth in his discourses occasionally, according to
> the pulse of the hearer.[13]

Though this is one of Herbert's shortest discourses on the
parson's character, it is perhaps the one most generally honored

in the subsequent style of Anglican pastoral care. For the clergy have generally eschewed—in those wonderful phrases—"everlasting droopings" and "perpetual severity." In fact, it may with more justice be said that there has been a greater tendency to err toward a "pleasantness" too much in accord with "the pulse of the hearer."

There is in Herbert, nevertheless, an exhibition of that desire "to drawen folk to heavene by fairness/By good ensample." Again, however, as was seen to be the case with Donne, this following the dominical and apostolic pattern rests, for Herbert also, on sacramental ground as the effective means of grace in pastoral care. Here is where the empowerment is discovered and made effective in the life of Christians. Chaucer did not mention this in his catalogue of character traits, but for him the sacramental base as the means of grace was assumed, whereas by the time of Donne and Herbert it was very much a matter of controversy. Herbert is as unequivocal as Donne in laying the liturgical and sacramental ground of pastoral care open to our view:

> Love bade me welcome: yet my soul drew back,
>   Guilty of dust and sin.
> But quick-ey'd Love, observing me grow slack
>   From my first entrance in,
> Drew nearer to me, sweetly questioning,
>   If I lacked anything.
>
> A guest, I answer'd, worthy to be here:
>   Love said, You shall be he.
> I the unkind, ungrateful? Ah my dear,
>   I cannot look on thee.
> Love took my hand, and smiling did reply,
>   Who made the eyes but I?
>
> Truth Lord, but I have marr'd them: let my shame
>   Go where it doth deserve.
> And know you not, says Love, who bore the blame?
>   My dear, then I will serve.
> You must sit down, says Love, and taste my meat:
>   So I did sit and eat.[14]

In conjunction as presbyterial types of pastoral care in classical Anglicanism, Donne and Herbert set an early pattern, some of which will continue to obtain throughout the period, some of which will be recovered in a subsequent period, but part of which will, by the end of the classical period and throughout much of the next, be obscured or lost—and that precisely is the sacramental base of pastoral care.

By way of transition to the troubled middle years of the classical period we may mention two other figures who contributed much toward setting the style of Anglican pastoral care. The first is a bishop, Lancelot Andrewes (1555-1626), and the second a deacon, Nicholas Ferrar (1592-1637). In his own time Andrewes's fame was principally based on his reputation as a preacher. Theologically, he was one of the foremost developers of a distinctive Anglican alternative to the rigid Calvinism of the Puritan faction in the Church of England. He bequeathed to the Church a rich heritage of devotional literature (not published in his lifetime). As a scholar (Hebraist) he shone forth as one of the principal translators of what became the King James Version of the Bible, having indefatigibly chaired the fifth of the commission responsible for Genesis through II Kings.[15] His persuasive pastoral style as an educator and administrator successively in the sees of Chichester and Winchester stands in marked contrast to the well-intentioned but pastorally coercive bent of William Laud (1573-1645) as Archbishop of Canterbury.[16]

Yet it was Laud who, in 1626, ordained Nicholas Ferrar to the diaconate. Ferrar had been deputy-treasurer of the Virginia Company (dissolved 1624), but he turned his attention to the gathering at Little Gidding of an extended family community that lived, through the self-supporting cottage industry of bookbinding, a rigorous life of prayer and work based on the piety of the *Book of Common Prayer*. His community was also pastorally active in educating the children of the neighboring countryside and in the care of the sick and the poor.[17] Though the community survived Ferrar's death by several years and might have proved a model for diaconal ministry in the Church, it achieved both favorable notice by King Charles I and was subsequently branded as *The Arminian Nunnery* by the Puritans and forcibly disbanded by Cromwell's troops in 1646.[18]

As has already been indicated, life during the Commonwealth/ Interregnum was not easy for those formed in, and loyal to, the Anglican tradition of pastoral care during the early part of the classical period. One example will have to suffice. For a variety of interrelated reasons—theological, liturgical, and social—the victors in England's civil strife banned the observance of

Christmas. John Evelyn (1620-1706), devout Anglican layman and diarist, relates an event of 25 December 1657:

> I went to London with my wife to celebrate Christmas-day, Mr. Gunning preaching in Exeter chapel, on Micah vii. 2. Sermon ended, as he was giving us the Holy Sacrament, the chapel was surrounded with soldiers, and all the communicants and assembly surprised and kept prisoners by them, some in the house, others carried away. . . . These were men of high flight and above ordinances, and spoke spiteful things of our Lord's nativity. As we went up to receive the Sacrament, the miscreants held their muskets against us, as if they would have shot us at the altar; but yet suffering us to finish the office of Communion, as perhaps not having instructions what to do, in case they found us in that action. So I got home late the next day; blessed be God![19]

In consideration of this passage we may say two things. First, that worship according to the *Book of Common Prayer* was illegal and, therefore, that pastoral care of this nature (though Cromwell occasionally winked at it) had usually to be exercised *sub rosa*. Though the tradition was at risk, the faithfulness of such pastors as Peter Gunning and the devotion of such laity as the Evelyns and many others was strong enough to hazard the consequences.

There is, however, a darker side to the picture. On the Restoration of monarchy, episcopacy, and a new *Book of Common Prayer,* Gunning received the reward (of sorts) for constancy by consecration to the see of Chichester. Not all who have suffered, when the tables are turned, find themselves above revenge. Though noted for an impeccable personal life, Gunning became the hammer of dissent and Nonconformist worship after 1662:

> He often disturbed meetings in person [and] once finding the doors shut, he ordered the constable to break them open with a sledge.[20]

After 1662 Nonconformity was in fact a permanent feature of English Christianity. The theory, however, was that all the people of the English nation were under the pastoral tutelage and care of the Church of England and her clergy. The social position of these clergy remained long a potent one—as late, for instance, as 1832 (though their numbers were greatly reduced), fully a fourth of the Justices of the Peace in England were clergy.[21] One pastoral inheritance from the late classical period that obtained throughout the second and most of the third period (as these have been previously delineated) was to invoke against dissent the legal penalties of the Clarendon Code,[22] especially when the Established Church was felt to be under threat. The clergy also were liable to use their social position to obstruct or harass the religious life of Dissenters, particularly in arranging and recording baptisms, marriages, and burials. Of larger social consequence was the Church's monopoly on education until the developments and reforms of the nineteenth century. In this area there was every attempt (on all levels, from village to university) to hinder schooling through any other means, regardless of quality, than that offered under Church auspices.

But as has already been remarked, much more than the politics of toleration (or the lack of it) worked by the end of the late seventeenth century to effect a change in the style of Anglican pastoral care.[23] The extensive pastoral writings of Jeremy Taylor (1613-1667) attest to the fact and stand as a clear harbinger of that which predominated in the century to come. Taylor had served as a chaplain in the Royalist army during the Civil War until his arrest and brief imprisonment in 1642. Following his release, he removed to Wales and found employment as chaplain to the household of Lord Carbury. From then until he was consecrated Bishop of Down and Connor in Ireland (1660), to which was added the see of Dromore in 1661, he produced what have come to be regarded as a series of classics in Anglican pastoralia: *The Rule and Exercise of Holy Living* (1650); *The Rule and Exercise of Holy Dying* (1651); a treatise on sin and repentance, *Unum Necessarium* (1655); and a comprehensive manual of casuistry for the guidance of clergy in pastoral care, *Ductor Dubitantium* (1660).[24]

The form and linguistic style of these works are very much consonant with efforts we have already seen. In large part they have helped Taylor's works (with the exception, perhaps, of *Ductor Dubitantium*) win continuing approbation and even republication in our time. Beyond this, Taylor's contributions to the enrichment of Anglican worship have received renewed attention.[25]

Taylor has, however, also received weighty criticism in our time, to the effect that his writings betray a double standard, namely, one set of pastoral advice for the general mass of Christians and another for "the best Christians."[26] Without reproducing the intricacies of the controversy here, we can yet see in the following passage from Taylor's introduction to *Holy Living* a subtle doctrinal change from, say, Donne or Herbert, that will issue in a different kind of pastoralia in the age succeeding Taylor:

> A man does certainly belong to God who believes and is baptized into all the articles of the Christian faith, and studies to improve his knowledge in the matters of God, so as may best make him to live a holy life; he that, in obedience to Christ, worships God diligently, frequently, and constantly, with natural religion, that is of prayer, praises and thanksgiving; he that takes all opportunities to remember Christ's death by a frequent sacrament, as it can be had, or else by inward acts of understanding, will and memory (which is spiritual communion) supplies the want of the external rite; he that lives chastely; and is merciful; and despises the world, using it as a man, but never suffering it to rifle a duty; and is just in his dealing, and diligent in his calling; he that is humble in spirit; and obedient to government; and is content in his fortune and employment; he that does his duty because he loves God; and especially if after all this he be afflicted, and patient, or prepared to suffer affliction for the cause of God: the man that has these twelve signs of grace does as certainly belong to God, and is His son as surely, as he is His creature.

> These are the marks of the Lord Jesus, and the characters of a Christian: this is a good religion; and these things God's grace hath put into our powers, and God's laws have made to be our duty, and the nature of man, and the needs of commonwealths, have made to be necessary.[27]

Though the style is reminiscent of the earlier period, the theology behind it begins to betray a subtle shift that will usher in the age of moralism. If the two parts of our basic model of pastoral care "on the pattern and in the power" of the Lord who says to the Apostle, "Feed my sheep," must be held together, then what we discern in Taylor is a shift of priority from the latter to the former part of two elements, which must be kept in a dynamic tension to result in authenticity. This is not to accuse Taylor of having lost his balance in this matter, but to note that his contribution to Anglican pastoralia is transitional and strikes the theme of the time to follow. Later the sacramental base of pastoral care will be at the least obscured, if not nearly lost. We can see the implications for the exercise of pastoral ministry by the clergy in a final, short citation from Taylor:

> The work of the ministry consists in two things, in threatenings or comforts. The first is useful for the greatest part of Christians who are led by the spirit of bondage, and fear to do evil, because of wrath to

come; which grows out of love to themselves. The second is fit for the best Christians, that are led by the spirit of love; who endeavor to do righteousness. . . .[28]

Having now noticed what has been gained and what has been lost in the development of Anglican pastoral care in its classical period, we turn to the century of exhortation "to do righteousness" and the late rediscovery of the prior question, "By what means may we do well?"

II. Old Establishment and New Experiment
1688-1789

At the very inception of this period we can appropriately turn our attention to a new experiment on the part of the now old establishment. Through the agency of one priest in particular, this tack has the advantage of bringing into view the pastoral situation of England's American colonies as well as evidencing the quality of that moralism which has been identified as characterizing the period's pastoral care. We refer here, then, to Thomas Bray (1656-1730), founder of the Society for the Promotion of Christian Knowledge (SPCK, 1698) and the Society for the Propagation of the Gospel in Foreign Parts (SPG, 1701). In addition to his work in these societies, Bray also served briefly as the Bishop of London's Commissary in Maryland (1699). In organizing the pastoral ministry of the Church of England in America he advised the parishes to accept no clergyman off the ship from England unless the vestry were satisfied

whether . . . he gave no matter of scandal, and whether he did constantly read prayers twice a day [the Daily Offices] and catechize and preach on Sundays, which, [a little tongue-in-cheek?] notwithstanding the usual excuses, I know can be done by a minister of any zeal for religion.[29]

Though the passage may say more about the motives and the quality of clergy inclined to serve in the American colonies, Bray was concerned for their advancement in pastoral character. To this end he published in 1697 *Bibliotheca Parochialis,* subtitled:

Or, A SCHEME of such Theological Heads both General and Particular as are More peculiarly Requisite to be Studied by every Pastor of a Parish. Together with a Catalogue of BOOKS Which may be Read upon each of those points.[30]

This work gives us some indications of what was thought to be necessary for the equipment of pastors in that age, even though its immediate and practical point was to appeal for funds to support that ministry:

> Now, in reference to our Foreign Plantations, the Subject of our present Concern . . . there is scarcely any more effectual way to testifie our Love of God, or the Souls of Men . . . than by imparting something towards the providing of such *Libraries* therein, whereby the Clergy sent thither, may be enabled to instruct those People in the [NB] Doctrines of sound Belief and good Morals; the two great constituent parts of Christianity.[31]

These libraries were to be replete with "such books as treat of all the Sacred Truths of Christianity"; included, therefore, beyond commentary on Scripture, were the published works of Anglican divines and the Fathers of the early Church. As a director of pastoral studies, however, Bray was attuned to the age in which he lived. He therefore brought to bear on the matter more than his concern for a learned ministry (as we have seen, a constant theme in the pastoral ideal):

> For besides that we live in a very Inquisitive Age, wherein Persons of all Ranks and Professions have arriv'd to great Attainments in all the parts of Knowledge; and it is not a little indecent to see a Gown Man [clergyman], whose very Garb denotes him one Devoted to Study, outdone by any ordinary Laik [layman], in *Philology, Philosophy, Mathematicks, Antiquity,* or any part of useful Learning . . . besides this, I say, the Business of a Divine is of that comprehensive extent, that good Skill even in Nature [science], Mathematicks and Laws, which may seem most remote from his Business, is not only Accessary and Ornamental to his Profession, but of exceeding great use for the Explication and Proof of some of the principal Subjects he is to Discourse upon to the People, and also for the Defence of the most *Fundamental Articles* of Faith, that he is to maintain against the *Atheist* and *Anti-Scripturalist.*[32]

And so in an age of enlightenment when not only the doctrines but the morality of traditional Christianity were increasingly subjected to the critical scrutiny and challenge of new learning, this was to be the shape and content of the pastor's, of the parochial library.

Bray's plan was not only for "this Curious and Incredulous part of the World [America]"; it also reflected on the Mother Church:

> So that it is very requisite, that every Pastor of a Flock . . . should give himself up to farther Enquiries into Universal Learning, still making this his Rule, that he spends most of his Time and of his Thoughts upon what is essential and immediately necessary to Man's Salvation, *viz.* the Terms of the Covenant of Grace. . . .[33]

One who stood out in this period as giving the "Terms of the Covenant of Grace" renewed consideration was William Law (1686-1761). With Law we see an entire large category of pastors in the Church of England which obtained in all the periods under historical examination here, namely, chaplains to the households of the aristocracy or landed gentry. As a nonjuror, Law was legally deprived of his ordinary clerical living and spent some ten years before retirement in the household of the Gibbons family in Putney, serving principally as tutor to the father of the famous historian and critic of Christianity Edward Gibbon.[34] Within a year of joining the household as chaplain, Law published his classic *A Serious Call to the Devout and Holy Life,* which stands as an attempt to ground the moral life of Christians not just in homiletical exhortations to the practice of virtue but, rather, in a mystical and ascetical vision of the covenant of God's grace.

> Most of the employments of life are in their own nature lawful; and all those that are so may be made a substantial part of our duty to God, if we engage in them only so far, and for such ends, as are suitable to beings that are to live above the world, all the time they live in the world. This is the only measure of our application to any worldly business . . .; it must have no more of our hands, our hearts, or our time than is consistent with a hearty, daily, careful preparation of ourselves for another life. For all Christians, as such have renounced this world, to prepare themselves by daily devotion, and universal holiness, for an eternal state of quite another nature. . . .[35]

Now the first line of this citation is very reminiscent of Donne's Christmas sermon (already noticed), in that Law is focused on the various callings of human existence, but it is (and in marked contrast to Donne) scarcely centered in a radical apprehension of the Incarnation's graceful effect on human beings and their several societies. In other words, one wonders about the source of such grace as may enable those who heed the "Serious Call" to bring the matter to good effect. In this respect Law is a child of his age, setting forth the pastoral ideal of living "on the pattern" of Jesus Christ. But the "power" to do so—at least by Law's measure—is to be found in a rather individualized mystical and ascetical vision. There is here, then, a tendency toward the privatization of the spirituality that informs pastoral care. This is borne out by the consideration that although he was politically a High Churchman, Law had little "appreciation for the spirituality of the Book of Common Prayer [and] no sense of corporate worship."[36]

In terms of the type of pastor presently under examination, namely, the chaplain to aristocracy or gentry, we are possessed of two marvelous literary examples that illustrate the two aspects of William Law as, on the one hand, the High Church defender of the Establishment and, on the other hand, as moralist. Taken together these eighteenth-century literary examples fairly represent the nadir of Anglican pastoral care, whether in this period or as the temptation to either has been yielded to in any age. The first is from Henry Fielding's *The History of Tom Jones, A Foundling,* published at midcentury; the second, from Jane Austen's *Pride and Prejudice* (written by 1797 but not published until 1813).

In Fielding's novel we find the Reverend Mr. Thwackum (so aptly named as the intrepid hammer of the Establishment against all enemies), chaplain to the household of the virtuous Squire Allworthy. Along with Mr. Square—self-styled skeptic, Enlightenment philosopher, and, as it turns out, *bon vivant*—Thwackum serves as tutor both to Allworthy's nephew, the dreadful Mr. Blifil, and to our hero Tom Jones. Square and Thwackum are constantly engaged in debate, but in one vociferous exchange on the nature of "honor" and "religion" (their relation, if any, and the priority of one over the other) Thwackum delivers the following at his most pompous and stuffy best:

. nor is religion manifold, because there are various sects and heresies in the world. When I mention religion, I mean the Christian religion; and not only the Christian religion, but the Protestant religion; and not only the Protestant religion, but the Church of England.[37]

The reader is spared explicit drawing of conclusion to the arrogant argument implied by Thwackum's reduction of true religion. It is but a fine manifestation of the old question, "Is there salvation outside the Church of England?" To which the answer is, "Of course, but no *gentleman* would avail himself of it!" In setting forth the Established Church (or successors to it), Anglican pastoralia cannot, lamentably, claim innocence of attitudes here reflected in the mirror art holds up to reality.

Our second example brings into view the Bennet family of Jane Austen's *Pride and Prejudice*. Genteel but of limited means, Mr. and Mrs. Bennet reside at Longbourn, Herts., with their five as yet unmarried daughters. In the absence of a male heir, the family property is entailed upon a cousin, the Reverend Mr. Collins. He has, however, achieved substantial preferment early in his clerical career at the hands of an overbearing lay patroness, Lady Catherine de Bourgh, who has conferred on him the rectorship of Rosings, near her estate in Kent. Collins presumably serves that congregation and yet spends most of his time and effort in utterly obsequious attendance on the whims of Lady Catherine, whose schemes intermingle with the Bennets' lives.

But plot intricacies need not detain us from noticing toward the end a fair sample of pastoral advice proffered by Collins to Mr. Bennet in view of his youngest daughter's elopement and subsequent marriage to an unscrupulous militia officer. Writing principally on the matter of another daughter's better matrimonial prospects (disapproved by Lady Catherine), Collins yet takes time breathlessly to interject the following:

> I am truly rejoiced that my cousin Lydia's sad business has been so well hushed up, and am only concerned that their living together before the marriage took place should be so generally known. I must not, however, neglect the duties of my station, or refrain from declaring my amazement, at hearing that you received the young couple into your house as soon as they were married. It was an encouragement of vice; and had I been the rector of Longbourn, I should very strenuously have opposed it. You ought certainly to forgive them, as a Christian, but never to admit them in your sight, or allow their names to be mentioned in your hearing.[38]

"*That*," exclaims Mr. Bennet, "is his notion of Christian forgiveness!" Indeed, and we may here remark in addition the all-too-frequent end of such pastoral care as exhibited in Mr. Collins' or any other age, namely, the utter bankruptcy of a moralism that so confounds class habits with the practice of Christian virtue in human interaction or society.

Even so, it was implied by the title of this section that "new experiments" as well as "old establishment" were characteristic of developments in pastoral care during this era. For these we must refer to the influence of Continental pietism and the concomitant English expression of a similar reaction to ecclesiastical formalism or rationalistic moralism as either or both attempted to stem the tide of social and intellectual challenges to Christianity in the Enlightenment. For the care of souls involves far more than the defense of social arrangements sprinkled with holy water or the duties of belief and morals made clear by the rarer forms of ratiocination; authentic pastoral care must speak also to the heart.

With the nascent industrial revolution of the eighteenth century came the beginnings of a social revolution. Not only was there a general increase in population, but with better agriculture came enclosures of land once common and a rise in prices that precluded the economy of small farming. Manufacturing centers (steel and textiles) grew in the English midlands and proved a magnet to the rural dispossessed. One result of these developments was the growing mass of unchurched people. The parochial system—largely in place from the Henrician reform in the Church of England—could not cope with this situation. Add to this milieu the feeling among many who were churched that something was lacking in their spiritual nourishment, and the scene was set for the revivals and awakenings in England and America associated with the names George Whitefield (1714-1770) and John (1703-1791) and Charles (1707-1788) Wesley.

John Wesley's famous religious experience of May 1738 need bear no recounting here. What he did with his converted and strangely warmed heart bears more scrutiny in terms of pastoral care. By 1739 he had accepted the invitation of George Whitefield to join him in Bristol for a series of open-air sermons.

> In the evening I reached Bristol, and met Mr. Whitefield there. I could scarce reconcile myself at first to this strange way of preaching in the fields, of which he set me an example on Sunday; having been all my life (till very lately) so tenacious of every point relating to decency and order, that I should have thought the saving of souls almost a sin, if it had not been done in a church. . . . At four in the afternoon [on a later day] I submitted to be more vile, and proclaimed in the highways the glad tidings of salvation, speaking from a little eminence in a ground

adjoining to the city, to about three thousand people. . . . At Baptist-Mills . . . I offered the grace of God to about fifteen hundred persons from these words, "I will heal their back-sliding, I will love them freely."[39]

From there the story goes on to say that in the face of pastoral need John Wesley, priest of the Church of England, could "look upon all the world as my parish; thus far I mean, that in whatever part of it I am, I judge it meet, right, and my bounden duty, to declare unto all that are willing to hear, the glad tidings of salvation."[40] These glad tidings, as preached by John Wesley and George Whitefield, once again brought together the pattern and the power with respect of pastoral care. Horton Davies has aptly summarized the content while reminding us that an appreciation of the context must be a work of active imagination:

> The modern reader is at a serious disadvantage in trying to identify . . . imaginatively with these princes among preachers. . . . In brief, for us moderns the *mise-en-scène* is missing. [But] the chief topics on which both preached were the practical doctrines of experimental religion which are the hallmarks of Pietism to the degree that they require an inner verification in the heart, but are also the great doctrines in the Pauline, Augustinian, Lutheran, and Calvinistic traditions. Wesley, however, while accepting the doctrine of Election, stops short of Predestination in the interest of universal salvation.[41]

Neither the content nor the context, however, met with a high degree of acceptance in the Church of England. It is one of the ironies of history that the eighteenth-century Church of England bishop-theologian remembered for his apt defense of Christianity against its intellectual despisers, namely, Joseph Butler (1692-1752) in his *Analogy of Religion* (1736), was also the man who officially denied Wesley's claim to ministering pastoral care wherever he found need for it. In a 1739 interview between the Bishop of Bristol and the Reverend Mr. Wesley, Butler is recorded by Wesley as saying:

> Mr. Wesley I will deal plainly with you. I once thought you and Mr. Whitefield well-meaning men; but I cannot think so now; for I have heard more of you . . . . Sir, the pretending to extraordinary revelations and gifts of the Holy Ghost is a horrid thing, a very horrid thing . . . . You have no business here. You are not commissioned to preach in this diocese. Therefore, I advise you to go hence.[42]

John Wesley did, indeed, go hence from this fateful *faux pas* that set Anglicanism and Methodism on separate paths in England and America. The heritage of the latter has not, however, been without effect on the character of Anglican pastoral care. Though John Wesley's sermons and methods have not retained currency, the profound hymnography of his brother Charles has continued to shape the piety of subsequent generations of English-speaking Christians. If in nothing else than their rare ability effectively to link the objective theological elements in the Christian economy of salvation with the hearts and minds of assembled worshippers, these hymns stand forth. In them, too, we witness the renewal of the Incarnational and sacramental base for Anglican pastoral care.[43]

But beyond this and within the Church of England the new experiments of this era remain largely in the purview of the Evangelicals. They represent the vital force of Christianity by the end of the period, and whatever their ecclesiology may have lacked in concern for catholicity and apostolicity was surely made up by their renewing concern for holiness and sanctification. In this regard we have especially to mention the pastoral examples of the so called Clapham Sect, named for the parish of Clapham in southeast London around which the Rector, John Venn (1759–1813), drew so many notable lay persons whose social endeavors, though exercised from a privileged and conservative outlook, nevertheless brought the Gospel to bear on questions of the day such as the (ultimately successful) abolition of slavery in the British Empire. In this respect also, it is well to mention the contributions of a deacon, Henry Martyn (1781–1812), who was inspired by the Evangelical founder of the Church Missionary Society, Charles Simeon (1759-1836), to serve as a missionary to Persia and India. Martyn proved himself not only a patient and effective preacher, but he translated the New Testament into Persian and Hindustani and the Book of Common Prayer into the latter as well. This, too, on the verge of Anglican participation in the nineteenth-century globalization of Christianity can be seen as an exercise of pastoral care—at its best an *informed* zeal for souls characterized by authentic *humilitas*.[44]

III. Challenges and Cataclysm
1789-1918

The continuing effects and implications of three revolutions—the French, the Industrial, and the American—worked throughout this period radically to alter the structures of human society and existence (and, therefore, the political, intellectual, and moral context) in European and American life. The Christian churches, however, though still entrenched in their time-honored divisions and willing to expend energy on the maintenance thereof, were yet constrained by a common cultural heritage to acknowledge themselves self-consciously as a "Christendom."

Thus, on the one hand, the churches were inescapably affected by the challenges of this century, but, on the other hand, they were more and more reluctant to realize the need for, much less undertake the necessary, restatement of theology. I say "necessary" because Christian theology is nothing if not ordered and articulate reflection on the continuing experience of God's redemption of human beings and society through Jesus Christ. The principal locus of that enterprise, of course, is the Church.[45] If, then, the theological enterprise remains static or becomes defensive in its posture, while the very context within which the pastoral care based on that theology is exercised radically changes, the situation of the churches—of Christendom, in this case—is increasingly imperiled. That is precisely what transpired in this period, and Anglican theology and pastoral care represent no exception to the rule. It is to the support of this claim—and to the highlighting of those remarkable exceptions that serve to prove the rule—that this historical essay of Anglican pastoral care must now turn before a conclusion can be offered.

If one were to ask about the state of the theological enterprise in the early decades of nineteenth-century Great Britain and request a short, descriptive phrase, the words "high and dry" would very well meet the need. The referent of "high" is not a particular ecclesiastical party but rather the character of theology as it was shaped intellectually by the prevailing *rationalism* inherited from the eighteenth century, or as it was molded practically by the *moralism* of that age. The aridity suggested by the word "dry" intimates a desert scene in which the winds of circumstance forever blow the sand—the content of theology—

into various, perhaps even interesting, configurations. Nevertheless, it is the same sand. Futhermore, such a shifting on the surface of the theological desert may be just that—superficial. For what life or growth the desert fosters lacks abundance, contenting itself with the expenditure of its energy for survival. To the wanderer in the desert, such shifting configurations and what life exists there may appear simply as testimonies—*evidences* of a firmer pattern and a more luxuriant growth. But evidences, however interesting, are scarcely the realities of which they speak.

To characterize the state of theology in the late eighteenth and early nineteenth centuries as "high and dry" is to refer primarily to its academic aspect. In a broader definition of theology, one directly involving the implications of pastoralia, we of course have to mention the continuing and growing influence of the Evangelicals "as upholders of the vital force in religion, and exponents of its spiritual power."[46] In spite of a certain Biblicism and a rather rigid Calvinism, Evangelicals in the Church of England had been profoundly influenced by the devotional and spiritual warmth of that Methodism which, as we have seen, the Church at first had mothered in response to the metaphysical coolness and moral calculus of eighteenth-century rationalism.

It has been more than once remarked, however, that Evangelical theology *per se* was defective. In congruence with the temper of the age, communal aspects of Christianity were neglected in the overwhelming concern for individual salvation. Emphasis on the ecclesial marks of catholicity and apostolicity suffered for a stress on holiness. A deficient doctrine of creation and incarnation resulted from an understanding of atonement as effecting salvation *out* of the world. Echoing the observations of many other scholars, Horton Davies offers a compendium of these criticisms by remarking that the proper claims of the mind were often sacrificed to the concerns of the heart by Evangelicals, whether within or without the Church of England.[47] If one wanted to discover the locus of Evangelical theology, one would find it not so much in learned treatises as in extensive volumes of collected sermons, in the Cheap Repository Tracts of Hannah More (one of the Clapham Sect) that were sold and reprinted over and over again, and in the hymnody of the movement—particularly in *"Rock of Ages."*

But the formal theology that was proffered to undergird pastoral care is principally to be found in two works of

Archdeacon William Paley (1743–1805): *A View of the Evidences of Christianity* and *Natural Theology*. These works set forth what has been called "evidential theology." The moral and metaphysical point of evidential theology was to meet the religious skepticism of the rationalistic temper. To this end, Paley made the concept of "miracle" central to his discussion: (1) The object of Christianity is to enforce obedience to God's will by sanctions; (2) the discipline of theology exists to promote the object of Christianity; (3) it should be obvious to any impartial observer that miracles brought the first generation of Christian believers into existence; (4) being central to the revelation of God, miracles such as the New Testament records are evidences of the divine origin and truth of Christianity; and (5) divine evidences ought, therefore, to satisfy anyone's spiritual quest for eternal verities and simultaneously to provide the basis for all moral duties, whether of an individual or of an entire society.

Given the (to us) remarkable first assumption about the purpose of Christianity, the whole pattern is quite compact and the argument lucid. Paley himself was little hindered by the metaphysical and moral problems of "miracle," but as a consequence evidential theology was revealed as progressively incapable of meeting the new situation of the nineteenth century. First, it was an increasingly inadequate vehicle for the doctrinal formulations of a Church and an ecclesiastical establishment threatened by reform. The failure of evidential theology, second, rests precisely in that it had ceased, by the early decades of the nineteenth century, to be attractive or compelling. The practical power had departed from it because it purported to deal only with the *evidences* of spiritual realities or eternal truths and not with the realities people were seeking. As it failed to mediate grace it was disclosed as indeed "high and dry"—it had less and less appeal to men and women, or to a society perplexed with rapid and unprecedented changes in all areas of life. As F. D. Maurice (1805-1872) put it in the same year Karl Marx declared religion to be the "opium of the people":

> The one thought which posesses me most at this time and, I may say has always possessed me, is that we [the clergy] have been dosing our people with religion when what they want is not this but the Living God . . . .[48]

Increasingly, then, the spiritual alternatives in this pastorally critical situation seemed to many to have been either an uncritical and theologically defective Evangelicalism or unbelief. The rejection of Christianity could take the form of a simple agnosticism, or it could be militantly atheistic. The former would express itself by indifference to the theological enterprise and nonattendance on the Church. The latter (in a British utilitarian manner, as opposed to the Gallic revolutionary manner) could in all candor and seriousness propose that the entire fabric of the Church of England be converted into a vast institute of science and industry befitting the new age.[49] But by 1833 the more palpable and immediate threat to the Church of England was reform imposed by Parliament. More than anything else this sparked the political reaction, theological reform, and pastoral renewal of the Oxford Movement (1833–1845).

Though the Movement was occasioned by a perceived political threat to the Church, those who formed it became a purposeful group for more than negative reasons. Churchmen, like the men of the Oxford Movement, who adopted some form of the early nineteenth-century romantic temperament, did so to do justice to the spiritual depths of human being—depths as it seemed to them, their age was in danger of losing by rejecting an organic conception of humanity in favor of that more mechanical and socially atomistic utilitarian philosophy which appeared so well to fit the requirements of an expanding industrial culture and nascently technological era.

The chief means, of course, of disseminating the positive, renewing program of the Movement beyond the confines of Oxford's ecclesial academia was through the series of *Tracts for the Times*. These tracts had a twofold purpose: to speak the authentic historical mind of the English Church and to awaken in their readers' hearts and minds a keen sympathy for the true life, sound thought, and effective practice of the Church. At first the tracts (by 1838 selling faster than the publisher could print them)[50] were little more than leaflets encouraging a serious consideration of such things as the Book of Common Prayer envisioned as (but by then were far from) normal in Church life.[51] Later tracts were weighty treatises aimed toward a recovery of doctrinal apostolicity and catholicity in the Church of England. But in all this the tracts took their cue from a platform clearly enunciated in the 1837 *Lectures on the Prophetical Office of the Church* by John Henry Newman (1801–1890).

By the historical recalling of Anglicanism to an appreciation of its apostolic and catholic character, the Oxford Movement served a pastoral end. Owen Chadwick provides an incisive view of the influence of the Movement that has reached far beyond its time and the confines of the Church of England:

> It would be too sharp a dissection, but not therefore without its truth, to say that Newman represented the moral and intellectual force in the Movement, [John] Keble the moral and pastoral, [E. B.] Pusey the moral and devotional. Newman left the Church of England, Keble and Pusey remained; and though this single fact is in no way a cause but only a symbol, the pastoral and devotional power in the Movement proved to be far more effective, in the long run, than its intellectual power.[52]

In this judgment we recognize a renewal of those pastoral ideals of parish priesthood under consideration in this chapter. This was, indeed, true of Keble (1792–1866) in his own faithful parish work at Hursley near Winchester over the years. There was, too, in the Movement a recalling to the sacramental base of pastoral care. How far the Church of England had departed from that ground can be seen in that Pusey (1800–1882) was officially banned for two years from the university pulpit for having dared to preach a sermon entitled "The Holy Eucharist: A Comfort to the Penitent."[53] But from this practical renewal of the ideal of pastoral care based in community flowed a reinvigorated tradition that would express itself not only in traditional settings of parish life—whether in England or America—but later in the work of Anglo-Catholic priests in the slums of cities, among the human flotsam and jetsam of industrial society.

It is, however, one of the Movement's ironies that for all its emphasis on apostolicity, the vast majority of England's episcopal bench proved intractable. The bishops—lords spiritual of the realm—did not easily see their way to becoming those successors to the apostles envisioned by the Oxford presbyters. To their credit, nevertheless, the bishops did undertake with greater regularity to leave London and venture into their dioceses for the purpose of Confirmation. This was in itself ironic, more to be credited to the growing network of railroads than to the influence of the Oxford Movement.[54]

Concomitant with this development there was a certain practical gain in the recovery of an apostolic quality of the episcopate in the United States. The shock of disestablishment after the American Revolution occasioned a longer period of recovery for the new Episcopal Church as formed from the remains of the colonial Church of England in the nation. By 1835, however, ECUSA had selected its first missionary bishop, Jackson Kemper, for nearly all of what we now call the Midwest. This appointment initiated a notable succession of bishops whose character and indefatigible pastoral labors under the most adverse conditions in vast areas resulted, by the end of the nineteenth century, in the establishment of dioceses that were coterminous with the expansion of the United States itself.[55]

But these pioneer bishops were in a sense exceptional, as is evidenced by developments in the Episcopal Church leading up to and surrounding the disposition of the 1853 Muhlenberg Memorial to the General Convention. It was incumbent on American Anglicans to rethink the relationships between church and state, Christ and culture. The heritage of an established church tradition could at once ignite and dampen the pastoral impetus to mission. The Muhlenberg Memorial was a case in point. As with the Oxford Movement, the presbyterate of the church presented a challenge to the episcopate: William Augustus Muhlenberg (1796–1877) and his colleagues petitioned the bishops to seize the initiative in the still new situation of the United States. They were directly called on to act as apostles in ordaining ministers of other traditions (especially on the frontier) without binding them to the Thirty-nine Articles and all the rubrics of the *Book of Common Prayer*. The Memorial met with some enthusiasm as an incisively pastoral and incipiently ecumenical proposal, but—alas—no practical action in the face of a nation and churches increasingly divided by sectarian and moral questions in the pre-Civil War era. The pastoral principles of that Memorial have, nevertheless, formed part of an inheritance that is actively remembered in today's ecumenical engagements.

What stands between that past and our present—as already noted—are radical changes in society during the nineteenth century, culminating for the churches in the end of Christendom by 1914–1918. In the Occidental World, at least, the nineteenth century was a period during which the traditional foundations of society on all its levels were tested and found wanting. Consequently, it abounded in diverse philosophical and ideological restatements, along with radical (as well as superficial) social experiments. Long before midcentury in Great Britain (and later in America), the fact that intellectuals and the new laboring classes were criticizing Christianity had been evident to all but the most obtuse. The British census of 1851, however, forcibly revealed to the ecclesiastical world the practical effects of these facts in an unprecedented manner. Included in that survey was a "Census of Religious Worship." Though the statistics published in 1854 were not always reliable, some broad outlines appeared. And, as Owen Chadwick has rightly observed:

> It finally established the impossibility of treating the establishment as privileged on the ground that it was the church of the immense majority of the country.[56]

The Registrar-General of the religious census could not, however, resist the homiletic opportunity presented by the overwhelming nonattendance on the Church of England relative to the size of the population. He proceeded to compliment the middle classes for having maintained their high degree of "devotional sentiment and strictness of attention to religious services," and noted (with obvious approval) that "regular church-attendance is now [!] ranked amongst the recognized proprieties of life" with respect to the upper classes. But then came the blow of the census under sermonic exegesis:

> But while the *laboring* myriads of our country have been multiplying with our multiplied material prosperity, it cannot . . . be stated that a corresponding increase has occurred in the attendance of this class in our religious edifices . . . . These are never or but seldom seen in our religious congregations; and the melancholy fact is thus impressed upon our notice that the classes which are most in need of the restraints and consolations of religion are the classes which are most without them.[57]

It is important to note well the words "restraints" and "consolations" in respect to religion as applied to the working classes increasingly bereft of pastoral care. It was remarked in a previous section of this chapter that a change in the character of Anglican pastoral care was harbingered as early as Jeremy Taylor in the late seventeenth century. Taylor had spoken of the ministry as consisting primarily of two things: "threatening or comforts." Here we meet with his concept of pastoral care fully developed. In our own time we understand the "comforts" or "consolations" of religion proffered to the "laboring myriads" as the occasional respite from the adversity of their social and economic conditions, or perhaps the present contemplation of a future bliss compensatory for their present political powerlessness. More pointed, however, are the "restraints" of religion to which we are referred.

For contemporary Anglicans it requires an act of rigorous imagination or the vigorous suspension of disbelief to perceive with any comprehension the prevalence in nineteenth-century preaching of the threat of everlasting punishment. Of help in setting forth the evidence on which such acts of imagination or will can be made is Geoffrey Rowell's *Hell and the Victorians*.[58] This work demonstrates the twofold social function of such preaching: (1) to provide through the medium of a theology of future rewards and punishments the moral underpinnings of society, and (2) to keep the social, political, and economic aspirations or agitations of the working classes for redress of grievance or relief of conditions very much under control.

Pastorally speaking, the sharpest critique and most lasting theological alternative to such a theology and its homiletical exhibition came from F. D. Maurice. In his seminal ecclesiological work *The Kingdom of Christ* (1842), Maurice set forth an analysis of the requisites for authentic Church life and identified the historical-theological elements necessary to the development of contemporary Anglicanism's ecumenical vocation. Maurice's 1853 *Theological Essays* directly challenged the regnant propositional theology with its concomitant moralism sanctioned by the threat/promise of future punishment/reward. The author did great pastoral service by recovering for Anglicans the older theological tradition that appreciates eternity as qualitatively distinct from time (and, therefore, not to be conceived as time extended infintely). But by Maurice's social engagements, as represented in his leadership of the Christian Socialist Movement from 1848 to 1854, he demonstrated in practice the principles of a theology grounded in the worship of a loving God in Trinity of Persons and Unity of Being.

On these principles Maurice showed himself (to the surprise of working men) a clergyman who not only sympathized with their plight but actively listened. He was, to be sure, a pastor who could act on behalf of the working classes, but (and more importantly) he was also a theologian who would seek for the "laboring myriads" an education that could raise them into such freedom as is the very condition of moral agency. The character of such pastoring affirms and respects the dignity of persons, rather than making them objects of ministry or charity. And this, indeed, is the direct implication of Maurice's theological restatement that perceives Christ as the true head of all humanity and the Kingdom of Christ as comprehending human society properly constituted.

Maurice's real and lasting achievement for Anglican pastoral care was the recovery of that radical incarnationalism which was presented as typical of early Anglicanism, only now adapted or adaptable to the conditions of contemporary society. The old formalism, especially in worship, is rejected in favor of a deeper practice:

> I hope you will never hear from me any such phrases as our 'excellent or incomparable' Liturgy, or any of the compliments to our forefathers or ourselves which are wont to accompany these phrases. I do not think we are to praise the Liturgy, but to use it. If we find that it has been next to the Bible our greatest helper and teacher, we shall shrink with the modesty and piety of pupils from assuming toward it a tone of patronizing commendation. When we do not want it for our life, we may begin to talk of it as a beautiful composition: thanks be to God it does not remind us of its own merits when it is bidding us draw nigh to Him.[59]

Maurice's appreciation of the sacraments as basic to pastoral care at least matched that of the Tractarians, but he did not confuse (as did some of their successors) the means of grace with grace itself. By maintaining the distinction, he prevented himself and any who would follow his pastoral lead from yielding to the temptations of antiquarianism or exclusivism. In brief, Maurice provided for Anglicanism a much needed reconnection of the elements of "pattern" (the moral principle and example) and "power" (grace communicated through incarnation). When appropriately integrated, these elements make for authentic pastoral care in the life of the Christian community and an effective exercise of its mission in the world.

All this is not to say, however, that the regnant theology and moralism of the age, as reinforced by its eschatology of fear or favor, disappeared overnight. Hints of the pastoral possibilities were, nevertheless, given some exhibition as the century wore on toward its conclusion. One thinks, for example, of the Maurician restatement as it influenced B. F. Westcott (1825-1901), who managed to combine the vocation of theologian and noted New Testament scholar with that of a chief pastor (Bishop of Durham). In the latter position he distinguished himself in meeting the pastoral demands of the new age by his successful mediation of the 1892 coal strike.[60] Such pastors were, nevertheless, largely exceptional, for the crisis of the old social order had not yet reached its culmination.

Though it was not really seen with any clarity until much later, the Church of England had also inherited a situation that would increasingly militate against its pastoral effectiveness. As John D. Gay has noted:

> The history of the Church of England over the last three-hundred years has been one of gradual movement away from the centre of national and social life . . . . The processes of industrialization and urbanization, coupled with transformation of the countryside resulting from the disappearance of the self-sufficient village, have rendered the old patterns of pastoral care obsolete . . . . The real problem is that the Church of England is still geared to a stable and static pre-industrial, pre-urban society.[61]

When one has made the necessary changes and noted the exceptions, some similar conclusions can be drawn about the exercise of pastoral care among Episcopalians in the United States, at least through the decade of the 1950s. But at this juncture, one further consideration on our side of the Great War will provide us with a concluding occasion.

Conclusion

The pastoral career of yet another Bishop of Durham, H. Hensley Henson (1863–1947), spanned the worlds on either side of the watershed of the Great War. Indeed, his life exhibited many of the possibilities within Anglicanism. Coming from a Nonconformist and strictly evangelical background, Henson served as the Anglo-Catholic vicar of a slum parish in Bethnal Green, becoming later a strong defender of Establishment when many Anglo-Catholics had surrendered any hope for that position, and concluded amidst the suspicion from many quarters that at best he was an agnostic Modernist! But as shown in Owen Chadwick's recent, magisterial biography, Henson realized that a "plea of consistency could only be made if he resorted to personal history."[62] This remark in itself justifies the autobiography Henson undertook late in his life (even if it does not warrant the manner in which the bishop brought forth the result in three uneven and, by intention, occasionally misleading tomes).

But the larger point here should not be missed, namely, that the attempt to enter such a plea is probably the only methodology that will provide a canvas adequate for portraying the character of Anglican pastoral care (warts and all). It is precisely that which, in fact, I have been writing about in this historical presentation of the subject. It is for the other chapters in this volume to essay whether or to what degree this lively and personal inheritance is apt for, or can be adapted to, the pastoral requisites of the Church in our age—a Church set in a world remarkably different from anything previously experienced, but nonetheless a Church in the midst of a contemporary society composed, as always, of a humanity created in the divine image and redeemed from its many distortions in the power and on the pattern of Jesus Christ.

Toward the end of his biography of Henson, Chadwick summarizes the contents of what he regards as Henson's best book, *Ad Clerum*, published in 1937. It is a collection of Henson's episcopal charges over the years to candidates for holy orders on the evening before their ordinations. Even Chadwick's summary of that passage cannot be cited here, but it is more than interesting to note with Chadwick that Henson sets forth to the ordinands a character for the true pastor "in an authentic tradition of the English pastoral ideal, from Richard Hooker to George Herbert, from John Keble to Richard Church."[63] I would, in conclusion, claim of the passage even more than Chadwick does, since it appears exactly—point by point—to correspond to the pastoral ideal indicated as early as Chaucer's exhibition of the good parish priest. It was this last discovery—made serendipitously long after the thesis of the present chapter was conceived—that gives me confidence and hope for the present and future exercise of Anglican pastoral care. It is my further hope that what has been here essayed to this end may also serve for others.

2

Spiritual Direction and the Struggle for Justice

Kenneth Leech

It is over twenty years since Martin Thornton wrote that spiritual direction was the Church's greatest pastoral need.[1] Written in the same year as John Robinson's *Honest to God*, his words were not in accord with the prevailing mood of the time; nevertheless, many believed their day would come. In 1984, the year of Robinson's death, Thornton returned to the theme with a practical introduction to the ministry of direction, based on several years' experience of training spiritual directors in the Diocese of Truro.[2] What has happened in the intervening years? I discern two shifts, one of them highly desirable and to be encouraged, the other distinctly unhealthy and worrying.

The first shift has been the rediscovery of the riches and dynamic potential of the Christian tradition, the rediscovery of traditional wisdom. This rediscovery has occurred at a number of levels. Many of those Christians who espoused "radical causes" in the 1960s did so without any clear sense of their rootedness in a tradition of Christian dissent. This was particularly unfor-

41

tunate and dramatic in the case of Anglicans in England, where there had been a radical and revolutionary tradition of social and political action, rooted in orthodox theology, going back to the Church Socialists of the Stewart Headlam and Thomas Hancock era and continuing to World War II. Yet by 1963 John Robinson needed to go to continental Lutherans in revolt against their own dualistic tradition to recover a unity of sacred and secular that has been the norm, rather than the exception, in Anglican social thought from F. D. Maurice to William Temple. During the 1970s there was a recovery of some of the riches of this social tradition.[3]

In relation to the life of prayer and the pastoral ministry, the 1970s saw a growing unease at the cult of modernity, the assumption that nothing that occurred in Christian history before the '60s was of any value. In the words of T. C. Oden:

> We have bet all our chips on the assumption that modern consciousness will lead us into vaster freedom, while our specific freedom to be attentive to the Christian pastoral tradition has been plundered, polemicized and despoiled.[4]

The movement to recover lost or neglected insights in pastoral care was already under way by the mid-60s. In 1965 a symposium of Protestant and Catholic writers on the spiritual life included a call for a nonauthoritarian, empirical, and much more tentative type of spiritual guidance.[5] The late '60s saw the growth of a counterculture with a vigorous spiritual dimension, oriented mainly to the exploration of non-Christian traditions of meditation, mysticism, and enlightenment.[6] By the 1970s, Christians in increasing numbers were recognizing the urgent need to dig deep into their own spiritual roots. By the end of the '70s and early '80s, there was a veritable epidemic in the United States of writing on, and interest in, spiritual direction.[7]

In relation to the quest for roots both in providing nourishment for Christian activists and in enriching the inner resources of pastoral ministry, the motivation was similar: a combination of a sense of deprivation and undernourishment, and of a recognized need for a more unified, integrated approach to social and spiritual theology. There has been, however, a second, and less attractive, shift, occurring over the same period—a shift toward a spirituality of escape, withdrawal, and entirely private piety. This shift, which has affinities with earlier gnostic movements, offers an extremely popular cult of "spirituality" as a kind of diversion from the struggles of the world, a spirituality of retreat to a private realm. It values personal comfort and inner growth more than social struggle and the cries of the oppressed. It manifests itself in Catholic and Protestant forms. Through it undoubtedly has helped many individuals in their personal searches, its contribution to the redemption of the world is marginal.

It is essential, therefore, in reflecting on the contemporary quest for spiritual guidance, to recognize its ambivalent character. The spiritual world is not universally benign, and there is a major task of discernment, of discrimination, between true and false spirituality. At its best, the Christian understanding of spiritual direction has laid great emphasis on this work of discernment and critical scrutiny.

In this essay I shall first summarize the ministry of spiritual direction as it has been understood in the various Christian traditions; second, discuss the connections between direction and, on the one hand, counselling and psychotherapy and, on the other, sacramental confession; third, attempt to summarize the nature of this ministry today and the qualities required for its effective exercise; and, finally, relate direction to the struggle for justice in the world.

Spiritual Direction in Christian Tradition

Historically, the growth of spiritual direction as a distinctive form of Christian ministry was associated with early desert monasticism. The *pneumatikos pater* (spiritual father) was central to desert spirituality, whereas the quality of discernment, *diakrisis*, was central to the spiritual father's role. In the desert tradition, the spiritual father was an example rather than a controller of lives. The guidance he gave was a result of a life of silence and striving after purity of heart. In the sixth century, St. Isaac the Syrian emphasized experience as the essential quality of the guide:

> Confide your thoughts to a man who, though he lack learning, has studied the work in practice. Therefore follow the advice of a man who has himself experienced all, and knows how to judge patiently what needs discrimination in your case, and can point out what is truly useful for you.[8]

Similarly, St. Symeon the New Theologian, writing in the eleventh century, says that a spiritual father should be "an experienced teacher with knowledge of the passions."[9] The eastern spiritual writers do not prescribe direction for all people at all times. They do, however, stress the dangers to sanity and spiritual balance for those who seek to practice the way of interior prayer and *hesychia* (inner quietude) without adequate guidance. For, as the nineteenth-century Russian writer Macarius explained:

> Whenever we set out firmly to tread the inner path, a storm of tempta-
> tions and persecutions always assails us. It is because of the dark host
> that spiritual direction is profitable, nay necessary to us, whether we
> retire to a monastery or continue to live in the world.

Like Symeon before him, Macarius urges people to follow "the guidance of a wise man experienced in the fight."[10]

In the west, St. Gregory the Great in the sixth century called the guidance of souls the "art of arts." In the same period, the "soul friend" (*anmchara*) was a feature of Celtic church life. The saying "Anyone without a soul friend is a body without a head" became a well-established Celtic proverb. Some "soul friends" were women, and many were lay persons. It is possible that Celtic spirituality was influenced by the Eastern desert tradition. In the West, personal direction grew under the influence of lay brotherhoods and, later, of the mendicant friars. It was the friars who promoted spiritual direction through the confessional, and the fifteenth-century *Manipulus Curatorum* of Guy de Montrocher distinguished such confession (*confessio directiva*) from the ordinary sacramental practice (*confessio sacramentalis*). Earlier, St. Catherine of Siena (1347–1380) had laid down three basic principles of direction: a nonjudgmental posture; regular prayer for one's directees so as to become sensitive to their feelings and states and thus able to offer support and encouragement; and the recognition that everyone is led to God by a unique path.[11]

After the Council of Trent, spiritual direction underwent both expansion and a narrowing of perspective. Key figures are St. Ignatius Loyola (1495–1556), whose *Spiritual Exercises* introduced a whole new approach to methodology within the personally directed retreat, and St. John of the Cross (1543–1591), who was particularly concerned with nourishing and guiding the transition to contemplative prayer.[12] Recent Roman Catholic writing has moved toward a view of direction as friendship, an approach followed also in some Anglican writing.[13] At the same time, there has been a revival of interest in the Ignatian Exercises, and St. John of the Cross has rightly been seen as holding a central place in the spiritual director's resources.

Within the Anglican tradition, personal guidance was a central feature of the Caroline period, and "it would be hard to find a writer of this age to whom personal spiritual guidance was not a normal and necessary part of Christian living."[14] Jeremy Taylor (1613-1667), in his *Ductor Dubitantium* (1660), sought to provide resources for the guides of souls. But his aim was that "men that are wise may guide themselves in all proportions of conscience." The spiritual guide was to be available, when necessary, "to untie the intrigue and state the question, and apply the respective rules to the several parts of it."[15] This attempt to combine guidance with a concern for personal freedom was central to Caroline "casuistical divinity."

It was the anxiety about authoritarian modes of direction and overdependence on directors that made the Tractarians wary of the concept of spiritual direction. Thus E. B. Pusey, who edited an English edition of the Abbé Gaume's *Manual for Confessors*, stressed in his preface that spiritual direction was "entirely distinct" from sacramental confession, pointing out that he himself had never been a director.[16] J. M. Neale similarly, though conceding that direction was sometimes expedient, believed it was "in many instances pernicious."[17] On the other hand, William Cunningham claimed the importance attached to the guidance of the soul was "a special characteristic of the Anglican communion."[18] In spite of the reservations of some nineteenth-century thinkers, spiritual direction did become more widespread through the Oxford Movement, and its spread was for many years restricted to those within the Catholic tradition.

In the English context, the situation as it stood in the 1950s can be summarized as follows. A minority of Anglicans, mainly within the Catholic tradition, went to confession on a regular basis. This was often, perhaps usually, combined with some kind of spiritual direction, however fragmentary. Because confession was voluntary, and therefore the numbers involved were not considerable (as was the case in the Roman communion), probably the majority of confessors felt some obligation to give advice and guidance. At the same time, it was not uncommon for direction of a more intensive kind to be given apart from the confessional.

The continuity of the Anglican tradition from the Caroline period did not encourage excessive dependence on a spiritual guide; on the other hand, the renewed interest in the inner life, generated by the Oxford Movement, led to an increased expression of the need for such guidance by many Anglicans. During the last thirty years, while the practice of confession has probably declined among many Anglicans who had been brought up to accept it as a *sine qua non* of Catholic life, it has increased among others who have felt able, in the more eirenical climate, to avail themselves of a ministry earlier considered taboo. In recent years, the need for more personal guidance has come to be recognized among Evangelicals, partly as a result of the opening up of new understandings of spiritual growth through the Charismatic movement.

Though it originated within monasticism, the ministry of spiritual direction within a Christian framework has over centuries come to be associated with people and communities seeking to lead lives of discipleship in many contexts. Though it has often concerned itself with techniques, methods of prayer, and ascetic disciplines, it is not primarily concerned with methodology. It is a relationship of companionship that will, from time to time, involve instruction and perhaps help over personal life-crises. But it is not essentially a problem-solving or "crisis-intervention" facility, and, in spite of the evident areas of overlap, must be clearly distinguished from pastoral counselling and from psychotherapy.

Counselling, Therapy, and Confession

Much pastoral theology in the last two decades has been dominated by a counselling and clinical model. The late Robert Lambourne, a physician as well as a priest, was a memorable critic of what he called "hang-up theology," a problem-solving approach to human progress.[19] Recently Martin Thornton has spoken of "the ambulance syndrome,"[20] and Alastair Campbell, who has played a central role in developing ministries of pastoral counselling in Britain, has complained:

> The tendency in recent pastoral care literature to focus almost exclusively on "counselling skills," and to encourage the development of a cadre

of professional "pastoral counsellors" must be viewed with some alarm.[21]

Campbell points to the military language used in much of the early pastoral counselling manuals, language that "makes the patient into an inert battlefield across which the rival forces of treatment and disease relentlessly march."[22] Though much counselling has occurred within a Christian framework, its categories have not, on the whole, been drawn from Christian theology or the Chrisitian spiritual tradition. Of course, there are close similarities with spiritual direction, and some have seen direction as a kind of intensified counselling; but the association of counselling mainly with states of emotional distress, pain, and upheaval, its location in the clinic or the office, and its excessively personal orientation, are in marked contrast with spiritual direction with its concern for the ongoing Christian life, its location in the context of church and sacraments, and its rootedness within the common life of the Body of Christ.

In recent years, there has been a marked shift within some schools of psychotherapy toward a concern with spiritual wholeness. In the 1960s R. D. Laing was speaking of the experience of God and of the common ground between priests and physicians: "Among physicians and priests, there should be some who are guides, who can educt the person from this world and induct him to the other."[23] Viktor Frankl was speaking of the need for therapists to recognize the spiritual dimension.[24] The psychotherapist Sheldon Kopp was speaking of his role as that of a guru,[25] and Theodore Roszak was arguing that "psychiatry is itself being transformed by all it touches and borrows into a syncretic, salvational discipline."[26]

Two points, however, need to be made about these shifts. First, clearly they are not typical of most psychotherapy, still less of most of what is termed psychiatry in Britain and the U.S. Second, where psychotherapists do move toward a stress on spirituality, it can be argued that what is happening is not that therapy is superseding spiritual direction but that it is recognizing its own limitations as a discipline. Of course, there is an area of overlap where spiritual directors gratefully make use of therapeutic insights and where therapists act as spiritual guides. But certain distinctions need to be maintained. Psychotherapists may or may not be concerned with spirituality or with God (however conceived).

Spiritual direction, in Christian understanding, is *essentially* concerned with these realities. Spiritual directors may or may not be concerned with psychological breakdown, but their fundamental concern is theological. To put it crudely, the Christian spiritual director is concerned with the relationship of a person to God through Christ, and, at the end of the day, as spiritual director, that is his or her only concern.

With this primary concern, the spiritual director will often be a person who receives sacramental confession and who, if a priest, absolves the repentant sinner. Within Anglicanism, spiritual direction has often taken place within the confessional and, since the *Ordo Poenitentiae* of 1974, Roman Catholics have been restoring an element of direction to the ministry of reconciliation. It is wrong, however, to identify direction and confession, for, though intimately connected, they are not the same. The purpose of confession is to receive forgiveness, not spiritual counsel or advice, valuable as it may be. (Anglican priests are often prone to give advice to penitents even when they are not asked for it, and many seem to regard it as a necessary part of the sacrament.) The framework of the confessional is not necessarily appropriate for direction that calls for a more relaxed and perhaps lengthy encounter. Again, not all spiritual directors are priests, a tremendously important fact being rediscovered in all parts of the Church. On the other hand, sin is such a major element in the human person that it is difficult in practice to keep confession and direction apart. Thus, though it is perfectly proper (and common) to confess one's sins and not seek or receive spiritual direction, it seems to me difficult to sustain a relationship as intimate as that of direction unless there is a confrontation with sin. This raises an important, and on the whole unfaced, problem about lay direction and the restriction of the ministry of absolution to priests.[27]

The Nature of Spiritual Direction

We are now in a position to clarify the role of the spiritual director in the Church today. In *Confession*, published in 1958, Max Thurian defined spiritual direction thus: "Spiritual direction, or the cure of souls, is a seeking after the leading of the Holy

Spirit in a given psychological and spiritual situation."[28] Though some may question the identification of direction with the cure of souls (which surely involves other areas of ministry), the twofold emphasis on mutual seeking, and on the specificity of each situation, is right. Both director and directee are fellow pilgrims, companions in spiritual journeying and spiritual warfare. How then can we summarize this relationship of spiritual direction?

First, it is freely chosen. It is not a relationship that can be imposed, whether by a bishop, theological seminary, or other church authority. It is essential to this relationship that an individual, after much thought and prayer, chooses a director and that the director, after much thought and prayer, agrees to accept the relationship. This dimension of freedom must remain. A particular relationship of direction will not last forever, and may not in fact last very long at all. If the two individuals do not "click," the relationship should be abandoned without any ill feeling on either side.

Second, the relationship is temporary. People outgrow one another, cease to serve or need each other. We need and use various people, as friends, companions, directors, at various stages in life. It is important that both people maintain an awareness of the need constantly to evaluate and review the relationship.

Third, the relationship is not authoritarian, not an imposing on another of one person's route to God. For, as Augustine Baker wrote of the spiritual director:

> . . . his office is not to teach his own way, nor indeed any determinate way of prayer but to instruct his disciples how they may themselves find out the way proper for them, by observing themselves what doth good and what causeth harm to their spirits; in a word, that he is only God's usher, and must lead souls in God's way and not his own.[29]

The director is not an exponent of a method, still less the holder of a secret way. The director is not one who moves the individual along clearly defined routes, but one who, humbly and in solitude, waits on the spirit and seeks to guide and to recognize guidance.

Fourth, spiritual direction is concerned with the whole of life. It does not see "spirituality" as a subdivision of Christian faith, the intensely personal and interior part of life, but as the whole life of the human person oriented Godward. It is therefore a relationship that cannot limit its concern to what happens in the moments of devotional practice. It is the whole person, this living, struggling, sexual, political, human creature, with which spirituality and spiritual direction are concerned. Anything less moves inevitably in the direction of yet another leisure-time interest.

Fifth, within the relationship of direction there is a combination of support, teaching, struggle, and discernment. The support element is very important, and it becomes increasingly mutual, for both persons are "fellow travellers, friends and comrades on this journey."[30] It is not, however, the only element. The spiritual director is a teacher, a theologian, one who seeks to enable an individual to see himself or herself against the background of the Christian tradition. Thornton defines spiritual direction as "the application of theology to the life of prayer."[31]

But more fundamental than either support or teaching is the process of struggle with illusion and of discernment of the working out of God's purposes. The confrontation with illusion and unreality in the self, a confrontation in which both persons involved in direction take part, is at the heart of the quest for purity of heart. As Henri Nouwen says:

> It does not allow people to live with illusions of immortality and wholeness. It keeps reminding others that they are mortal and broken, but also that with the recognition of this condition liberation starts.[32]

The process of spiritual direction is marked by upheaval and inner turmoil. Though its aim is unity and interior *shalom*, it recognizes the rough and dangerous country through which the heart in pilgrimage must travel. Along this pilgrim way, surrounded by many conflicting voices and by demonic threats both to sanity and to survival, it seeks to discriminate between voices, to discern the voice of God. *Diakrisis* (discernment) is in many respects the key word in the literature of spiritual direction in East and West. It involves struggle, but it also calls for attention, watchfulness, inner quietude of spirit, and that sensitivity of soul by which we learn to see and feel with the eyes and heart of God.

What qualities are called for in those who exercise such a ministry? One could produce lengthy lists, but I will single out three characteristics that seem to me to be of central importance. First, the spiritual director must be a person of deep prayerfulness, one who is seeking to grow in holiness of life, and who approaches this ministry with humility and a sense of his or her own unworthiness and poverty. A broken and contrite heart is a necessary mark of the spiritual guide. In the words of St. Gregory of Nazianzus:

> A man must himself be cleansed before cleansing others; himself become wise that he may make others wise; become light and then give light; draw near to God and so bring others near; be hallowed and then hallow them.[33]

The ministry is not so much a skill to be acquired as an overflow from a life of prayer and waiting on God. It calls for continual self-scrutiny and self-criticism, for the building up and nourishment of spiritual resources, and particularly for the cultivation of solitude and of a receptive, contemplative spirit. The director must be one who listens to the inner voices, the obscure motions of the soul, and this can only happen as a result of the practice of contemplation and recollection.

Second, the ministry of spiritual direction calls for persons of experience in the inner struggles and upheavals of the spiritual journey. It calls for an experience of suffering and of solidarity in suffering. As with the psychotherapist, the spiritual director's ability to enter into the personal depths of the other will depend to a considerable extent on his or her experience of pain and on the recognition of a solidarity of inner struggle. "Therapist or Abba, it is only the experience of inner confusion, tension, synthesis, and meaning that enables one to be of any service to those seeking guidance."[34] The person who has wrestled with God in the night and has emerged wounded from that conflict has much to give from the depths of a wounded heart. For it is by our wounds that others are healed, or rather, as Christian believe, by our identification with the wounds of Christ, our sharing in his passion. The ministry of direction is thus a passion-centered ministry. It is a real solidarity in suffering, not only in the physical and emotional distress of people but in that alienation from God which was the experience of Christ on Calvary. Thus our "effectiveness" will depend not on acquired skills and regular refresher courses but on our continued closeness to the Crucified. Nowhere is it more true than in this ministry that we bear in our body the marks of Jesus (Gal. 6:17).

In the life of the spirit, integrity comes through brokenness, resurrection through death. The experiences that shape spiritual guidance are often those of affliction; they wound and heal us. And no amount of study can compensate for the lack of interior struggle with the ensuing pain. But much of our pastoral practice seems designed not to lead us to this prospect of interior struggle but to deflect us into the pseudoresolutions of rhetoric, efficiency, and confidence. So by the fluency of our preaching or the charm of our social graces, we disguise the vacuum, relying on reports of what others have said about experiences long past.

> The priest dealing with questions of meaning, of intimacy, and of death is stripped naked because spirituality is the one area where it is impossible to go on constantly faking it (as we do more or less successfully in other areas of our ministry). It is often the priest who hesitates, who is reticent, who feels himself inadequate in his task, who is haunted by failure, who is able to express most directly the mysteries of the inner life. Eloquence is not the primary gift we seek but faith and love.[35]

Faith is a way that passes through darkness; love can be so profound as to be inarticulate.

Third, this ministry calls for people who are steeped in the tradition of spiritual theology. Of course, learning and professional competence are not enough, but they are necessary. It is unwise to rely only on one's particular temperament and style. If we are to respond to, and minister to, the greatly varied people God puts across our path, we need to be familiar with a wider spectrum of Christian experience and understanding. The spiritual director must always remember that God is the true Guide and leads individuals by various routes. A sense of our rootedness in a living and rich tradition helps protect us from idolatrous attachment to our own methods, our own way.

To regard spiritual direction as a high priority in pastoral practice is to act against many of the prevalent conventions of the Church. Studies of pastoral ministry suggest that the work of personal guidance, and indeed theology itself, is treated as relatively unimportant by many Church members.[36] Thus we find that "the clergy feel called to ministry for one type of function but are likely to spend their time and energy performing quite a different function. The cure of souls is one thing. Making a parish a howling success is another."[37] It follows, then, that to place personal spiritual guidance at the center of Christian ministry is to demand a major shift in priorities and in pastoral strategy. Attention must be shifted from an emphasis on quantitative growth and visible success to a concern with inner, qualitative growth and life in God.

Personal Growth and Social Transformation

Does this revival of interest in personal spiritual guidance have any sociopolitical dimensions? At one level, the answer is obvious: No man is an island; all individuals involved in spiritual direction are also parts of a wider secular community and are therefore politically involved. At the same time, it is easy to use "spirituality" as yet another diversion, another escape from the harsh realities of life, a way of becoming neutral. Religious devotion can be, and often is, as Marx saw, an opiate, an analgesic administered in response to a pain-filled world.

It is important, therefore, to return to the two motivations of the contemporary spiritual quest I referred to earlier. For some, spirituality is a way of escape, of retreat. Personal transformation is placed over the cries for justice in the world. For many others, however, there is an integral bond that unites the concern for personal *metanoia* and that for social change. The fate of the soul and the fate of the social order are one. It is this sense of the integral unity of spirituality and social justice that is perhaps the central feature of the current renewal.

How is this sense reflected in spiritual direction? I suggest three basic Christian themes as being of central importance to this question: (1) the orientation of Christian spirituality toward the Kingdom of God; (2) the incarnational basis of spirituality and spiritual direction within the body of Christ, the extension of the incarnation; and (3) the character of contemplative prayer as essentially subversive of illusion and falsehood.

First, Christian spirituality is a spirituality of the Kingdom. It is a spirituality of movement and progress, a spirituality for pilgrims rather than settlers. Its end is not personal adjustment or enlightenment but "new heavens and new earth, the home of justice." (2 Peter 3:13). It is over sixty years since P. E. T. Widderington wrote of the Kingdom as the "regulative principle of theology" and claimed that the recovery of its central place in Christian thought would lead to a new Reformation.[38] His prophecy is seeing its fulfillment in our day. The Kingdom of God is an integrative, unifying symbol of the inward and outward dimensions of Christian struggle. The recognition, in much recent theological reflection, that the Kingdom includes both personal and social transformation is a major point of convergence for Christians of differing confessional backgrounds. It is significant that the renewal of concern for social justice, for peace, and for human liberation has gone hand in hand with a renewal of prayer and spirituality. The false polarity of a theology of "two kingdoms" (one spiritual and inward, the other sociopolitical and external) is increasingly being rejected.

Within the framework of a Kingdom theology, spiritual direction must be seen as a necessary purification and a necessary illumination. It is a purification, a catharsis of spirit, by which we seek to become disaffiliated from captivity to oppressive, worldly structures. Spiritual direction is about finding our direction, and that direction has already been outlined in the baptismal liturgy: the turning to Christ, the repentance from sin, the renunciation of the realm of evil. It is an illumination, an opening up of our consciousness to the demands of our baptismal commitment within a world-order based on conflicting principles. Hence the necessity for discernment in relation to social trends and demands.

> The discernment that is required of those who would grow in themselves includes a discernment of where they stand in the system of things in an order which can oppress or set free—and which mostly oppresses.

To seek direction is thus a social act within a social context, as the quest for sanctity is itself a quest for a *vita socialis*. In Augustine's words, "How could the City of God . . . begin at the start of progress in its course, or reach its appointed goal if the life of the saints were not social?"[40]

The awakening consciousness of the demands of the Kingdom of God, however, is certain to lead to an intensifying of the conflicting demands of a church that seeks the Kingdom of God, and the prevailing sociopolitical order. Jim Wallis has argued that the recovery of the centrality of the Kingdom of God in our evangelistic preaching would have disturbing social consequences:

> One of the effects of such evangelism would be the spread of social deviance. The priorities of God's Kingdom are at such variance with the ruling assumptions and structures of our day that the simple proclamation of the Kingdom will undermine the economic system and present the risk of being charged with political treason.[41]

Spiritual direction, which seeks to deepen and guide the Christian disciple beyond the experience of conversion, is similarly likely, in the present climate, to have the result of nourishing a community of deviants. Hence the contemporary relevance of its origins in the desert movement. For the desert is, above all else, the training ground for the prophetic spirit, the place where resistance and fidelity are strengthened in the rigorous climate of solitude.

If spiritual direction occurs within the context of a commitment to the Kingdom of God, it occurs also within the extension of the Incarnation. It can never be purely "spiritual" or purely "personal," nor can it properly be exercised in a detached, clinical way. Its context is the Christian community, the flesh and bones of Christ's living body. It is a social act, directed to the building up of that body. It is necessarily messy and untidy, and involves close and intimate sharing of loves and wounds. Its aim is not conformity or adjustment but the sanctification of all the members of Christ.

As well as this essentially social character, direction derives from its incarnation basis two other characteristic features. First, it will seek to direct disciples away from the Church to the streets, to find the incarnate Christ in the bodies of the neglected, the voiceless, and the poor. Sensitivity to that real presence of Christ in the poor is a necessary outcome of sound spiritual guidance. Second, it will not be able to separate the "spiritual dimension" from other aspects of human life. Thus an Anglican incarnational approach to spirituality and spiritual direction will be deeply suspicious of attempts to separate the life of prayer from the rough and tumble of life in the world. It will view spiritual direction as a ministry concerned with all life oriented Godward. Orthodox Christology, believing in the taking of humanity into God and insisting that what has not been assumed has not been healed, must reject dualistic spiritualities and divisions into spiritual and social.

Thus the Incarnation is the theological root and basis of the Anglican spiritual tradition, a tradition that sees human life and society as fundamentally deiform, created to reflect the image of the triune God. The Incarnation unites spirituality and social action in a christological unity. The formation of Christ is us, our "Christification," and the recognition of, and service of, Christ in others, are parts of one process, the transfiguration of human life and society.

Finally, spiritual direction is concerned with deepening the contemplative spirit, a spirit that includes a critical, subversive element, what Thomas Merton called the "unmasking of illusion." Contemplation involves seeing reality and seeing through illusion and falsehood. It involves an intensity of love that undermines stereotypes of one's enemies, and a freedom from worldly attachments that calls into question the values of a consumer society. Contemplation is, therefore, in Daniel Berrigan's words, "a deeply subversive activity."[42] It knows by "unknowing," sees by darkness, and places all idols under the most radical critique. Idolatry is, as Theodore Roszak has written, "a mistaken ontology, grounded in a flawed consciousness."[43] Contemplative prayer is the prayer of transformed liberated consciousness, set free from the tyranny and limitations of idols. In our idolatrous culture, contemplation is deeply and fundamentally subversive.

Christians in the West are currently living in a transitional era in which Constantinian establishments are crumbling and churches are becoming increasingly marginal to the mainstream culture. That political regimes that claim to be Christian appropriate a Christian vocabulary to disguise manifestly anti-Christian positions serves only to emphasize the marginality of the Christian witness. In this situation, the work of spiritual direction as a tool of the Kingdom, as a testimony to the Incarnation, and as a force to strengthen contemplative awareness, is more urgent than ever before.

3

Secular and Religious
Models of Care

Ruth Tiffany Barnhouse

The human predicament is basically ambiguous. Robert Neale, professor of psychiatry and religion at Union Theological Seminary, describes it as follows:

> Because we are not gods, we become physically ill, mentally sick, and spiritually diseased. Because we are not animals, we are both aware and intolerant of our condition. What is a human being? One who experiences anxiety and hope: a creature who desires to be healed.[1]

Clergy and psychiatrists are not exempt from this description, even though both are, in different ways, healers. Healers are themselves in need of healing; good training systems for both professions take account of that—nor is the process ever assumed to be complete. In fact, we know that psychiatrists who claim they are "thoroughly analyzed" and so have no countertransference problems, no personal difficulties beyond their understanding, or clergy who claim to have conquered sin and so live the nearly perfect life—these are people with serious problems!

We know the horror stories from both professions, of which the Jonestown tragedy is only the most notorious. The list includes: the Californian minister who refused to permit an eventually successful suicide to have any treatment other than prayer and listening to taped sermons; those whose sexual problems have been aggravated (if not actually caused) by religious instruction or outright seduction by clergy; the unfortunate people whose ability to process various tragic or difficult events in their lives has been seriously obstructed by clergy who tell them these events are God's will or, still worse, punishment for their sins. Every psychotherapist has seen at least one such case, and some have seen many.

On the other side is the rising problem of psychotherapists who have sex with their patients. And there is the widespread abuse of electric shock and drugs. More subtle, but just as damaging are the therapists who so closely identify with a particular theory that they ignore anything the patient presents that does not fit. Still worse, they sometimes interpret such manifestations as resistance calling for further analysis. Many clergy have been called to the rescue in such cases.

As Pattison has pointed out, "Compliance with religious beliefs, attitudes and practices, can be a tremendous force for *either* good or evil in human affairs."[2] We must not forget that the year that saw the Jonestown tragedy also saw Mother Teresa receive the Nobel Prize. Nor must we forget that psychiatry can also be a tremendous force for either good or evil. For either side to maintain its prejudice against the other by generalizing from horror stories is tempting but counterproductive.

There are "diploma mills" for both clergy and psychotherapists, and even among accredited institutions some are marginal. Further, there are differences in the degree of accountability required of practitioners in both professions. They depend on institutional policies, and also on how isolated, either by circumstance or temperament, a given practitioner may be from his or her colleagues.

I shall address the issues of care as they arise in the Episcopal Church, the mainline Protestant Churches, and the Roman Catholic Church. On the other side, I shall mainly be considering psychiatry, including psychoanalysis (derived from Freud) and analytical psychology (derived from Jung). Clinical psychologists and some others without medical training often do psychotherapy that is indistinguishable from the parent discipline of psychiatry, and their work is included in what follows.

The Problem of Healing

The concepts of salvation and healing are etymologically related, and the words for the two are identical in many modern languages. This fact illustrates the well-known, ancient connections between healing and practical theology that have become separated only in the last few hundred years. Important similarities remain. Both psychiatry and pastoral care are concerned with change. Both perceive themselves as leading people to a better state, however "better" may be defined. But there is a difference in the attitude now taken by the practitioners of each discipline. Nearly all clergy, with varying degrees of sophistication and expertise, are aware that, in addition to their overtly religious duties, they are involved in mental, emotional, and sometimes physical healing. Psychiatrists, with very rare exceptions, do not realize that regardless of their personal beliefs, they are perforce physicians not only of the mind but of the soul.

According to Abbott, "Early clergy pastoral theory saw everyday life problems instrumentally, as aids to salvation."[3] Many psychoanalytic theories take a similar view. If you come to understand your problem, you can be better than you were before you had it. The definition of neurosis as an unsuccessful attempt to provide self-healing expresses this attitude. From the standpoint of the meta-process, then, both systems, in at least some instances, see the problem itself as instrumental in healing.

When limited to traditional religious vocabulary and uninformed by psychological insight, however, much pastoral intervention not only did not work but in many instances aggravated the problem. Furthermore, psychiatry has a great deal more to say about work, leisure, sex, and friendship than does religion. We have no comprehensive, widely disseminated practical theology of those subjects; and yet, they are the practical problems of everyday life, occupying at least 90 percent of most people's waking hours. No wonder psychiatry and its daughter specialties have gradually taken over their interpretation and control. This is why later pastoral theories, those evolved over the last thirty years, have for the most part abandoned any traditional theological base and have been almost exclusively inspired by psychiatry. This is a serious error for many reasons.[4]

The Problem of Personal Religion

In evaluating mental states, psychiatrists first ascertain whether persons are oriented as to time, place, and person. Do they know what day and year it is? What time of day it is? Do they know where they are? Do they know who they are? Can they correctly identify other people? Accurate answers to these questions are the indispensable prerequisites for any grasp of reality. In a similar way, religious health depends on the answer to those same questions, posed on a different scale. How does one perceive oneself in relation to time with a capital T, to all the time there is—Eternity? What is one's place in the total scheme of the universe? Who is one, in relation to all of this? There is no known culture, however primitive, that has not evolved at least rudimentary answers to those questions, and there is no person, however isolated or individualistic, who has not thought about them. The set of answers a person has arrived at, with or without reflection and in however limited or negative a way, constitutes that person's religion. As William James remarked about a young atheist at Harvard, "He believes in No-God and worships Him." One is dealing here with that which is in principle unknowable, at least in terms of any modern definitions of knowledge. The fact that *all* human beings consider these questions is remarkable, but it is a psychological fact, one psychiatrists ignore at their peril.

Most psychotherapeutic systems claim not to deal with religion, except, perhaps, in its floridly pathological forms. In fact, however, some psychological theories do make claims about religious questions, if only to declare that the traditional transcendent formulations of theology are mere epiphenomena of the human psyche. Such declarations are not denials of religion, they *are* a religion, since they make a claim about the ultimate system of orientation.[5]

Theology is quite different. Each of the many theologies is a symbolic system, often highly elaborate, through which its adherents try to deal with the mystery of the Unknowable and to tolerate its paradoxes. In terms of this symbology, the believer answers the questions of meaning and purpose. Thus, theology has two components: (1) the symbols themselves and (2) the speculations about their importance.

Both religion and theology can be purely private, highly idiosyncratic, although it is rare for a person to develop a completely private symbolic system. (It is usually seen only in persons with identifiable psychopathology, where it surfaces as religious delusions.) Symbols and mythological speculations about the cosmos are often remarkably similar from one theological system to another, and both normal and psychotic persons often dream in symbols identical to those of religions they know nothing about. Private and highly individual variations on established systems, however, are common. These facts do not speak to the objective truth or falsity of any system, but they are part of the large body of evidence that suggests that the religious function is instinctive, part of what constitutes our humanity. Jung was a pioneer in this field, and a few others from differing theoretical bases are carrying the work forward.

Ana-Maria Rizzuto has written a book she describes as "a clinical, psychoanalytical study of 'postulated superhuman beings' as experienced by those who do and do not believe in them"[6] She says, "In Freud's understanding of the subject, and in my own, there is no such thing as a person without a God-representation." Her research establishes that not only the father, as Freud thought, but the mother contributes to the formation of the young child's God-representation. In believers, its development is inextricably linked with self-representation. In unconflicted unbelievers, the God-representation is enmeshed with the repressed parental representation while the self-representation continues to develop.

Rizzuto adds, "My method enables me to deal only with psychic experiences. Logic does not permit me to go beyond a psychological level of inference." In the 1937 Terry lectures, Jung described the ubiquity in dreams of symbolic representations of God. He adds,

It would be a regrettable mistake if anybody should take my observations as a kind of proof of the existence of God. They prove only the existence of an archetypal God-image, which to my mind is the most we can assert about God.[7]

Both Rizzuto and Jung exhibit a rare discrimination. They

know they are not talking about the Unknowable itself, as do theology and religion. They know their investigations can only describe, more or less specifically, the psychological ways of processing experience of, or ideas about, the Unknowable. Freud and most of his followers have not been so careful; based on their observations of what their patients did with religion, they presumed to criticize religion itself. It is as though one were to criticize the "nature" of automobiles on the basis of how they are driven by some people.

But it is possible to be still more specific about individual religious manifestations. In a detailed study—modeled to some extent on the developmental work of Piaget, Erikson, and, particularly, of Kohlberg—Fowler has demonstrated there are six stages of faith development.[8] I shall review them very briefly. Stage 1 is *Intuitive/Projective,* "the fantasy-filled imitative phase in which the child can be powerfully and permanently influenced by examples, moods, actions and stories of the visible faith of primally related adults."

In Stage 2, *Mythic/Literal,* "the person begins to take on for him or herself the stories, beliefs and observances that symbolize belonging to his or her community." Here everything is taken literally, symbols are one-dimensional. This is most characteristic of schoolchildren but is sometimes seen in adolescents and adults. The phenomena described by Freud, Rizzuto, and others are mainly situated in these first two stages.

Stage 3 is *Synthetic/Conventional.* It is typical of adolescents, but many adults have stopped there. It is:

> a 'conformist' stage in the sense that it is acutely tuned to the expectations and judgments of significant others and as yet does not have a sure enough grasp on its own identity and autonomous judgment to construct and maintain an independent perspective. . . . At Stage 3 a person has an 'ideology' . . . but . . . has not objectified it for examination and is . . . unaware of having it . . . . Authority is located in the incumbents of traditional authority roles . . . or in the consensus of a valued . . . group.

Stage 4 is *Individuative/Reflective.* Young adulthood is an appropriate time for its development, but often it does not appear until one's thirty's or forty's, if at all. This is a "demythologizing stage," in which the capacity for critical reflection on one's identity and ideology develops. There is an explicit conceptual system of meanings. A great many people remain at this stage within their religious institution. It is also characteristic of the educated secular classes, which have abandoned traditional theological symbols but not speculation about meaning and ethics, or commitment to love of neighbor.

When the transition to Stage 5 occurs, it is precipitated by "disillusionment with one's compromises and recognition that life is more complex than Stage 4's logic of clear distinctions and abstract concepts can comprehend." Stage 5 is *Conjunctive,* using a "both/and" way of thinking rather than Stage 4's "either/or." It is characterized by what Ricoeur calls "second naïveté," in which "symbolic power is reunited with conceptual meaning." It is at home with paradox, with truth in contradictions, able to unify the opposites in mind and experience. It is open to the strange truths of others. Reaching this stage is unusual before midlife.

Stage 6 is very rare. Fowler describes it thus: "Their sense of an ultimate environment is inclusive of all being . . . . [They are] living with felt participation in a power that unifies and transforms the world . . . their community is universal. Life is both loved and held loosely. Such persons are ready for fellowship with persons at any of the other stages and from any other faith tradition." He cites Gandhi, Martin Luther King, Mother Teresa, Abraham Heschel, and others as representative of this stage. Fowler is at considerable pains to insist that, from the religious point of view, no stage is closer to God than any other. But from the human point of view it is highly desirable that fanatics in the earlier stages not assume positions of power over others. The Ayatollah Khomeini and Jim Jones both make that clear (with superimposed psychosis in the latter case).

Some religions seem tailor-made for certain stages of faith development. Fundamentalist denominations and sects favor Stages 2 and 3, and from their vantage points persons in later stages are likely to be perceived as heretics. Mainline Churches accommodate a wider range of stages because their leaders, in most cases, are at least at Stage 4. Most forms of Judaism strongly facilitate development to Stage 4 or beyond. Certain smaller but very influential groups, such as the Quakers, attract persons who are able to reach Stage 5 or Stage 6.

Another factor is psychological type, according to Jung's description and as measured by the Myers/Briggs test. This factor assesses the relative strengths of introversion and extraversion and the four basic functions of thinking, feeling, intuition, and sensing. Preliminary research suggests that the types are not randomly distributed throughout the various denominations, especially not among the clergy.[9] Roman Catholicism is far more protean in its manifestations than any Protestant denomination, and so all psychological types and faith stages are likely to be found there.

Thus we see that *all* persons have at least a rudimentary religion, though it may be unhelpful or otherwise unsatisfactory. The poet e.e. cummings said, "Not to decide is to decide." Those who refuse *all* decisions end up as catatonic schizophrenics—ironically, a drastic decision. In a parallel way, not to believe is a form of belief. Those who refuse *all* religious belief, not only the standard formulations of theology but their consequences for conduct in the human community, suffer from spiritual pathology because they are trying to deny a basic human instinct. Nobody can succeed at this rejection entirely, since there is always an image of deity he or she daily rejects, and to abandon religion absolutely entails the abandonment of one's fellow creatures as well. Those who travel very far along such a path are recognizably sick even by secular standards and are generally considered untreatable. Pastoral care may have more to offer in such cases, since no one is beyond salvation. And by pastoral care I do not mean the modern, truncated "mini-shrink" version but the original, faith-based search for the lost sheep.

Both psychotherapists and clergy could be more effective than they usually are if the universality of the religious function and the factors that affect the form it takes in particular people were more fully appreciated. Almost no psychiatrists systematically inquire about the religious life of their patients. Rizzuto believes it is unfortunate that psychiatrists in their own analyses (and therefore in that of their patients) do not deal with the nature and significance of their own God-representation, whether they believe in it or not. This unanalyzed but very important part of the psyche may lead to blind spots, especially to the failure to deal adequately with the religious and moral dimensions of their patients' lives. In extreme cases, psychiatrists' own committed secularity may lead them to view any upsurge of overt religious interest on the part of their patients as manifestations of neurosis requiring further analysis.

Rizzuto includes in her book a questionnaire for taking a religious history. She has designed it for psychiatric use, but it could be adapted by clergy, particularly pastoral counselors and spiritual directors, when a sophisticated understanding of a person's beliefs is required. Pastoral interventions could then be more closely tailored to the seeker's actual needs, including many that may not be fully conscious but could be helpfully elucidated by the appropriate use of Rizzuto's work (and that of Fowler). In addition, pastoral counselors are equipped, as psychiatrists almost never are, to distinguish normal from pathological religious ideation. But there are still further challenges. In her review of Rizzuto's book, Ann Ulanov says pastoral counseling

> possesses the equipment to examine God-images both theologically and clinically. In this way, Pastoral Counseling might finally come into its own secure professional identity, no longer aping therapeutic or medical models. Indeed, one of the reasons Pastoral Counseling as a profession has kept its identity a bit blurry has to do with the great impact on theology such analytic clarity would exert. Theology would have to pay more attention to the connecting links between personal, idiosyncratic God-representations that are alive, and the living stream of official doctrine and dogma . . . . For many—both clergy and laypeople—official religion is failing. It is not alive . . . . Rizzuto gives us data to see what that failure of religion is—the loss of connection between the official and the living God.[10]

The Problem of Science

Psychiatry has felt superior to religion, believing the latter to be at least unscientific, if not actually a manifestation of neurosis. Religious professionals, on the other hand, have generally felt themselves to be either above or beneath science. Pastoral counselors who believe they are above science draw on psychiatric theory and technique in a selective and haphazard way that usually makes no sense and often makes mischief. Those who have capitulated to science are frequently credulous and sycophantic in their approach to psychiatry, and even if they avoid that pitfall they may inappropriately abandon their specifically pastoral function.[11]

But psychiatry is not—as it generally considers itself—a science but, along with religion, a metaphysical system. Recently Burra has reminded us that the distinction between science and nonscience is a matter of convention. Citing Karl Popper's criterion of falsifiability, he finds that psychoanalysis and the other "talking therapies" fall on the metaphysical side of Popper's line of demarcation. He adds that "all psychotherapy rests importantly on the basis of a mutual agreement between therapist and patient as to how reality is to be construed."[12]

But science and the scientific method are based on something quite different. Christou points out that the matter of science is delineated "by a philosophical act that separates and abstracts reality into mind on the one hand and body on the other; while [that] of the common man is based on no such presupposition but presents itself as a whole that includes much that science and philosophy have seen fit to exclude."[13] The scientific method is designed to deal with those phenomena that either occur spontaneously in nature or can be produced for artificial study in the laboratory. It is essentially a statistical method, one that depends for its efficacy on expressing numerical probabilities. But the whole world of quality cannot be dealt with in this way without doing violence to the material. Science is, therefore, not equipped to deal with ends, but only with the means to those ends. It cannot deal with what *ought* to be, but only with what *is*. Its predictive ability is limited to a more or less reliable assessment of what may happen *if* the system under study continues to operate in the same way. To be sure, when it foresees an undesirable end, its methods can be of help in devising means to reach a different end. But science itself does not clarify the ultimate questions of value, the decisions about which ends we choose. Now scientific method can often be of great help with means, but it cannot tell us anything about ends. Religion is supremely concerned with ends, and with their relation to quality and value. To give an example, psychiatric *technique* (which is to some extent scientific) may be able to assist us in improving a sufferer's capacity to love, but psychiatric *theories* do not deal with ultimate questions of meaning and so cannot tell us anything about why love (especially when it involves self-sacrifice) is in principle desirable.[14]

According to Christou, though "the method of psychological investigation is more or less objective, in the sense that it can be learned and applied by different people, the proof is subjective, in the sense that confirmation of the predictions made on the basis of the method are to a great degree a matter of personal experience." An apt comparison is to religious categories of testimony and witness rather than to scientific proof. This is why so much of the effort to establish the efficacy of psychoanalysis or therapy using research methods is doomed to fail. What actually happens simply cannot be fully studied by such methods. Even to begin to reduce the material to statistically manipulable units, it has to be taken out of its natural context and distorted, and the mesh of the research net is so wide that the most significant things may slip through. Unique psychological events are likely to be overlooked, and the individual will get lost in categories that are much too general to be helpful. That which cannot be measured gets ignored when people are too firmly wedded to the scientific mindset.

Religion, on the other hand, is greatly concerned with unique events, both in our sacred myths and in our pursuit of each individual life journey. It was when religion began to be intimidated by science that it first doubted an important class of unique events—miracles. Until the last decade, most clergy were extremely skeptical of private religious experience. Before then, God help the psychologically normal person who was foolish enough to report having seen a vision! Immediate referral to a psychiatrist was common.

Jerome Frank has written about psychotherapy as the restoration of morale and cites the fact that "any form of psychotherapy yields significantly better results than the so-called spontaneous improvement rate."[15] He points out that the patients who can be described as suffering from lowered morale are the ones who get better in all systems. Syndromes included here are anxiety, depression, and other neuroses in which a prominent symptom is low self-esteem or a feeling of helplessness. In such cases, the experience of guilt is almost invariably an issue, consciously or otherwise. Frank thinks all schools of psychotherapy have some common features responsible for raising the patient's morale, and they are more important than the influence of specific therapies on specific symptoms. Among these common features are the "trusting, confiding, and *emotionally charged* relationship with the therapist." But Frank also includes the rationale, or conceptual scheme, about which he says: "The rationales of Western psychotherapy resemble those of primitive ones in that they are not subject of disproof—they cannot be shaken by therapeutic failure." It is not necessary to consider such rationales "primitive," but to do so is a typical Stage 4 outlook.

Nevertheless, what Frank says about psychotherapy is just as true of religion—the continued presence of evil and suffering, not only in the world but in committed members of religious groups, does not invalidate the system. He goes on to say that "the rationale must be convincing to both the patient and the therapist; hence it is linked to the dominant worldview of their culture."

There is no question that the dominant worldview of our culture is scientific. Psychiatry stands with one foot in the medical sciences and the other in the social sciences. I have no quarrel with the medical side, believing it essential to the task of keeping the whole person in view. Doctors, especially psychiatrists, know that mind and body are inextricably linked, each influencing the other. It is rare for symptoms to appear either psychologically or physically isolated, though some may be relatively unimportant. At one level, psychiatrists know that the mind/body split is an artificial construct with no correlate in experience, but they are not consistent about implementing this insight. Because of their wishful misperception of themselves as scientists, many are succumbing to what they call the "re-medicalization of psychiatry," which is partly responsible for the current popularity of drug therapy.

The same theoretical problem surfaces in religion. The mind/body problem is only a subset of the spirit/matter problem central in nearly all theological systems. It was the subject of intense debate in the first four centuries of Christianity and is one issue underlying such theological metaphors as the doctrine of the resurrection of the body as well as the soul, or the insistence that Jesus was fully human as well as fully divine. But Christianity has also been inconsistent here, frequently erring on the side of the superior character or truer reality of spirit. Judaism has not made this error; from the beginning it has insisted that a human being is an indivisible psychophysical unity. This is one significance of the meticulously detailed Jewish law: Every possible activity or relationship has physical *and* spiritual meaning, indivisible one from the other.

The problem lies not with psychiatry's roots in medicine, but with social science. In a recent consultation for university faculty on "Religion and the Intellectual World," Robert Bellah described the situation.[16] He noted that the intellectual assumptions of mainstream social science are derived from seventeenth-century English social thought, particularly as exemplified in Thomas Hobbes's writings, and from the French Enlightenment. The four main assumptions are *positivism, reductionism, relativism,* and *determinism.*

According to *positivism* the methods of science are the only approach to valid knowledge. Psychotherapists do (or should) know better, since the ways in which they and their patients arrive at transforming insights are not exclusively based on this type of knowledge. *Reductionism* explains the complex in terms of the simple, no matter how complex the original. Systems theory is beginning to make a dent in this view, but unfortunately many who espouse systems theory in such fields as family therapy do not realize it is philosophically incompatible with reductionism, which they continue to believe in at other levels. *Relativism* is "the assumption that matters of morality and religion, being explicable by particular constellations of psychological and sociological conditions, cannot be judged true or false, valid or invalid, but simply vary with persons, cultures and societies." Such a view is a heavy contributor to the existential anxiety so characteristic of our times. Finally, *determinism* is the "tendency to think that human actions are explained in terms of [measurable] 'variables' that will account for them."

Bellah contrasts these assumptions with those of religion: "the traditionally religious view found the world intrinsically meaningful. The drama of personal and social existence was lived out in the context of continual cosmic and spiritual meaning. The modern view finds the world intrinsically meaningless, endowed with meaning only by individual actors, and the societies they construct, for their own ends." He then adds, "Most social scientists . . . are largely unaware of the degree to which what they teach and write undermines all traditional thought and belief."

I would go further. I believe this "unawareness" is actually a repression, in the technical sense of the term. I connect it with Fowler's Stage 4, which, you will recall, is a demythologizing stage whose strength is, in the author's words, the "capacity for critical reflection on self and ideology." But Fowler goes on to say that the danger of this stage is "excessive confidence in the conscious mind and in critical thought and a kind of second narcissism in which the now clearly bounded, reflective self overassimilates 'reality' and the perspectives of others into its own world view." A succinct example of this attitude is Freud's famous dictum glorifying rational consciousness: "Where id was, let ego be."

Thus, the Stage 4 mentality does not even see the point of trying to differentiate between various religious manifestations, or to understand them; they are all banished to the realm of irrationality. At best they have peripheral significance.

The historian William Thompson, from the vantage point of his years in the humanities department of M.I.T., described the whole scientific enterprise as a dangerously one-sided runaway development of masculine values.[17]

> Bellah sees the scientific attitude as related to the liberation . . . of the modern ego. It's linked up psychology and metaphysics with the notion of separation of self from world. The 17th century is the time when the distinctness between subjectivity and objectivity appears as a central dimension of modern thought. Psychologically, what is happening is a cultural expression of the liberation of the male from the mother, and the celebration of separateness, of ego-boundary and self-boundary. I'm afraid that conception is linked to a conception of domination, that we are no longer integrated with Nature, Mother Nature, but we stand outside it and control and dominate it.[18]

Yes, but with every passing day we are revealed not as true masters but merely as sorcerer's apprentices.

Ricoeur makes a similar point, saying, "The uncomfortable position of women in the scientific world is in no way a trivial thesis . . . . By uncovering the ideology of 'maleness, research, and prestige' which rules scientific research, we start putting some limits to the claim of this scientific worldview to be unidimensional —precisely as being male dominated."[19] Many women scholars see a primary feminist task to be that of reintroducing the values of context, community, and friendship into an enterprise now dominated by the narrow, overly focused preoccupations of male-dominated research. These values are precisely those associated with the ethical prescriptions of religion, now relegated to the background as not being relevant to the "hard" concerns of the "real world." By "real," obviously, is meant "male."

From this vantage point, Jung's insistence that the upper reaches of male maturity could not be reached without reintegration (rather than repression and projection) of the feminine principle, the *anima,* begins to look more like prophecy than mystification. But in the scientific view, representing as it does a crystallization of masculine values, religion after the Enlightenment gradually came to be perceived by educated, increasingly secular people as a vestigial repository of the nonrational, something soft, for women and children, presided over mainly by men whose own masculinity was seen as at least second-rate. Jung's interest in religious phenomena, taken together with his insistence that women cannot be understood in terms of a univocal model of humanity based on the male, led to his devaluation in the eyes of the psychiatric community, usually on the grounds that he was not sufficiently scientific. Now, however, the cracks in the foundations of science as a sufficient philosophy, rather than merely a useful method to study some (but not all) things, are beginning to be obvious, and many intellectually respectable voices are raising questions. Those questions are often the very same ones Jung raised forty and more years ago, but most contemporary writers seem to be unaware of that fact.

The Problem of Evil

Until the development of depth psychology less than a hundred years ago, all human behavior was evaluated in moral terms. Attempts were made to convict people of their sins, to induce remorse and repentance, which was then expected to result in changed lives. Failures of this process were attributed to more sin. As we all know, this approach frequently did not work; in fact, it often made matters worse. That it was not Our Lord's way of dealing with human failings was inexplicably overlooked.

Both psychiatry and pastoral care are concerned with facilitating the personal development of individuals and their adaptation to human community. Both do so via the problem of evil and suffering. But it is precisely here that it is urgent for pastoral counselors to relinquish the uncritical way in which most of them now appropriate psychiatric material.

The difficulty stems from the fact that in our culture the concept of sickness has been substituted for that of sin, and health has replaced virtue. But human nature has not changed, even though our vocabulary has. Nor has our basic attitude to human error, as witnessed by the modern expression of disgust, "That's sick!" which is identical to the old expression, "That's wicked!" The concept of mental and emotional illness should instead have been used to illuminate some of the ways by which we avoid sin, and to bring mercy and understanding to the ancient devices of confession and penance. And it should always have been understood that health results from grace, not virtue.

The old ways of thinking and talking about sin are largely responsible for the fact that modern pastoral counseling has in practice capitulated to this substitution. Judgment had frequently come to be seen as an end in itself; it had deteriorated from being true *judgment* to being merely *judgmental*. Still, we must not forget that there are many people who experience a trusted authority calling their behavior sinful as a real relief. This is because they know that, at least in their own case, the attempt to deal with the problem in psychological terms exclusively is beside the point, if not, as in some instances, dangerous nonsense. Recalling the intimate connection between salvation and healing, we may say that true judgment corresponds exactly to medical diagnosis. The doctor does not tell a patient, "You have pneumonia," and then walk out of the room. Instead, a course of treatment is suggested. In the same way, religious judgment should be propadeutic to a course of spiritual treatment. Judgment is not an end in itself, any more than diagnosis is.

Every psychiatric theory has two important components— philosophical and instrumental. There is an underlying anthropology, view of the nature of evil, and an attitude to teleology and to transcendence. They are often unstated and not infrequently seem to be unexamined (even by the author of the theory). Resting on, if not actually derived from, this base, there is also a more or less elaborate technique for effecting psychological change in the patient. (It is in this technique, and in the systems for classifying disorders, that psychiatry uses various scientific methods, without, as stated before, being intrinsically a science.) Some of the underlying philosophies are radically unchristian—even, one might say, radically opposed to *any* genuinely religious outlook. Eric Berne's "transactional analysis" is a case in point, as Robert Coles remarked in his *New York Times* review of Berne's popular book *Games People Play*. The Christian message is *not* "I'm OK, you're OK," but "I'm not OK, you're not OK, but that can be OK."

Psychiatric technique, as distinct from psychiatric theory, does have something to offer. It recognizes that everyone who has a problem serious enough to require sustained intervention is frightened. The sufferer is aware of symptoms, but the conflicts and complexes underlying those symptoms are largely unconscious, precisely because to admit them to consciousness would provoke too much anxiety. This is because the patient does not know what to do about the real problem; he or she has repressed it in order not to feel utterly helpless. But the urge to recover is also strong, and it produces symptoms as an attention-getting device. Jung expressed this by pointing out that every neurosis is a substitute for legitimate suffering. Therefore, even when the therapist is quite sure of the diagnosis, it is bad technique to convey it immediately and directly to the subject. The patient will not get better just because the *therapist* knows what is wrong; the *patient* must know it—and not just intellectually—or change cannot take place. It takes considerable building of trust, and sustained, gentle patience, to bring the sufferer to this point.

When pastoral theology was limited to the old religious categories, such factors were largely unappreciated. There was much talk about the will, and the failures of will were perceived as sin. This approach was far too intellectual, for it was ignorant of unconscious processes. It was therefore quite likely to increase rather than decrease the sufferer's burden. Just as doctors may withhold diagnosis from a patient in the interest of effective therapy, the sophisticated pastoral care-giver (whether specially trained in pastoral counseling or not) will often need to soften or withhold religious judgments temporarily if real *metanoia* is to occur. Pastoral care has learned this lesson, and those trained in it are most unlikely to repeat the old mistakes.

Many pastoral counselors, dazzled by the apparent simplicity and short-range efficacy of some psychotherapeutic techniques, do not realize that these techniques are in part (if not totally) contaminated by the antireligious base on which they rest. Counseling, therefore, often runs directly counter to the counselors' original vocation to ministry, leading to trouble not only in their dealings with their counselees but in their own spiritual lives. The following is just one of many examples I could cite. At the end of a year's Clinical Pastoral Education (CPE) training, a woman's supervisor asked about her immediate plans. She replied that she was going to a convent for a retreat. The supervisor got extremely angry, accused her of being absolutely determined not to learn the lessons of CPE, adding that prayer was nothing but mental masturbation, and he hadn't done it in years. We may presume that his belief in his understanding of psychological theory as a ''scientific'' system, and his uncritical acceptance of its underlying philosophy, had contributed to this sinful attitude.

It was not until some years after World War II, when the numinously awful story of the Holocaust was revealed and the specter of nuclear destruction began to loom over us, that it became impossible even for relentless secularists to hold (without major self-deception) that science might yet solve the problem of evil. But thirty years ago there were high hopes, especially that the insights of psychiatry, combined with modern educational and mental health efforts, could have a measurable effect. We are now forced to recognize that, if anything, things are worse. Psychiatry, having succumbed to empirical science and materialistic rationalism, operates from deficient premises. Pattison describes its outlook thus:

> There is no sin or evil in the world—only more or less adaptive behavior. Maladaptive behavior is primitive, adaptive behavior is mature. Health is homeostatic adaptation that promotes survival. Psychoanalysis in general has been a major legatee as well as promoter of this naturalistic image of Man.[20]

Freud himself was troubled by evil, and he was both an idealist and a realistic pessimist. His followers have stressed the idealism and so have virtually abandoned his death-instinct theory. And yet, out of their own experience, psychiatrists ought to have a more realistic picture of humanity. They talk about primary narcissism as the basic condition to the infant that must be outgrown if severe pathology is to be avoided. They also aver that all of us retain some of it, if only in isolated pockets of our personalities. I do not see that anything has been gained by substituting a concept of original pathology for original sin, especially when the underlying philosophical assumptions make it reasonable for people to ask on what grounds it is proposed that they take the trouble to grow up. (Norman O. Brown is perhaps the most sophisticated proponent of the "why grow up?" school, but the idea is now abroad in our culture.) The substitution is particularly unfortunate since the analytic ritual of absolution through the transference-produced surrogate parenthood of the analyst is not accessible to everyone. But forgiveness by grace of the God-parent is. This point stands, even without considering the efficacy of the respective methods.[21]

Bellah says that the social-science portrait of Man is taken from

Hobbes's *Leviathan,* which shows the atomistic individual who loves and seeks self only. This view is identical with the picture of natural, unredeemed Man in St. Augustine's treatise *The City of God.* Bellah quotes de Tocqueville, who, more than a hundred years ago, expressed the fear that "a society of such isolated self-regarding individuals would be unable to sustain free institutions and would fall victim to despotism." He thought religion or secularized mores might avert that disaster.

Such a view is echoed by Jung, who asserts that people need a reference point outside the self and transcending the human plane in order to avoid being at the mercy of the collective, the State, or other tyrannical authority. He says:

> It is possible to have an attitude to the external conditions of life only when there is a point of reference outside them. The religions give, or claim to give, such a standpoint, thereby enabling the individual to exercise his judgment and power of decision.[22]

But this has to be a real religion, not just a nominal creed, by which he meant religion at the service of the state. He adds that mere intellectual perception of the threat is no help; "it lacks the driving force of religious conviction, since it is merely rational." He enumerates at some length the parallels between religion and the claims of totalitarian states, which he explains in these words:

> . . . a natural function which has existed from the beginning, like the religious function, cannot be disposed of with rationalistic and so-called enlightened criticism. You can, of course, represent the doctrinal contents of the creeds as impossible and subject them to ridicule, but such methods miss the point and do not hit the religious *function* which forms the basis of the creeds. Religion, in the sense of conscientious regard for the irrational factors of the psyche and individual fate, reappears—evilly distorted—in the deification of the state and the dictator: *Naturam expellas furca tamen usque recurret*[23] . . . . As can easily be seen, 'community' is an indispensable aid in the organization of masses and is therefore a two-edged weapon. Just as the addition of however many zeros will never make a unit, so the value of a community depends on the spiritual and moral stature of the individuals composing it.

Sartre discusses the same issue from the other side:

> The existentialist is strongly opposed to a certain kind of secular ethics which would like to abolish God with the least possible expense . . . .

> The existentialist, on the contrary, thinks it very distressing that God does not exist, because all possibility of finding values in a heaven of ideas disappears along with Him: there can no longer be an *a priori* Good, since there is no infinite and perfect consciousness to think it . . . . Indeed, everything is permissible if God does not exist, and as a result man is forlorn, because neither within him nor without does he find anything to cling to . . . . I find myself suddenly alone, without help, engaged in a world for which I bear the whole responsibility.[24]

By inference this passage shows that the problem of evil does not exist in isolation but is linked to the problem of good. Good is generally taken for granted, and we are willing to own, even to claim it. Evil is something we prefer to deny or repudiate, seldom finding the courage to acknowledge our evil acts. From the formal point of view, however, the existence of good is just as mysterious as that of evil. Good is probably accepted because it is so central to human community, whereas evil disrupts it. But any satisfactory theory of evil must order good and evil together. Some psychiatric schools deny individual failure, claiming people are innately good and are deformed by society only. This just puts the original pathology in a different place—out in the world rather than in each person. Such ideas are illogical because society is precipitated out of the consciousness of persons and has no autonomous existence. To claim otherwise is the first step toward totalitarianism or other forms of mass-mindedness. Whatever good and evil may ultimately be, they are found *together* and cannot be successfully dealt with apart from one another. The extreme Calvinists who emphasized the idea of "total depravity" made the same mistake in religious terms, and we are still suffering from the aftereffects. Each of these mistakes makes it harder than it need be, and God knows it is hard enough, to deal with evil.

The Problem of Guilt

Closely connected with the theoretical problem of evil is the practical problem of guilt, which is extremely important for pastoral care. As mentioned earlier, feelings of guilt are always present in people who present themselves—whether to clergy or to psychotherapists—for care. These feelings may not be conscious, but sooner or later during treatment they come to the surface and must be dealt with. Therefore, it is crucial *for both professions* to have a clear grasp of the distinction between *real* and *neurotic* guilt. Psychiatrists tend to see people whose guilt is largely neurotic, that is to say, guilt either inappropriate to the putative offense or out of proportion to its actual gravity. Theologians have known about this kind of guilt for centuries, referring to it as "scrupulosity." It is true, however, that their understanding of it was defective and their methods of dealing with it inadequate.

The psychiatric focus on neurotic guilt has led in many quarters to the mistaken notion that all guilt is bad and to be gotten rid of. One of the most frequently heard criticisms of religion is that it promotes guilt. Now, even in religious circles, people are likely to respond to any accusation of wrongdoing by saying, "Don't lay a guilt-trip on me." Self-examination followed by restitution would all too often be a more appropriate response. And yet, the Nuremberg trials and the Eichmann trial were the attempts of an outraged civilization to deal with people who did not feel guilt when they should have. Elsewhere I have dealt at greater length with this question, attempting to show that the real issue is not guilt but responsibility.[25] Feelings of guilt are only a signal that something is wrong, either emotionally or spiritually (sometimes both), in the same way that fever is a signal the body is sick. Fever itself is not the disease. Such diverse authors as Jung, C. S. Lewis, and Hillman have demonstrated that the fundamental construction of the psyche includes the capacity to feel guilty and that it is anterior to the development of the moral code.

Freud thought deviant acts were "the product of the great human capacity for choice and so ultimately have a moral quality."[26] Many contemporary theorists repudiate this view in an effort to undermine the idea that people are responsible for their behavior. Religion is under attack for precisely the same reason. But the issue of responsibility is ultimately metaphysical, not scientific. The mechanics of how people experience and carry out responsibility can certainly be studied scientifically, but the nature and extent of responsibility itself cannot; it belongs in the realm of values. Science can tell us nothing about the base on which values rest. Only religion has the capacity to do so, even though it often fails.

Religion knows far better than psychiatry about how to deal with *real* guilt. Furthermore, when properly understood and applied (as they increasingly are), these techniques can be enormously helpful in preventing real guilt from festering in the psyche and developing damaging (to self and others) neurotic over-lays. In his monograph "Transformation Symbolism in the Mass," Jung points out that confession is central. He believes that the Mass is the rite *par excellence* of the "individuation process" (progress to full consciousness and maturity), since one cannot change that which one does not acknowledge as being part of oneself. In the confession, sins are first acknowledged, then sacrificed (entirely given up) on the altar.[27] Following closely on confession is forgiveness—by God, of others, and of self—the three inextricably linked, as shown in the Lord's Prayer.

The Problem of Ritual and Symbolic Language

Ricoeur discusses contemporary language theory which holds that religious language is meaningless because it is not falsifiable. This view relates to Popper's criterion (cited earlier) for the distinction between science and nonscience, but it also rests on the assumption that nonscience is ultimately meaningless. Ricoeur disputes this view, defending "natural language." He quotes the German linguist von Humboldt's definition of language as "an infinite use of finite means." Religious language, he says, belongs to the sphere of natural language, and its strength lies in that all its terms are polysemic, i.e., for every sign there is more than one meaning. "The strength of a polysemic language resides in its sensibility to contexts." he remarks.

Psychotherapists spend their time deciphering just this kind of language, as well as using it themselves. Rarely is their task to help patients express themselves logically, either in thought or action; most often it is to help them see the multivalence of the language in which they have described their troubles. This is because the symptoms covertly *express* those aspects of the patient's meanings that have been *repressed.* Thus, patients suffer from a univocal interpretation of their own formulations, since, when fully understood, the language they use may also contain the creative possibilities for improvement. As Ricoeur puts it, "indeterminacy and creative power appear to be wholly in-separable." When patients can be brought to see the indeterminacy of their statements, their creative and healing potential can be unleashed and new directions chosen for their lives.

Symbolic religious language operates on precisely the same principle. To be sure, religious language can be neurotically (and sinfully) restricted to a unidimensional or literal meaning, but that inhibits its correct use and is a perversion of the original intent. Interestingly enough, the fundamentalist theologies can be shown to be the bastard child of religion and science, representing the interpretation of symbolic, contextual religious statements as though they were unidimensional, scientific ones. In Urban Holmes's words, "Biblical literalism may be the only new heresy."[28]

Metaphor, according to Ricoeur, "is one of the strategies thanks to which language is compelled to transgress its previous limits, and become able to bring to language the not yet said." Psychiatrists, in their eagerness to be scientific, have often not appreciated that the language of all psychoanalytic systems, following Freud's example, rests chiefly on a base of metaphor and mythology—myths being, among other things, very extended metaphors.

Rituals are also important. In religion they offer the possibility of forming (in Ulanov's words, quoted earlier) a "connection between the official and the living God." Putting the same idea another way, they can be understood as a participatory psychodrama that provides the believer with a fuller appreciation of dogma than can be gained by mere theoretical exposition of it. In Jung's words,

> dogma expresses an irrational whole by means of imagery. This guarantees a far better rendering of an irrational fact like the psyche . . . . Any sacral action, in whatever form, works like a vessel for receiving the contents of the unconscious.[29]

This kind of symbol, in the words of dogma or the action of ritual, makes it possible for people to deal with conflicting feelings and other ambivalences without having to stuff some of them still deeper into the unconscious, unacknowledged and therefore unattended to. Perhaps even more important is that this process can work *even when the participant does not articulate what happened.* The evidence for the effectiveness of this process lies in improved attitudes and changed lives.

At least in the diluted form of prescribed ceremony, psycho-therapists also make use of ritual. The use of the analytic couch and the rigid exclusion of any self-disclosure by the analyst serve this purpose. These rituals are designed to facilitate the emergence of the patient's unconscious contents. (Whether or not, without other undesirable side-effects, they actually accomplish that purpose as often as claimed is another issue.)

Mutual understanding between the two disciplines would be greatly enhanced if the similarities in their use of semiotic language, metaphor, mythology, and ritual were fully appreciated. The next important step would be for both sides to recognize that religious use of these devices covers far more territory than does that of psychiatry. Psychiatry is concerned only with the re-orientation of sufferers to their immediate inner and outer circumstances. Religion, as stated earlier, is concerned with orientation to all that is, including the Unknowable. Thus for religion, psychiatry can be a good servant but a bad master. But religion must not forget that without intelligent and appropriate use of that servant, its house is likely to be in some disorder.

The Problem of the Individual's Relation to the Community

The central human problem may be to find a balance between the needs, rights, privileges, and duties of the individual on the one hand, and the needs, rights, privileges, and duties of the community on the other. American culture is pathologically over-balanced in favor of the individual. Other cultures (Russian and Chinese, to give only the most outstanding examples) are overbalanced in favor of the community.

Few secular models of care *in the West* (as distinct from Japan, as well as Russia and China) consider anything beyond the sufferer's immediate social context. In extreme instances this is perceived only as the family of origin, but few therapists nowadays continue to operate under this impractical limitation. The *natural* community itself is seldom seen as a therapeutic adjunct. In group or milieu therapy the patient is extracted from the natural com-munity and dealt with in an *artificial* community of other sufferers. This is one reason why the attempt to empty the mental hospitals and return patients to the community has failed. It also expresses the paradox that the most individualistic of all cultures (ours) is the one least able to assimilate deviants from its (usually unstated) norms. The Chinese-American anthropologist Francis L. K. Hsu says, "Individualist man is . . . moved by the constant pressure of lack of human intimacy." He believes that in the West "psychosocial homeostasis" (PSH) is inordinately difficult, and relates this problem to psychotherapy as follows:

> Without intending to disparage Freud and psychoanalysis (I have learned much from them), I see psychoanalysis as one way for the individual man to achieve and maintain his PSH. It compensates for his lack of intimacy with humans in less artificial circumstances, in conditions under which he can be off guard, dare to reveal his worst without the fear of rejection, and receive help and sympathy without accepting 'charity.' Regrettably it is a relationship for which he must pay and which, from the point of view of the analyst, is marked by role and not affect; consequently it is an asymmetrical relationship.[30]

He goes on to include T-Groups, Esalen, and related phenomena in his indictment.

When psychotherapists do pay attention to the community of which the sufferer is a member, they are frequently uncritical, and they often see their task as helping the patient "adjust" to that community. They seldom consider that the community itself may be an important contributor to the sufferer's apparently individual problem. They are therefore unable to understand reformers, especially not when these patients are overwhelmed with the magnitude of the problem that distresses them. They also have trouble understanding those who are socially disadvantaged. The inability of psychotherapy (as distinct from somatic—especially drug—therapies) to deal with sufferers from the lower classes is notorious.

Gregory Baum, in a lecture addressed to the National Guild of Catholic Psychiatrists in Canada, said:

> *Ignorance of the social causes of present suffering has dangerous social consequences . . . .* People who are not excluded from basic material resources or from the symbols of public respect easily think of their life as a personal journey. What they seek is personal growth, maturity, fulfillment, and inner richness. Does this mean then that psychiatry and psychotherapy in general, aiming as they do to enhance people's self-realization, embody—unbeknownst to themselves—a middle-class political perspective?[31]

There are now some psychiatrists who are concerned about large social issues, and their efforts deserve our admiration and support. Most notable is the organization called Physicians for Social Responsibility, many of whose most articulate spokesmen are psychiatrists. But the issue that has engaged them is the specter of nuclear war. Their attention has been caught, and their energies mobilized, by something that threatens *all* classes.

There are a few, but only a few, exceptions to this narrowed focus. The most notable is Robert Coles, who for thirty years has been working with, and writing about, those who have been traditionally excluded from "the American dream." It is no accident that he is a deeply religious man.

At least as an ideal, Christianity holds that the entire human family constitutes the community. Without such an ideal, no such thing as foreign missions would ever have been conceived. For the Christian, the ideal community is symbolized in such images as the Kingdom of Heaven, the New Jerusalem, or the Communion of the Saints. It extends not only through space but through time. Further, each person has some responsibility for the whole of that community. Of course, these ideal views are all too often more honored in the breach than in the observance, but they still exist. Baum describes the implementation of the ideal as follows:

> Christian theology distinguishes clearly between self-realization and self-centeredness. Since the center of Man is outside of himself (the expression is Rahner's), the closer we come to self-realization and self-possession, the more we are able to love other people, serve the society to which we belong, and open ourselves to the divine mystery. If self-realization is understood in this manner, then it comes very close to what we have meant by the subject character of human being.

Most psychiatrists do not consider the patient's relation to the wider community, except superficially, because to do so necessarily involves values. Therefore, they only take into account that truncated community which consists of the family of origin (and its social milieu) and those with whom the patient preferentially relates *now* (or in whose midst he or she is forced to live or function). Without that limitation, psychotherapists would have to deal with "what ought to be," not just "what is." They can deal somewhat better with members of oppressed minorities *after* they have managed to form political pressure groups. These people are then no longer perceived as dysfunctional losers but as applicants for inclusion in the mainstream of the middle class. The problem can then be conceptualized in culturally acceptable terms such as the guarantee of individual rights, "without regard to race, creed, or color." It thereby becomes part of "what is." A social-science assumption enters here also. If enough people are doing or saying something, then it must have merit. This is the (notoriously unsatisfactory) statistical approach to morality.

Psychiatry has a much harder time dealing with the *individual* who is a genuine reformer and sees a new problem, the solution to which requires what Christians would call a "prophetic stance." This is linked with the obverse problem, dealing with *individual* members of oppressed minorities who have not formed a politically effective pressure group but are nonetheless victims of social forces. There are some exceptions, of course, but usually not until the psychiatrist in question has achieved professional "Grand Old Man" status. Karl Menninger can talk in that vein—he can even talk about sin!—but the new resident cannot do so without being accused of "acting out with the patient." R. D. Laing is an important exception to this attitude, but I do not think it irrelevant that he is the product of a stern Scots Presbyterian upbringing. I believe that is why he was able to deal with such issues even as a young man, but it also helps explain why he was considered such a maverick. Now he is reaching "Grand Old Man" status and is well listened to.

In his concept of the *collective unconscious,* Jung expressed his belief in the essential totality of the human community (past, present, and future). His evidence and his formulation are psychological, but the same underlying idea can be put theologically; "Who is our neighbor? Every human being who has ever lived, is living now, or who will live in the future." It is significant that this concept is a crucial reason why Jung's views were rejected, often with considerable virulence, by Western psychiatry.

Conclusion

Jung once said that at bottom every neurosis is a moral problem. This brings us full circle to the relation between sin and sickness, which has yet to be fully explored.[32] But it is obviously a crucial problem for those who believe that salvation and healing may be congruent, and surely overlap. The opinion that the psyche can be ultimately dealt with apart from its religious component is mistaken, as Jung knew over fifty years ago. Not everyone will want to pursue the increasingly apparent connection through Jungian categories, but of course that is not necessary; there are, and always have been, many paths to truth.

Robert Neale, with whose words I began this chapter, says that "healing is not just enhancement of being, but the discovery that we live between the promise and the reality of salvation." Religion and psychiatry have much to contribute to each other, if they can learn to relate in truly complementary ways. Only thus can we do the best for those in our case—which includes ourselves. "Healing and humility make good companions."

4

Theology and Pastoral Care

James E. Griffiss

In this chapter I want to explore several dimensions of the relationship between how we who are Christians express our faith in God and how we hope to care for one another and for other people. I shall do that first by looking at some of the ways we have of talking about pastoral care; then I shall discuss several methods of pastoral care and suggest how they might deepen our understanding of what we are doing when we care for one another as Christians. Finally, by examining some biblical and theological themes I shall hope to show how those several models can be integrated with one another in the pastoral life of the Church, especially in terms of our spirituality and our understanding of the Christian life.

The main focus of the discussion will be provided by two considerations: first, by the emphasis Anglicanism has frequently placed on pastoral care as the chief function of the ministry; and second, by an incarnational and sacramental understanding of the Christian life as it has developed in the Anglican theological tradition. It is certainly true that those two considerations are neither exclusive to Anglicanism, nor are they the only considerations to have guided Anglican clergy and lay people in the pastoral care of others. They have, however, characterized one understanding of the pastoral ministry that developed historically from the Caroline divines and the Catholic Revival in England and the United States in the nineteenth century; and, I believe, those considerations are still valuable for us in the latter part of the twentieth century, even though we face new problems and have new resources for the exercise of pastoral ministry. They are still valuable because pastoral care must be grounded in what we believe about God and our fellow human beings; it must be pre-eminently *theo*logical. Hence the reaching out of God to us in the Incarnation and his indwelling presence in human life by the Spirit ought always to be the doctrinal context for speaking of God's care for us and our care for one another.

I

Caring is an ordinary human activity; human beings care for one another and for the world in which they live. We also fail to care for one another and our world. The ways in which we care have taken many forms; they are reflected in the biblical tradition as well as in literature derived from a variety of religious and nonreligious sources. We also care for the tradition and the memory of human history, of which we are the custodians. We care for it by remembering it and by passing it along through language, myths, symbols, and stories. In recent years we have become more conscious of caring for our world, which, according to many religious traditions, was committed to the care of human beings. Our caring for the world or our failure to do so has become a major concern because of our increased awareness of the environment, provoked by our misuse and exploitation of the things of nature and by our new concern for animals, especially as they are more and more subject to profiteering and experimentation. Also, because of the threat of nuclear holocaust we have become conscious in a new way of the necessity to care for the future of this planet and of civilization, not to destroy what we have been given from the past, in order that we may pass it on to future generations. Caring is characteristic of what it is to be human, just as our failure to care is that denial of our humanity which the Christian tradition calls *sin*. As far as we know (although some of us might want to include those animals that have closely associated themselves with human beings), human beings are the only members of the created order who *intentionally* care for others and who would regard the failure to care as a fault.

Because caring is fundamental to our humanity, it would be helpful to look first at the nature of caring itself before attempting to say anything about the particular kind of caring we who are Christians call *pastoral care*. What do we mean when we speak of caring for something or for someone else?

I have found helpful an image used by Henri Nouwen, who speaks of care in terms of reaching out to others.[1] To reach out to others and to care for them in some way we must, he says, develop an inner space, a quiet place in ourselves, where we can be hospitable and welcoming. Caring means protecting or being the custodian of another, not by enclosing it or locking it away but by making a larger space for it. The custodian of a painting, for example, cares for it by making it available to others so they can see and appreciate it. Custodians of museums must occasionally lock away a painting, but the impulse of a good curator is to show a painting in the larger space of a gallery. Good custodians or curators want to share with others; they must be the kind of people who are generous with possessions and hospitable to others so they also can enjoy what is being cared for. They must love the things they care for.

So also caring for another person is a form of love because it allows for freedom within oneself and for those for whom we care. When we care for another person we want to allow that person to grow and to be shared with others. Our caring, then, is both a welcoming into ourselves and a sending forth. That is why I find the image of reaching out and hospitality so helpful. The hospitable person is one who welcomes another out of love and concern in order that the person may in turn be hospitable to others, just as a painting must be welcomed and shared. To be a caring person is to be one who reaches out and who allows another person to enter in. Thus, caring has a double dimension. We care for others by welcoming who they are now, what has made them who they are, their past, in other words; but we also want to enable them to become something more than they now are—to become people who can, in turn, care for others by sharing with them.

The opposite of caring is holding on, smothering, keeping a

person to oneself, using another person to reinforce oneself—
what the Christian tradition has called lust and concupiscence:
making oneself an idol to be worshipped by others. If we care
for ourselves in the wrong way we shall care for others in a similar
manner. That is, if we do not have in ourselves the quiet place
where we can be hospitable and welcoming to another, then we
shall either refuse hospitality or lock the door behind the person
who comes into our lives. Therein lies the meaning of a common
description we make of certain people: "He cares only for himself." To care only for ourselves—and all of us are such people
much of the time—is to substitute fear, control, and rejection for
caring.

Another image for caring that can be helpful is that of being
aware of something or someone. While riding in a crowded train
or bus I have often thought about the relationship between caring
and awareness. In a crowd I can be aware of other people in
several ways: as a possible threat to my life, which is a reaction
of fear; as an inconvenience when they push against me, which
is annoyance; and merely as other bodies, which is indifference.
But there can also be those rare occasions when I am aware of
someone as a person for whom I care or could care or ought to
care—an elderly person or one who is ill, or one who seems
attractive and interesting. Usually, in a crowd, awareness of
another person offers no opportunity for caring, but in other
situations, to become aware of someone creates the possibility for
caring. Awareness can lead to caring; unawareness is the opposite
of caring. So also is forgetting. To be unaware of a person or
to forget him or her is the opposite of caring because it means
I am refusing to welcome another; I am choosing not to reach
out or to remember or hope for another. To be unaware is to
refuse to offer myself to another person because he or she is only
an object for which I have no concern except as it may be an
annoyance, a threat, or an inconvenience. In a similar way, as
I shall discuss more fully later, being unaware of the past or the
future can also be a refusal to care for them, and so it can lead
a person to become isolated in a hopeless present.

Caring, I believe we can say, has to do with the kind of people
we are, not just with the techniques we may use to care. Nowadays
this is a criticism frequently made of the "caring professions"
(medicine and nursing, for example): All the techniques are there,
but no persons have the concern to care. It is also a criticism that

has frequently been addressed to the ordained clergy when they have put too simple a trust in techniques but have not developed in themselves that kind of hospitality, reaching out, and awareness which can only be found through the life in the Spirit.[2]

How we care for one another can give us an insight into divine caring, even though, as I shall discuss later in this chapter, for those who identify themselves with a religious tradition, divine caring ought always to form the context in which human caring takes place. Just as it does for human beings, God's caring has to do with who God is and how he is related to the whole created order, and men and women in particular. Classical theology saw that aspect of divine caring quite clearly. Thomas Aquinas, for example, understood God's providence and governance of the world as his care: first, for the whole creation that it might find its end and perfection in him who created it and sustains it in being, since God is the universal guardian of all that is; and second, for the rational creature in a special way, namely, in the exercise of human freedom through grace. God's care toward creation has, for Aquinas, three components: the beginning of all things in God, their end in him, and the exercise of graceful freedom in men and women. "Since, therefore, the providence of God is nothing other than the notion of the order of things towards an end . . . it necessarily follows that all things, inasmuch as they participate in being, must to that extent be subject to divine providence."[3]

Aquinas read his Bible differently than we do, but he and many others before and after him were able to find sufficient material in the history of salvation that runs through creation, redemption, and sanctification to justify such a point of view. Whether it is still a viable point of view or, perhaps, viable in a different way is a subject to which I shall return. But his insight is of fundamental importance for our understanding of divine caring: Caring has to do with who God is as creator, redeemer, and sanctifier.

II

Anglicans, along with other Christian communities, usually speak of *pastoral* care in terms of the ordained ministry of the Church. *Pastoral,* however, is a very ambiguous word, so we shall need to ask what meaning it adds to the way in which we care. A *pastor* is, of course, one who cares for sheep, but the sheep for whom a real shepherd cares are notoriously stupid animals who wander about aimlessly and frequently get lost. One of my students spent some time as a real shepherd, and from him I have learned that sheep can be cantankerous in many ways and that the shepherd's staff frequently has to function as a weapon against a belligerent ram. The pictures we have all seen of Jesus carrying a lamb on his shoulders may not convey the clearest image of what it means to be a pastor.

There is a further ambiguity in the word *pastor*. Shepherds are very far removed from ordained clergy. Like their sheep, they are not settled in one place but wander about. They are also both male and female. Certainly they have nothing to do with services of ordination. In the Church we have only begun to move away from the idea that pastoral ministry is limited to ordained persons settled in one place, but we still have far to go before we accept that it can also be done by unordained men and women wandering about with their sheep.

From *pastor* we derive the word *pastoral*. For most people *pastoral* means the rural and simple life, the bucolic vision of peace and tranquility, such as one finds in pastoral poetry, painting, and music. When it is not romanticized, however, by those who only visit the country occasionally, it can also mean hardship, poverty, and the grueling life of the rustic and unlearned peasant or, nowadays, the migrant farm worker. Those who do romanticize the pastoral life frequently contrast it to that of the city, which is wicked, crime ridden, and the source of much vice and corruption; when young men and women want to go astray, they leave the farm and go to the city. On the other hand, the city has frequently been the image of the urbane and sophisticated, the source of civilization and culture. The Judeo-Christian tradition makes use of both images: rural simplicity in contrast to the corruptions of the temple shrines and cities (Amos), but also the Heavenly City, the New Jerusalem, the place where God dwells as in a temple (Revelation). The ambiguity of the word *pastoral,* then, must indeed cause us to pause before we use the term *pastoral care* too quickly. It introduces some questions we ought to consider. What difference would it make in our caring if we were to talk about *urban care?* Would a change of words make a difference in our way of understanding caring itself?

For many in the Church today there is also a problem in the notion of a *parish* ministry. *Parish* is an equally ambiguous word. It connotes, especially for Anglicans, a lingering and nostalgic vision of a cure that is serene, ordered, and peaceful, one in which George Herbert can be the ideal of the country parson, carrying out a ministry to a well-ordered society in which traditions and moral values are respected and the past is remembered with affection. But the reality of parish ministry is often quite different: an urban congregation of many diverse people in a society that is challenging, chaotic, and questioning; a suburban congregation of those who want to forget the past in their frantic search for new values; and even a rural congregation in which sin and violence are not unknown. Do the various situations call for various kinds of pastoral care or for various techniques of caring, or simply for various kinds of people to carry out a pastoral ministry? For those who teach pastoral theology in the Church's seminaries such considerations can give rise to a most perplexing and difficult question: How do you prepare people for pastoral ministry when there are so many ways in which that ministry must be carried out?

But with all the ambiguities and difficulties of the term *pastoral care*, it is deeply embedded in the Christian tradition as a way of talking about ministry, and it is not likely to disappear. Nor, indeed, ought it to disappear, for it is pointing to something of great importance in our understanding of the Church and its relationship to the God who cares for his people.

There are at least two ways of thinking about pastoral care as it has developed in the Church's tradition. One has long been a dominant model. The other is now emerging as an important alternative or addition to the more dominant model, even though it may in fact represent a regaining of earlier ways of understanding how God cares for us and how, therefore, we care for one another. The more dominant model is what I would call a *Constantinian* or *Christendom* model; it has been, and to a considerable degree continues to be, the most customary model for pastoral care in the Episcopal Church and in other major American denominations. The other I would call a *liberation* model; it has begun to emerge in response to the changing ways in which people understand themselves, their society, and their world. It is a temptation to see the two in opposition to one another and to make one or the other prescriptive for pastoral care. I shall suggest, however, that they ought to be seen as complementary. When they are seen in that way, they can give us a clearer perception of how pastoral care can be carried out in the Christian community.

A Constantinian or Christendom model has its theological foundation in the doctrine of the Incarnation as it came to be formulated in the patristic period and in later doctrinal development. The doctrine of the Incarnation is certainly not to be identified with the model itself, but it, along with many other theological and sociological factors, provided a way to interpret and understand the relationship of the created order, and humanity in particular, to God; and it has encouraged a notion of pastoral care in terms of ontology, order, structure, law, and hierarchy. Logos Christology, for example, which was the major contribution of the patristic period to the development of the doctrine of Christ, provided a medium through which the early Church could incorporate the rational tradition of Greek philosophy into its theological understanding of Jesus Christ. Such a Christology required some serious alterations in both the Greek and Jewish doctrines of God, but it also allowed Christians in the milieu of Greek philosophy to interpret the difficult figure of a wandering, crucified Jewish preacher in the categories of Being and reason. The presupposition of Logos Christology is that the created order is now the order of redemption and salvation and that the Christian life is to be understood as the tranquil working out of God's providence through the Spirit in the Church. Augustine and the Reformers, with their emphasis on the radical nature of sin, introduced a *caveat* into an otherwise ordered intelligibility, but it was largely ignored in practice when the Christian community settled back into its routine.[4] The emphasis of the general Catholic tradition in the West has been on the natural order fulfilled and completed by grace, the sacramental structure of the Christian life, and the Church as hierarchically constituted both in its ministry and in its relationship to society at large. All of that development, whatever other sources it may have had, clearly reflected a Constantinian or Christendom view about the relationship of created nature to the divine nature.

As I have said, the model has been the dominant one in the Anglican understanding of pastoral care, even for those who might not accept all its theological presuppositions or who might want to identify themselves more closely with the Reformation. It is reflected in our moral theology and in the spirituality that appears in the most recent revision of the *Book of Common Prayer*. In spite of the criticisms that can be and have been made of it, the model has not been bad in every respect. Many people need to be cared for within an ordered structure of life; they need to learn how to work out relationships, crises, and everyday problems in terms of established structures and norms. One of the questions with which the pastor must frequently deal is how we are to care for one another in relationships that, even if they have gone awry, are still structures within which we believe we ought to live because they are thought to be good structures. Marriage counselling is an obvious example. Most people in the Church and even in the wider society still think marriage is a social and religious commitment that reflects the natural order of human relationships. And I suspect that for many people who are not legally and sacramentally married but live together, a structured and ordered commitment is an ideal and even a goal.[5]

Social ethics has been another area where a Constantinian model has been important: the achievement of justice for minorities, the care of the sick, the suffering, and the poor, and the rehabilitation of the criminal element in society. The assumption of those who are cared for and those who care often is that if we will but allow grace and goodwill to function, we will be able to sort out our social problems and create a better, that is, more just and ordered, society. In the previous chapter Professor Barnhouse discussed the various models of care that can be drawn from psychotherapy. I would suggest in addition that, as it is usually practiced and as it has influenced pastoral counselling, psychotherapy has as its goal changing the way in which people understand themselves in order that they may become more "adjusted" or "normal." Whatever term is used, the intention is that a person's life should be more ordered, should conform to societal expectations, that alienation can be overcome, and that the problems and crises of life can be dealt with by conforming to society rather than by bringing about a change in the structures of society—a theme to which I shall return.

In the Church such a model is also obvious, not only for interpreting the relationship of the Church to secular authority but for structuring the life of the institution. Most Western Christians and a great majority of Anglicans are committed to the idea that the Holy Spirit works in an orderly and structured manner—in the ordained ministry, the sacraments, preaching, and the development of the moral and spiritual life (matters also discussed elsewhere in this volume). Most pastors are distinctly uncomfortable with the wildness of the Spirit or the utter gratuity of grace, even though many of the parables of Jesus and the Pentecostal experience of the early Church ought to suggest we think otherwise. We can have great difficulty in caring for those who do not conform to the institution and its structures because we want grace to transform them, not radically change them by revolutionary upheavals. I confess to being a thoroughgoing Constantinian, but I sometimes have a suspicion that in caring for others something more may be involved. And my suspicion has sometimes been confirmed when I have discovered that other people, for whom I think I am being a pastor, have cared for me in ways I have not expected and when I have been surprised by the sheer gratuity of the Spirit. As one who teaches systematic theology in a seminary of the Episcopal Church, I am occasionally made uncomfortable by such discoveries, but like so many others I usually find ways of blunting my discomfort in order to continue on an easier and more accustomed course.

But how much longer shall we be able to do that? As all pastors are well aware, or certainly ought to be, the Constantinian or Christendom model is under serious pressure from both theology and politics. Theologically it is under pressure to be more aware of the eschatological dimension of Christian faith, which is so prominent in the New Testament writings, and to be more sensitive to the free working of the Spirit in the Christian community and the world at large. Politically it is under pressure from several sources: the harsh realities of war, famine, and injustice that impinge on us from the third World, where the tranquil ordering of providence becomes hard to discern; and from crises at home, especially in the cities, where the notion of law and order is becoming increasingly nostalgic, a condition only to be maintained by force. In addition, it has come under pressure from nontheological and nonreligious interpretations of history, such as Marxism and secularism, which offer alternative evaluations of human nature and society and which advocate radical change rather than gradual transformation.

A new form of theology has developed in response to those pressures, and it holds out the possibility of a new model for pastoral care. The new model would be less concerned with order and structure, and it would understand the working of divine providence in a different manner. A liberation model, as I have called it, has its theological grounding in the biblical image of God's eschatological Rule and Promise, but it has also emerged in response to changing images and concepts about human nature and society. Theologically the significance of the eschatological theme in the biblical tradition is that it does not represent a hierarchical or ontological interpretation of reality, nor does it identify reality with intelligibility, as did the classical formulations of patristic Christology. Rather, it interprets reality, and most especially the human condition, through historical and eschatological categories, namely, that the Rule and Promise of God, announced by Jesus and proleptically established in the resurrection event, impinges on the present as a now and not yet, and it calls for conversion, radical response, and an openness to God's future. When viewed in terms of God's Rule and Promise, the history of human beings is shown to be more responsive to the creative presence of the Spirit, who brings into existence what is yet to be rather than sustaining and preserving the ordered and rational structures of Being; in their history human beings are called into the freedom of the future and not into conformity to the Law, whether Law be understood in Greek or Jewish terms.

The eschatological motif did not totally die out in the Western understanding of the Christian life, although it certainly was obscured by the development of a hierarchical and ontological theology for the interpretation of the Church and the world. It reappears in the early Luther, in apocalyptic movements, and in spiritual renewal movements of a pentecostal variety. Only recently, however, has it received serious theological attention as a way of understanding Jesus and the Church. It has also become a central theme in the development of liberation theology.[6]

As a theological movement, liberation theology is interesting in itself. It has clearly had an impact on events in Latin America, and certain of its concerns have become common to North American theology as well: theology as critical reflection on praxis, consciousness raising, base communities, the need for a political hermeneutic of the Gospel, and solidarity with the oppressed and the poor. It has also helped to give theological articulation to a movement that has been occurring in the West since the Enlightenment—a shift from an ontological, substantive interpretation of human nature to one more functional, historical, and evolutionary. Now the implications of that shift have come to influence political and ecclesiastical institutions as well as the way in which Christian people evaluate their lives and determine what has priority for them in moral and political areas. I believe liberation theology can also help us articulate what we mean by pastoral care in significantly different ways. If we take liberation as an image or vision for caring, how would it affect our understanding of pastoral care?

Caring through liberation can represent an interpretation of the human condition, whether personal or political, concerned with the developmental, becoming aspect of reality, in which futurity, the proleptic, and the eschatological are more important than structures and norms. As a result, reason and Law can be called into question and cease to have a definitive authority, and social and ecclesiastical structures can be radically revised; they can be regarded as tentative because they always stand under the higher judgment of God's Rule and Promise. Because these structures can no longer be conceived as part of an established order, either ontologically or theologically, there is no imperative reason for preserving them when they no longer function appropriately. To illustrate the difference a liberation model might make for pastoral care, I want to look briefly at two areas in which new attitudes may be called for—human sexuality and medical ethics. Both raise questions with which Christians must deal.

By human sexuality I mean the concern for the liberation of men and women from customary stereotypes as well as the changing mores in our society in regard to sexual activity. Both can be very threatening to many people because they represent the overthrow of a hierarchical model and the denial of what has long been regarded as natural and lawful in society. As any pastor knows, however, just because such matters are threatening and disturbing does not mean they will go away or that we shall be able to return to what many like to imagine as a more "golden" age. Women who say it is not part of the natural order of things that they should be or act in certain prescribed ways need to be cared for and, in turn, to care for others in a manner that can enable them to realize something new about themselves. And those men who are more and more resistant to being classified and judged by received standards of masculinity need a different kind of caring than did their fathers. What it means to be a woman or man now appears to be something to be discovered or achieved on one's own terms, so that in a caring relationship there may be less concern for the past, that is, where a person has come from, and more concern for future possibilities. Certainly a concern for the future was always a dimension of serious pastoral care, but it has now become much more explicit and demanding.

Such changes are even more obvious in the standards we use to judge sexual activity. Both homosexual and heterosexual persons are increasingly resisting the idea that their sexual lives must be confined to only one pattern, even though many would not want to abandon all moral standards in favor of unbridled promiscuity. The traditional concepts of nature, the normal, and moral law by which judgments were made no longer appear to function in their customary way for people who think of themselves as becoming liberated in their sexual lives. How is the Christian community to care for a person in order that he or she may be freed from structures or laws that purport to be, but may no longer be, accepted as normative? What is needed, I believe, in this as in so many other areas, is for us to find a way between the absolute, normative authority of law and structure and the trivial solutions of "situation ethics" and moral and social anarchy. To discern such a way is not easy.

The questions raised by changes in medical knowledge are even more vexing: abortion, genetic manipulation, the right to die, the morality of expensive health care, to name only a few—all raise fundamental questions about the value of life and how it is to be regarded, questions that were not explicit to previous generations. Certainly they cannot be answered by a simplistic appeal to a norm or law that really does not address the more complicated issues the advances in medical science have created. The several "Baby Doe" cases that have caused so much concern recently are obvious examples. Babies who twenty years ago might have died naturally from physical deformities can now be maintained in life, although at terrific expense and with great emotional struggle. How is one to care for the child whose life certainly has intrinsic value but whose continuance in life is problematical? How does one care for the parents and medical staff who have to make a decision not only about life and death (a decision that always had to be made, although in a simpler form) but about the quality of life for the child, the family, and society? Such moral issues are ambiguous in new ways because of advanced technology and because the old norms no longer seem to apply. How does the pastor enable those for whom he cares to develop an informed conscience in the light of radically new problems?

But the issues have far wider ramifications and are especially relevant to the attitude toward human life and development that seems to be influencing our way of thinking about ourselves and others. The most important issue raised in medical ethics, I believe, is our notion of *personhood*—how we define what we mean by *person* and what consequences such a definition will have for the manner in which we treat people. Can we any longer define personhood in relatively static terms, or must we see it as an expanding notion in which potentiality and possibility need to be given primary consideration? That question is certainly at the heart of the debate about abortion, whether therapeutic abortion (about which there may not be as much controversy) or abortion used as a means of birth control. Is there, as many people would maintain, a legitimate sense in which an unborn child (and the use of the phrase "unborn child" rather than the term "fetus" is an indication of the problem) can be called a person? If there is, does abortion mean that terminating the life of the fetus is killing a person? On the other hand, if a person is one who has both rights and responsibilities for her or his body, then to what degree does the personal right of the mother extend beyond the personal rights of the potential or actual person she is carrying? The issue here, as in many other cases, is how to care for the future of a person, whether child or mother, when the norms for doing so seem to be undergoing radical change. And, of course, there are many ancillary issues: the anguish performing an abortion can cause to medical personnel, the equal rights of the poor to have abortions, and the like.

It is clear, I believe, that a liberation model of pastoral care cannot, any more than can the older model, give easy answers to such vexing questions, even though it may help us see those questions in a different and sometimes more helpful context. But the temptation of a liberation model for pastoral care is that, in its concern for development, future possibility, and freedom from norms and structures, it can allow us to cut ourselves off from any claim the past, the tradition, may have on us. Christians believe that the past, what has been given to us and what has been shown and revealed to us, cannot simply be forgotten or dismissed as irrelevant; to do so would not be to care for them. We believe, indeed, that Scripture and tradition have a normative value for us, even though the sense in which they do so may not be the same

for us as it was for Thomas Aquinas, nor even for our grand-
parents. Our contemporary task as Christians who care for both
past and future is to discover anew what the authority of Scripture
and tradition may be for us, without absolutizing the norms of
the past (which so often can be legalism) nor absolutizing liberation into the future (which could well lead to a new form of
antinomianism). In addition, to set up a conflict between a
Constantinian model and a liberation model could well lead to
the belief that Christ stands for law and authority, whereas the
Spirit stands for freedom and spontaneity. Such juxtapositions
have not been uncommon in Western Christianity, and they have
always had unhappy consequences. Jesus himself means freedom,
and the Spirit also works in structures and institutions. *Christian*
pastoral care ought to be in the name of Jesus Christ through the
power of the Holy Spirit, and it ought, therefore, to involve past
and future, order and freedom, law and grace.

III

   Earlier I discussed several of the ambiguities of the term *pastoral
care,* and I hope to have shown in the discussion of the two models
of pastoral care that both of them, though helpful in many
situations, do not solve all the problems; they leave us with further
ambiguity even while clarifying some of the issues. I believe,
however, that some of those ambiguities can be further clarified—
not finally resolved, for I would not want to make so ultimate
a claim—through an investigation of the roots of pastoral care
in the biblical and theological tradition. Christians engage in
pastoral care because of their beliefs about God and themselves.
Therefore Holy Scripture and the theological tradition are essential
to our understanding of pastoral care and our practice of it.
   The most obvious reason for our use of the term *pastoral care*
is that in the New Testament Jesus is often spoken of as a shepherd
and the images of shepherd and sheep are frequently associated
with his ministry (cf. Matt. 9:36; 25:32; 26:31; Mark 6:34 and
14:27). But such descriptions of Jesus might easily have become
dead images for a nonpastoral people were it not for the fact that
they point to something much deeper about the person and work

of Jesus. Jesus the shepherd, the paradigm of pastoral care, has remained a vital image not only because of what he was reported to have said and done but because of who he is and how he has been experienced by Christian people: God's care incarnate. That is the deeper reality in the image of Jesus the shepherd, and it can be helpful to us now, when the images of shepherding are no longer as vital as they once were, when we have conflicting ideas about the nature of pastoral care, and when we are faced with newly perplexing questions about ourselves and God.

The New Testament image of Jesus as the shepherd has its roots in the Old Testament, where, of the many images used about God, it is clearly of major importance. It expressed the relationship between God and his people, who are frequently spoken of as sheep in need of a shepherd. For example, as the people are about to enter the promised land after their flight from Egypt and the time in the wilderness, Moses shortly before his death asks that they be given a shepherd to lead them on lest they be as sheep which have no shepherd. God appoints Joshua and directs Moses to commission him (Numbers 27:12, ff.). Again in 1 Kings, the prophet Micah prophesies to the wicked king Ahab that because of his evil deeds the people of Israel are as sheep who have no master; they are scattered on the mountains. Because the king has failed in his duty, he is destroyed by God (22:13, ff.). On other occasions the people themselves are described as rebellious and stiff-necked sheep who, in spite of all that God has done for them, test him and go after false gods; yet God remains faithful:

> He chose David his servant, and took him away from the sheepfolds.
> He brought him from following the ewes, to be a shepherd over Jacob his people and over Israel his inheritance.
> So he shepherded them with a faithful and true heart and guided them with the skillfulness of his hands. (Psalm 78:70-72)

Elsewhere in the Psalms God himself is described as the shepherd of his people. In Psalm 23 God is the shepherd who cares for his sheep, leading them to pasture; but in Psalm 80 we find a passionate cry that the shepherd of Israel will restore His people and bring them out of desolate places: "Hear, O Shepherd of Israel, leading Joseph like a flock; shine forth, you that are enthroned upon the cherubim" (Psalm 80:1).

The most profound insight into the shepherding relationship

of God to his people is found in the thirty-fourth chapter of Ezekiel, in a passage that clearly lies behind the Johannine interpretation of Jesus as the Good Shepherd as well as those sayings in other Gospels where Jesus condemns the false shepherds of his own time. The passage has two themes. First, God, through the prophet, condemns those false shepherds who are destroying his people and announces that he himself will be the shepherd of Israel:

> Therefore, you shepherds, hear the word of the Lord: As I live, says the Lord God, because my sheep have become a prey, and my sheep have become food for all the wild beasts, since there is no shepherd . . . I will rescue my sheep from their mouths, that they may not be food for them. For thus says the Lord God: Behold, I, I myself will search for my sheep and seek them out. (34:7-8, 10b-11)

Second, God promises to set David over the people as a shepherd and to establish with them a covenant of peace: "And they shall know that I, the Lord their God, am with them, and that they, the house of Israel, are my people, says the Lord God" (v. 30).

Walter Eichrodt, in his commentary on Ezekiel, sees this chapter as having great significance for the messianic hopes of Israel. His comments are worth citing at length:

> [The one who is to come, David,] is much more intimately associated with Yahweh, and more definitely taken into his divine being than any other has been hitherto . . . . One can see Yahweh himself at work in this servant, and thus be assured of his effectual and saving nearness among his people. So the whole of the stress is laid on the way in which the other-worldly God actually approaches his own, in his real presence. This God expresses his humanity, his will to have the most intimate personal fellowship with his people, by the very fact that he exercises his own office of shepherding through his servant . . . . what Ezekiel chiefly means by his servant David is that he is to be regarded as the fully reconstituted image of God, in whom the will of God, already expressed in creation, for the very close fellowship in nature with the most excellent of all his earthly creation, is finally brought into effect.[7]

That Jesus is understood by the New Testament writers to be the shepherd and the one who fulfills the Davidic promise of the covenant of peace is, therefore, of striking importance for their belief concerning his relationship to God: He is the great shepherd of the sheep, the one in whom the God of peace establishes an eternal covenant (Hebrews 13:25); the shepherd and Guardian of our souls (I Peter 5:4); and in the Fourth Gospel the shepherd who gives his sheep eternal life (John 10:28). Indeed, it is this latter saying of Jesus that leads to his condemnation for blasphemy "because you, being a man, make yourself God" (John 10:33).

In addition, Eichrodt points out, the Ezekiel passage is replete with language of covenant.[8] It speaks of the blessings God will give to his people when the land has been purged and the covenant once more established. Thus the image of the shepherd, whether it be used of God or David (or finally of Jesus, in the New Testament), points to the most fundamental experience of Israel in its relationship to God, the one who has cared for them by leading them out of slavery, by giving the Law to Moses, sustaining them in the wilderness, and leading them into the promised land. Through their experience of salvation the people of Israel were shown that God is the only Lord, the one who creates heaven and earth, and that he continues to care for his people through his *hesed* (loving-kindness, steadfast love, or grace).[9] *Hesed* expresses one of the most important aspects of the covenant relationship between God and Israel; it is the act of loving-kindness by which God chose Israel and promised his blessing and salvation; it is the self-giving of God toward them, not only in the past but as a promise for the future. *Hesed* is, in other words, the eternal, unchanging act of God, his commitment to and his care for creation, a pledge given and not to be revoked even though Israel is stiff-necked and rebellious. Thus it points back to creation itself and ahead to the eschatological fulfillment of God's promise, when God will make a new covenant with his people: "Incline your ear, and come to me; hear, that your soul may live; and I will make with you an everlasting covenant, my steadfast, sure love for David" (Isaiah 55:3; cf. also Jeremiah 31).

But there is another dimension to the covenant relationship: A covenant is not one-sided. God's *hesed* in the covenant found its focus in the Law: The people must care for God and for one another as he cares for them. There is a relationship of mutual responsibility: God's faithfulness, his loving-kindness poured out on them, but also their responsibility to be a just and holy people (Exodus 20:6; Deuteronomy 7:12; Hosea 6:6). For that reason God's care for his people also means judgment expressed through prophets who recall Israel to its responsibility to care for God's Law and for one another. Caring is not sentimentalized in the Old Testament; caring for your people can also mean sending them into exile. There is the dark dimension of God's righteous anger and wrath toward his people when they forsake the covenant. But, as the great prophets saw, even when afflicting his people God is still faithful to his care; he will not take back his *hesed* but will write a new law in the heart (Jeremiah), create a new spirit and a heart of flesh (Ezekiel), and he will finally redeem his people (Isaiah).

For Christians God's *hesed* finds its fulfillment in Jesus the human embodiment of God's care. In the Gospels Jesus is remembered as one who cares for people as God cares for them: He eats with sinners and forgives them; he gives preference to human need above the requirements of the Law; he enables others to experience God's loving-kindness and mercy through his actions and in his parables. As E. Schillebeeckx has said:

> In the care he shows for man and his record of suffering, for publicans and sinners, for the poor, the crippled and the blind, for the oppressed and for people torn apart by "evil spirits," Jesus is a living parable of God: that is how God cares for man. In the story of Jesus is told the story of God. It is God himself who opens to us in the story that is the life of Jesus a new world, a different experience of reality and way of living.[10]

The memory of the words and actions of Jesus is very important in showing us how to care for others, but there can be a temptation for us to see his way of caring simply in terms of his doing good works and giving us an example to follow. We can trivialize his care for people if we only think of him as being kind and gentle and forget other aspects of his caring: the demands of the Kingdom he proclaimed, the fearful Day of the Lord, his judgment on those who were unfaithful or who oppressed others, and his denunciation of those who placed heavy burdens on others. Like the caring of God in the Old Testament, the caring of Jesus also has its dark side. Indeed, the dark side of the caring of Jesus is most clearly expressed in the Cross. His way of caring was his way of the Cross, because it aroused fear and anger in some and because it demanded a change of heart and repentance in those for whom he cared. The Gospel of John, for example, interprets the Cross of Jesus as judgment and light upon the world:

> And as Moses lifted up the serpent in the wilderness, so must the Son of man be lifted up, that whoever believes in him may have eternal life

> . . . . And this is judgment, that the light has come into the world,
> and men loved darkness rather than light, because their deeds were evil.
> For every one who does evil hates the light, lest his deeds should be
> exposed. But he who does what is true comes to the light, that it may
> be clearly seen that his deeds have been wrought in God." (John 3:14, ff.)

Paul also develops an explicit theology of care in terms of the Cross, and he draws together several of the themes we have been considering: grace, covenant, and law, through which God's care is expressed to Israel. Paul in his theological and personal development struggled with the Jewish understanding of God's *hesed* for his people and the new faith that had come to him in Jesus Christ. The Cross became for him the focus through which the two could be brought together. God's *hesed,* his *charis,* as Paul calls it, is made manifest and effective in the Cross because in his death Jesus shows that God cares ultimately and irrevocably. The care at the heart of God is expressed in the death of Jesus—his absolute self-giving and sharing of himself for our salvation. This is the central theme of Paul's Gospel as it is expressed in the fifth chapter of Romans: We have peace with God because Christ has died for the ungodly; he shows his love for us "in that while we were yet sinners Christ died for us" (Romans 5:8); and we have received the free gift of righteousness. What I believe Paul came to see here and elsewhere in his writings (cf. Galatians) was that who the God of the Old Covenant had always been is now made known concretely and historically in Jesus Christ. Grace in Jesus Christ is nothing new; it is the eternal loving-kindness, steadfast love, of God once and for all established in the resurrection and in which we now live through God's Spirit. In the death and resurrection of Christ we, through Baptism, are raised from the works of the flesh and the curse of the works of the law into the freedom of Christ and the fruits of the Spirit (Galatians 5). Now we can yield our members to righteousness for sanctification (Romans 6:19). In Christ we are God's temple and God's Spirit dwells in us (I Corinthians 3). Life in the Spirit, which Christ makes possible for us, is to live in the new age—that hope of Israel which, as we have seen, found expression in Ezekiel and elsewhere; it is an eschatological existence, the present sign of what is to come and the character and structure of the new life itself, that is, the freedom of the sons and daughters of God and heirs of his promise. Paul does not refer to Jesus by the title of shepherd or pastor, but the covenant of God with his people is fulfilled in him:

Jesus is the shepherd because he is the one in whom God's covenanted care is made present to us, and he opens for us our present life in the Spirit as the hope and guarantee of that which is yet to be (Romans 8:23; II Cor. 1:22 and 5:5; cf. also Ephesians 1:13-14).

Such an understanding of the relationship between Christ and the Spirit can help us see that Jesus cares for us and is the exemplar for our caring not simply as a figure in the past, one to whom we look back for an example to follow; he cares as the Risen Lord in the Spirit. There is good reason, then, why the image of Jesus as the shepherd has not died out and, indeed, why it ought not to die out. What is regrettable is that the image of the shepherding of God in Christ has become so dissociated from the work of the Spirit of God. On the contrary, the care of God is our redemption in Christ and our sanctification through the Spirit that dwells in us.

In Paul's theology of redemption and sanctification we can see the beginning of the development of the doctrine of the Trinity that began with the New Testament writings. In subsequent reflection on the experience of salvation in Christ, the Church was required to think more deeply about the relationship between Christ and the Spirit, in terms both of their unity and difference, and of their mutual relationship to the Father. That doctrinal development took several forms, reflecting various conceptual models and ways of describing the work of Christ and the Spirit. It is important, however, to recognize that the doctrinal formulations did not arise in the abstract; theology and theologians were necessary in the process of clarifying terms and concepts, but they did not invent the belief of the Christian community in the triunity of God. Such belief arose from the way in which Christian people understood and articulated the working of God in their lives and how they responded to him in worship and prayer. Those early doctrinal formulations, however much they may need clarification and restatement today, have continued to shape the Christian understanding of God as well as the nature and purpose of our life in the Church. Unfortunately, for many people in the Church the doctrine of the Trinity has become abstract and speculative, something that is recalled on Trinity Sunday in the Anglican calendar and that provides a formula for ending public prayers, but not a doctrine that expresses a deeply held belief about the nature of God. Certainly the vital significance of the triunity of God must be reclaimed in many aspects of the Church's life, for it is the Mystery at the heart of Christian faith. Here I want to focus only on one area in which our experience of God as Trinity and the doctrinal formulation of the experience can be of great importance, namely, our pastoral care for one another in Christ through the Spirit. What does our belief in the triune God say to us about ourselves as human beings and about the way in which we ought to understand our caring for one another?

The interpretation or elucidation of the doctrine of the Trinity that I have found helpful in thinking about this question is the one developed by Karl Rahner. Rahner's transcendental theology seeks to give expression to the fundamental belief of Christians in the absolute Mystery of the eternal God as one who, though beyond all human comprehension, is yet one who reaches out as Creator, Redeemer, and Sanctifier. His elucidation of the Mystery of God is essentially trinitarian, and not, as with some others in the theological tradition, only peripherally so, because he approaches it from the experience of the history of salvation, the working of the divine economies in the space and time of our existence.[11] God reveals himself in us and in our history through his free self-communication: What we believe about him is derived from what has been shown to us and created in us by Jesus Christ and the Holy Spirit. Thus Rahner can say, "The economic Trinity *is* the immanent Trinity . . . . [and] . . . no adequate distinction can be made between the doctrine of the Trinity and the doctrine of the economy of salvation."[12]

The self-communication of God as the Son and Logos in Jesus Christ is truth in history not only as a concept but as a lived truth: "Truth in the full sense is the *lived* truth in which someone freely deploys his being for himself and for others, manifests himself historically as faithful and reliable and makes this state ir-revocable."[13] Jesus Christ as the economy of the Son and Logos is at once the truth about God and the truth about our human nature; and he is the Savior and Lord who sets us free to love. The economy of the Spirit is God's self-communication as love: God's "outgoing, without self-seeking or gain, taking a risk with others because one is great enough freely to be small, is precisely what is meant by love, in the sense of the New Testament agape . . . . God's self-communication aims at the inner-most centre of the human person and is active there not only as the gift but as the power of the acceptance of the gift" (p. 176[1]). And he concludes:

As truth the self-communication takes place in history and is the offer of the free faithfulness of God. As love, it brings about acceptance and opens man's transcendence to the absolute future of God. Since the historical manifestation of God (the Father) as truth is only knowable in the horizon of transcendence towards the absolute future of God, and since the absolute future is manifested irrevocably as love by being promised in the concrete history of the faithful God (the absolute bringer of salvation), these two aspects of the divine self-communication are neither disjoined nor joined merely by divine decree. Without being identical, they form together the one divine self-communication which explicates itself as truth in history, beginning and offer, and as love in transcendence, towards the absolute future in acceptance.[14]

For Rahner the truth and love of God's self-communication in Jesus Christ and the Spirit is the explicit confession of Christian faith about the eternal nature of God; it is the substance and structure of life in the Christian community, the Church; and it is the ground for our eschatological hope. The Church is the community in which the faithfulness of God—his care, as I have called it—in Christ and the Spirit is both a present reality and a promise of the hope of our calling into the divine life.

Such a consideration can help us see the nature of pastoral care in a new way. Too often, I believe, we have thought of pastoral care almost exclusively as the work of individuals, especially those who are ordained. But the trinitarian structure of God's care enables us to see that the Christian community is the primary focus of God's care in Christ and the Spirit, and only in that context do we as individuals, whether ordained or not, care for one another. In addition, the notion of the Church as the community of care enables us to recognize that caring is both incarnational, the Body of Christ, and eschatological, our being called in the Spirit. The Church is the community where the creative love and freedom given us in Christ can inform our lives as persons and direct us to their end and fulfillment in God. In what follows I want to make some suggestions about how the Church exists as a caring community in the name of Christ and through the power of the Holy Spirit.[15]

The Church as judge of present reality. The Church is the community in which sin and forgiveness, brokenness and wholeness, the past of failure and the future of freedom are made concrete realities in the lives of human beings. By placing before us the moral and spiritual demand to be the holy people of God, a people committed in the covenant to God's righteousness and justice (cf.

Paul's discussion of the law in Romans 7), the community of the Church enables us to see our unrighteousness, our breaking of the law of God, and our failure to care for that which we have been given and for that which we are called to be. It does so in many ways—through preaching and hearing the Word of God, which discerns the thoughts and intentions of the heart (Hebrews 4:12,13), through proclaiming in word and action the call of Jesus to perfection (Matthew 5:48), and through the fact of community life itself in which we are opened to the command to love our neighbor (I John, for example). The constant pressure of God's presence to us in Christ as a call to holiness in the Spirit is the structure of the Church's life in word and sacrament; it is his judgment on his people.

But at the same time the Church is the community of forgiveness. The care of God who judges us is also a call into a new future. Christ judges our past failure, but he also creates in us, through the Spirit, a new possibility. Forgiveness is not just wiping away or forgetting past failure. If it were only that it would not be an act of caring for who we have been, the past from which we have come. It is essentially a new creation, a renewal and calling to what we are to become in Christ. Therefore, judgment and forgiveness mean taking the past seriously for the sake of the future into which we are called by the Spirit.[16]

The Church as the community called into holiness. As we have seen, God's care for us is his grace, *hesed,* the grace that is the gift of Christ and the indwelling of the Holy Spirit. Grace does not destroy or annul what we are in our unfreedom; it transforms and completes what we are in order that we may be free to love.[17] The Church is the community in which we experience in particular words and actions the reality of grace as a calling from unfreedom into the freedom of the sons and daughters of God (Galatians 5). Because in the Church we are made able to see ourselves as sinners yet forgiven, the Church is the community of grace in which our transformation and sanctification by the Spirit is indeed a liberation into holiness.

Many Christians have customarily spoken of that process as vocation. But vocation is a term that carries with it a certain amount of confusion. Often we have used it in an exclusive sense for those who believe themselves called to the ordained ministry, and one can still hear students in seminaries speak of "my vocation" as though it were a unique phenomenon, unknown to lay people. It can also conjure up thoughts of esoteric visions and voices that can be somewhat frightening to ordinary Christian people who have not, so they think, received a "call." But vocation is the common lot of all those who are baptized into Christ. It is, quite simply, the process of our sanctification, however it may be worked out in the life of an individual. It means being called from one place to another place, from one condition to another condition, from who I am now to what I am to become. And, therefore, when we speak of vocation we must take two things seriously—who it is who is being called and to what he or she is being called. Vocation begins with who a person is, with all his or her limitations, failures, sins, and weaknesses. It is not a conjuror's trick. The awareness of vocation may take place in a moment (as apparently it did for Paul) or be a long and painful process of growth and understanding (as apparently it was for Peter). By the grace of God, Paul says (I Corinthians 15:10), I am what I am, and even though his conversion was sudden, Paul went on to work out his vocation in terms of his somewhat difficult and cantankerous personality. In other words, the person *I am,* with all my quirks and problems, is the person who is called, not someone else; it is the person *I am* who is being made a new creature, not someone else. Grace, as I have said, by calling me beyond myself does not destroy who I am; it transforms *me.* Indeed, we might say that grace is the gift of being who we are, of being called beyond who we are, and of being able to give thanks for both. God cares by grace for *me,* not an imaginary person.

Earlier in this chapter I spoke of the dichotomy between nature, order, structure, and law and a calling to freedom, liberation, and becoming. But in fact the dichotomy is only apparent, not real: The grace of vocation means being who I am, but being called beyond that; of being obedient to the law, but called beyond that; of leading an ordered life in an ordered society, but being called beyond that. In every case we are *always* being called beyond where we are. Vocation means caring for the past out of which we have become who we are by grace, caring for the present in which we experience grace, and caring for the future into which we are called by grace. The sacramental life of the Church makes it possible for us to believe such things about ourselves and to act on the belief.

The Church as a sacramental community. To call the Church

a sacramental community is to speak first of the Incarnation of the Son/Logos in Jesus Christ, for Jesus is the presence of God with us in and through his humanity; he is the primordial sacrament because he is both the gift of the eternal God to us and the faithful response of our humanity to the gift, the shepherd who offers himself with his sheep. The Incarnation structures the life of the Church and of all Christian people; it enables us to believe God is present with us and we are present with him through the faithfulness of Jesus. In the sacramental economy of the Church God's gift of grace, his personal presence, calls us to the completion and fulfillment of our humanity in the humanity of Christ because his care for us in the Incarnation creates in us the humanity, the personal being, which in Christ we are called to share. It enables us to believe that every human nature is called to be open to the transcendent reality of God and to share in the divine life.

And that is the work of the Spirit in us. The Spirit makes the sacramental actions of the Church the effective sign of God's indwelling presence. The Spirit makes the water of Baptism the means by which we are cleansed from sin and incorporated into the Body of Christ, the community of his Incarnation: "We thank you, Father, for the water of Baptism. In it we are buried with Christ in his death. By it we share in his resurrection. Through it we are reborn by the Holy Spirit."[18] The Spirit makes the bread and wine of the Eucharist to be the Body and Blood of Christ: "Lord, we pray that in your goodness and mercy your Holy Spirit may descend upon us, and upon these gifts, sanctifying them and showing them to be holy gifts for your holy people, the bread of life and the cup of salvation, the Body and Blood of your Son Jesus Christ."[19] In the sacraments the Spirit calls and enables us to enter into God's eternity even in the present time of our existence; and God's eternity, made present to us now by Christ in the Spirit, creates in us the hope of our calling, namely, that our lives, hidden now with God in Christ, will find their end in unity with God. The Church in the sacraments recalls our redemption in the passion of Christ, as a reality present to us now by grace, and as the sign of future glory. What we are shown and what is made effective in us through the sacraments is that God's care for his people is not simply what Christ has done for us in the past but much more his continuing care for us in the Spirit until the Kingdom comes.[20]

The Church as a sent community. We have been thinking of God's pastoral care for his people, those who by Baptism now live in Christ and are renewed by his Spirit. But the care of God is not only for the Church; his providence, as Thomas Aquinas said, extends to all created being.[21] Therefore, the community that knows it lives within God's care is also called to extend and show his care to others who do not yet know it in their lives. Because we know God's judgment and forgiveness, his call to holiness, and his sacramental presence, we have a mission; the community is lived out in its apostolate and diakonia.[22] God's care in the Church calls the Church to care for the world by witnessing in word and action to the saving event of Jesus Christ and the hope of our calling in the Spirit.

There are many ways in which the Church, that is, all Christian people, can express and make concrete for others the care of God for his creation: missionary strategy, programs to feed the hungry, social-service agencies, political advocacy, and, perhaps the most important of all, simply being present to those in need. I would like to draw all those ways together under four categories, which, I believe, can help us see how we care for the world in the name of the triune God.

First, the Church is called to be a community that, even with its failures and sins, proclaims God's judgment and forgiveness. This very important responsibility is difficult to carry out in our complex world; it requires faith, patience, and understanding. How do we proclaim God's judgment and forgiveness to government leaders who talk about survival in a nuclear war, to corporations that exploit other people and the environment, or to the wretched, hopeless poor in a ghetto? But we must, unless we want to say that God does not really care about the pain and suffering of the world. If we believe God's care extends to all human beings and to all created being, then we must witness to his care in our judgment on human sin and in our practice of forgiveness. Finding the way to do so is the mission of all Christian people who care.

Second, we are to be poor. Most Episcopalians are reasonably well-off. Many other Anglicans and Christians in the world are desperately poor. But we are all Christ's people, and, therefore, all of us are called, each in our own way, to show where the foundation of life is and what is the hope of our calling. Even though I am secure and cannot really become as poor as those in Africa who are starving, or those in the United States who come to soup kitchens, I am called to show in my life that God cares. The only witness I have—and other Episcopalians along with me—is to show in my life that I know there is no security or comfort except in that which is given to me freely in the Cross and in the new life to which the Spirit calls me in the resurrection. So it is also for the Episcopal Church and the whole Christian community. The Episcopal Church will, in all probability, always be an affluent Church; it is difficult to imagine how it could not be. And, in all probability, it will continue to be a Church generous in its gifts to the poor. But that is not enough; being a caring community means finding the way to express God's care, and that, in turn, means witnessing to the Gospel of Christ, knowing our foundation and hope in Christ and the Spirit.

Third, we are to be a spiritual community. The suggestion that the Church cares for the world by being spiritual can be understood as contradictory to our mission to become involved in the poverty of the world. It can suggest an other-worldiness unconcerned with the realities of the human condition in Latin America, Asia, Africa, and even in the United States. The liberation theologians of Latin America have quite rightly rejected "spirituality" if it means only a "pie in the sky" attitude toward human suffering. But the authentic tradition of Christian spirituality means much more. The spirituality of the Church is the proclamation that belief in God, the transcendent reality of all that is, has consequences for human life and hope, that there is value and care in the order of things, and that morality is not simply capricious or subjective. By believing in the God who is incarnate in the humanity of Jesus Christ and who is present with us in the Spirit, Christian people are saying there is more to the world than the world is sometimes willing to acknowledge, namely, that material things, water and bread and wine, and human beings, are open to the presence of that which transcends the space and time of our created existence. Only with such a belief, however it may find expression in philosophical or theological terms, can we say that human life and hope and love have worth, that they are not simply expendable. To witness to the spiritual dimension of our humanity is not to solve the pastoral and moral dilemmas of abortion, euthanasia, warfare, and the like, but it is to say that those questions can only be dealt with in a context that asserts the essential value of human life because it is grounded in God.

Finally, we are to be a community that serves those in need. Those in need include all human beings, not only the sick and oppressed but the comfortable and secure, not only "the world" but those who believe (Romans 2). Serving those in need takes many forms. Here I want to speak only of the form that draws together all the others and is the particular Christian vocation: prayer. Because of our belief in the triune God, Christian prayer has a particular shape to it; it is always through Jesus Christ in the Holy Spirit. It is through Jesus Christ because he shares our human nature and offers what we and all men and women are to the Father. It is in the Spirit because only through the Spirit are we able to offer our prayers through him. To pray through Jesus Christ is to believe that, with all their complexity and sin, every human life is offered to the Father; to have the courage and hope to pray through Jesus Christ is a gift of the Spirit: "Likewise the Spirit helps us in our weakness; for we do not know how to pray as we ought, but the Spirit himself intercedes for us with sighs too deep for words. And he who searches the hearts of men [and women] knows what is the mind of the Spirit, because the Spirit intercedes for the saints according to the will of God" (Romans 8:26-27).

I find such a thought rather terrifying. It means that Christian prayer is not just individual, isolated petition. Rather, it is of the Body, of that Body which the Church is now and of which all men and women are by promise. My prayer carries with it, offers with it, the prayer—articulate or inarticulate—of every human being because we all share in the humanity of Christ. The pain and suffering, the need, as well as the joy of every person is present to the Father through my prayer, just as my need is present to the Father through the prayers of others. Because we pray through Jesus Christ, we are not just praying for others; we are praying with them, sharing with them who they are and who they are called to become. I—and we—can only have the courage to pray when I believe the Spirit dwells in me, teaching me to pray and enabling me to do so: The gift of the Spirit is hope, the belief that prayer is not in vain. Praying for the world and with the world is our care for the world because it is God's care in Christ and the Spirit; what he has done, what he will do, and what he is doing now.

Conclusion

I want to conclude this chapter with a very simple statement: Pastoral care has its foundation in the belief that at the center of all we know and at the center of all that is, there is One who cares, who in Jesus Christ has irrevocably committed his care to us, and who in the Spirit calls us to share in his eternal life. It is the belief that what God has begun in his creation he will complete, for the hope of our calling, the end of our beginning, is the God who calls us from our past to our future. The purpose of pastoral care is to enable others to have that belief as well.

5

Worship and Pastoral Care

Louis Weil

Symbols abound in Christianity. Some have been shaped by the historical nature of Christian faith, so that certain external symbols, such as those associated with particular saints, are reminders of events in saints' lives. More fundamental are the symbols that draw their energy from physical nature, as the *natural* symbolism of water undergirds its significance as the material element of Baptism. All symbols are called to reveal and to remind, to join some physical element or historical event with what is perceived in faith as an articulation of the grace and presence of God. This joining, this symbolizing or throwing together of visible and invisible reality, lies at the heart of the Christian revelation. It is the substance of a religion that centers on belief in an Incarnation, the presence of the living God revealed in the historical and human life of Jesus of Nazareth.

If symbol is so basic to Christian faith, if in its universal forms it becomes "an outward and visible sign of an inward and spiritual grace," the instrument by which God penetrates and transforms the created world, then the Church has a serious responsibility of stewardship in this deeply mysterious realm of spiritual and material union. When such stewardship has been lacking, history

115

reveals a trivialization of symbols, a drying up of the vitality of their external forms with an accompanying impoverishment of participation in their internal reality.

Our church buildings, the places in which the Church gathers because of its baptismal identity with Jesus Christ, often reveal this lack of stewardship. Excessive multiplication of symbols (in the windows, on the vesture, in the sanctuary) leads to a diminution of their power to proclaim. There is a loss of focus, a loss of what is really fundamental, and the liturgical action easily becomes detached from the human realities it is called to illuminate.

The great multitude of symbols one can find neatly catalogued in the various compendia on the subject are all derivative. If such symbols are to have religious value, it can only be as they are rooted in the essential symbols of Christian faith, those comparatively few external signs without which Christianity would be robbed of its authenticity. Religious practice, especially in the so-called liturgical churches, can become preoccupied with worship as a ritual routine and come to identify the Christian life with the performance of certain symbolic routines. In the more perverse instances, this can result in a kind of schizoid state in which religious practice and daily life are radically disjunct.

It is the purpose of this essay to explore how the integration of authentic worship with a sense of the imperatives of pastoral care can serve as a salutary corrective to this destructive schism. The celebration of the liturgy is the *work* of the Church; it is the doing of its identity. It is always the action of an assembly of people who gather because what Christian faith impels them to do must, in its most normative expression, be done together.

The gathering of God's people for the Eucharist on Sunday is not a convenient means for the fulfillment of individual spiritual needs. The fact that history reveals examples of this privatization simply confirms the imperative in every generation for the members of the Church to be *formed,* to be shaped by their shared participation in the risen life of Christ. In other words, we are shaped by the fundamental symbols of Christian faith as we participate in them, and those fundamental symbols, focused in the liturgy, embrace the whole human experience. "Christ . . . takes in His gospel net all the hue and cry of existence."[1] Anything less falls short of the mystery of God's action revealed in the Incarnation.

Symbols of Christ: Cross and Table

At the center of the Christian mystery there is a person. Ultimately there are two symbols that sum up and sustain the whole of God's act in Jesus—the cross and the table. On the cross hangs Jesus in the fullness of his vulnerable humanity. At the table this same Jesus both presides and serves. On the cross we see the total self-offering, the oblation of Jesus. At the table that oblation, that deeply internal giving over of himself, is identified by Jesus with basic elements of human nurture—bread and wine.

The essential act of faith is oblation. Without the offering of self, all the outward expressions of piety a person may practice remain essentially void because they are merely external forms if the reality they seek to articulate is not operative. The result is an empty formalism, an identifying of religious practices as the whole content of the faith. Jesus constantly warned his disciples against reliance on the performance of outward forms. His point was simply that, in the end, the only authentic act of religious faith is oblation. His life was such an oblation, and its totality finally led to the pouring out of that life on the cross. For Christians the cross is the great symbol of selfless oblation.

Yet Jesus made, on the night before his death, an identification between his body, to be offered on the cross, and the bread and wine he shared with his disciples. This connection has remained operative for the disciples of Jesus ever since that night. We continue to participate in the self-offering of Jesus, we unite our own faltering oblations of self with his in an act of profound simplicity, the sharing of food and drink—yet not merely ordinary food and drink but human gifts offered in union with God's purposes and then shared. The food I eat nourishes my physical body, but if this food is not shared, my body is nourished to the detriment of those who have nothing to eat.

The Eucharist is an astounding transformation of the act of nurture; it is in its meaning *essentially* corporate. The whole Body of Christ, the Church, is built up by its reception of the sign of nurture. All receive the same gift, whether ruler or beggar, rich or poor, privileged or deprived—here at the table we are all at the same level, all are the people of God. If we truly participate in this awesome symbol, we cannot leave the table unchanged. I do not receive the gift as a private believer but as a member of the Body. All the pain in the lives of the other members of this body is offered with my own to be shared, an unbearable burden were not all these pains, *when offered,* taken up by Christ in his oblation. So also are our joys offered and shared: All that is most fully human is the content of the Christian oblation.

The cross and the table are one; they are both symbols of the offering of Jesus, and they both summon us to participate in that offering. The link Jesus made in his own life between the cross and the table, between oblation and nurture, means that external liturgical rituals, even the most hallowed forms of the Eucharist, require a true oblation in the daily lives of those who would participate. Without this interior act of faith, the rituals point no further than to themselves.

The Physical and the Sacred

The natural symbol on which the Eucharist rests is the ordinary meal, food not taken in isolation but in union with others, my companions. The word "companion" points to this meaning: "Those who share bread." For a whcle range of complex reasons, as the medieval period progressed the liturgy became increasingly clericalized and eventually came under the absolute authority of the clergy. The laity were left only with passive forms of participation. This clericalized pattern of liturgical worship also became increasingly removed from apparent links with the underlying natural symbols of the sacraments. A type of minimalism of the outward signs emerged with an accompanying preoccupation with issues of canonical validity.

These developments suggest an anxiety about the capacity of natural aspects of human experience to be appropriate instruments of divine grace. Baptism became as unlike a human bath as can be imagined, and the meal dimensions of the Eucharist diminished to the point at which only the priest normally ate and drank the sacramental gifts of bread and wine. A break had gradually emerged in which the doctrine of Creation—the conviction that God is the source of all that is and thus that the physical creation is good—was obscured as the foundation on which a truly incarnational theology of the sacraments might be built.

Yet surely our understanding of the Eucharist is artificially and falsely sacralized if we can see the holy revealed only where the created physical world is viewed as a source of temptation and evil. The whole point in sacramental worship is that ordinary physical realities can be transforming instruments of divine grace. This view points to the more fundamental implication that the human person is called to be such a transforming instrument. Sacraments are thus reminders to us of what we are called to be. Saint Augustine commented in a homily to his people in Hippo, "You are the bread on the altar."

If we approach the meaning of sacramental worship in this way, it inhibits a privatized sacramental piety by its reference to the gathered community. But its implications are yet more far-reaching, for it points to the essential sacredness of the whole physical world. The more fully I am able to enter into and share what is authentically human, the more I find the signs of God's presence. The Incarnation must not be domesticated, held captive by ritual forms. Rather, the rituals should constantly hold before the gathered worshippers the reminder of the oblation of Christ "for the life of the world," not merely for card-carrying members.

Marcella Hazan, the well-known authority on Italian food, has written that "what people do with food is an act that reveals how they construe the world."[2] This is as true of the Eucharist as it is of cuisine. In its dazzling simplicity, the Eucharist reveals everything we are, and as we enter more deeply into its essential symbol, we find this sacred meal to be the focus of the most intense mutuality within the family of faith. But our highly individualized approach to the Eucharist cuts off its manifest link with the mutuality our humanity cries out for in the meal we share with those we love.

In sum, all that is human comes into focus and finds its unity in the basic symbols of Christian faith. This is why, if we allow these symbols to enter and transform our lives, we are sent from worship to serve the human community. Pastoral care is the inevitable service of a worshipping community that has embraced the full dimensions of the symbols of faith. A liturgical mentality that is turned in on itself, preoccupied with the niceties of ritual details, is perverse. It fails to undertake the lifestyle, our incorporation with others, that the rites are called to articulate.

The Role of the Catechumenate

A discussion of the catechumenate might seem to be more appropriate to an essay on Christian education than on worship. But the classical catechumenate of the fourth and fifth centuries involved far more than merely the learning of information prior to Initiation. The catechumenate was an extensive period of preparation for participation in the life of the Church, its worship, its service of those in need, its common life.[3] Although the specific details of the early catechumenate cannot be taken over directly into the life of the Church today, its underlying purpose is essential not only for us but for the Church in every generation.

The gradual disappearance of the catechumenate, with the increasing frequency of infant baptism, is one of the greatest tragedies in the history of Christianity.[4] Its loss is indicative of an insensitivity to the fundamental role of formation—the making of a Christian—in the life of every believer. Its loss corresponds, interestingly, with the first stages of an emerging clericalism and the reduction of the laity to second-class status in the Church. The process of formation represented by the catechumenate is a critical ministry of the Church in nurturing into Christian maturity persons coming to faith.

The ministry of mature Christian formation is thus an utterly appropriate subject for an essay on worship and pastoral ministry. It is precisely because of the general absence of this ministry that the great majority of laity see little relation between worship and their daily lives, nor between their own baptism and a call to service, nor between their membership in the Church and an authentically Christian lifestyle. The catechumenate is where these connections are to be made, and without it people are left wondering what Christian faith is all about. Whether it is called by the traditional title "catechumenate" or not, the important thing is that such a process of mature formation be a normative ministry, available to candidates or members as a standard ministry of Christian nurture.

During my years as a member of a seminary faculty, I have realized that the three-year process of seminary formation is for many students a dislocated process. Many people who come to seminary are actually seeking faith. They come to the seminary community with questions and yearnings that would be far more appropriately ministered to in the parish community. Further, this ministry is needed not merely by persons seeking ordination but by the laity as a whole. Seminary should be a place where a different formation takes place, one built on the foundation of the process traditionally known as the catechumenate. Our situation creates a mutual dilemma for both parish and seminary. Because of the loss of the catechumenate from the general ministry of the parish community, the laity are often disposed toward an individualized consumer model of Christian membership. Integrated with this model is a "sacrament machine" model for the ordained clergy, who are seen as the professional suppliers of the religious program. Whether the work of the clergy is seen in the realm of preaching or of sacramental services, the basic problem is the same: This is a diseased model of the Church.

From within this context, some individuals are moved to seek something more. There grows a sense that faith calls one to a life of more active commitment. And so faith does; but given the familiar parish model, active commitment seems to imply a call to Holy Orders. Commitment should be characteristic of all the baptized, and the catechumenate in the parish is where that commitment is appropriately nurtured. Under present circumstances, with the general absence of the catechumenate in the dioceses of the Church, such people are drawn toward seminary training. For most of these candidates, an authentic vocation to Holy Orders emerges within the seminary experience, but the seminary is, in the process, often obliged to perform a role to which it is not suited. The seminary community becomes the place where a kind of catechumenate process must take place while the appropriate special areas of preparation for ordination must also be accomplished. Perhaps until the catechumenate is restored to its rightful place, it might be wise for seminary curricula to be designed with the catechumenate in mind, especially during the first year.

The true goal, however, must be the recovery of an integrated process of mature formation as a normative ministry within every Christian community. By "integrated process," I mean a substantial, unhurried program in which a person is enabled to discover the fundamental connections between membership in the Church, worship, service, and lifestyle. This implies the development of an ability to reflect on one's history as an arena of God's activity and thus to see one's life in its essential union with all God's people. It is crucial for Christian maturity that a person come to see the gift of salvation as a corporate gift, that God's work in one life is a particular image of the work God is accomplishing in all. A mature faith leads to a commitment to this saving work in all its expressions. The gathering of the members of the Church to celebrate the Eucharist on Sunday thus becomes an event of the highest priority in the life of a Christian: It is the reunion of the assembly of believers to hold up and celebrate the great signs of the faith that unites them; it is the occasion on which the memory of God's great acts is proclaimed and shared; it is the place of our identity from which we are sent forth as "other Christs" to continue his all-embracing ministry in the world.

Formation for Membership

Baptism has come to be perceived by vast numbers of Christians in both encapsulated and trivialized terms. It is encapsulated in the sense that it is perceived as a self-contained sacrament, often dislocated from the full implications of membership in the Body of Christ. The individualization and privatization of baptism have nourished a folk theology of private salvation, identified in very narrow terms with the pouring of water in the Name of the Holy Trinity. The narrow identification of this water rite with "necessity for salvation" led to its celebration in an uprooted situation, cut off from the context from which it draws its salutary significance. Ironically, this encapsulation contributes to a trivialization of the rite as a brief, minimalized ceremony, performed generally apart from the assembly of the Church, a ritual to be gotten through, with utility and convenience as the primary priorities.

The recovery of a healthy theology of Christian Initiation sets up a whole new pattern of priorities. Baptism is seen again in its biblical and patristic framework as an *ecclesial* sacrament, a Church sacrament that reveals the Church's identity and nature. Baptism is seen again as the culmination of a process of formation for participation in the Church's corporate worship. Baptism is seen again as entrance into the fellowship whose common faith is proclaimed not only in its assembly each Sunday but in lives of service in the world day by day.

The recovery of such priorities is a slow and painful process. It goes roughly against the grain not only of religious individualism

but of a complacent acceptance of the world's moral standards. This recovery of Christian integrity, this holistic understanding of the relation of all aspects of Christian faith, requires patience and effort. It is far easier to find excuses for allowing the encapsulated model to persist.

The alternative, the slow and painful process that must be undertaken, is the path of conversion, a radical change of mind and heart, a rediscovery of authentic Christianity. No shortcuts or magic will effect this transformation. Because of their role as leaders of the Christian community, ordained clergy must be committed to this process for it to bear fruit. This is not a way of reintroducing clericalism through the back door; it is, rather, the honest recognition of the critical role played by the clergy in shaping the Church's pastoral priorities. There is ample evidence already available that the opposition or indifference of the clergy to this process is likely to undermine its potential for the transformation of parish life. Yet there is also evidence that, where undertaken, this process is abundantly fruitful in the renewal of the Church's life.

The goal of the process of mature formation is participation in the death and resurrection of Jesus, a sharing in what is often called the "Paschal Mystery." This is the fundamental event of Christian identity. The event itself may take place at any time or at any age. It may occur at the beginning of what will be a very long life, or it may occur in advanced old age, at the threshold of death. It is always an event initiated by God, who reaches out through the Church to draw the whole human race, all cultures and all nations, into one fellowship.

Our human response to this divine initiative always implies that the normative candidate is an adult, one who can make a genuine act of deliberate choice.[5] The great frequency of infant baptism has had the effect of confirming the idea of individual salvation, but any mature act of commitment requires an adult either as the candidate or as the one who will undertake the responsibility of spiritual oversight for an infant candidate. Whereas infant baptism speaks convincingly of God's initiative, it does not absolve the Church of its duty to nurture the child to the point that such a mature commitment may appropriately be engaged. Thus, whether it be before baptism (in the case of an adult) or several years after baptism (in the case of an infant), the Church's ministry of formation stands as a fundamental task of pastoral care.

Structure and Goals

Conversion requires the disintegration of a world. A grasp of the implications of such a disintegration requires a maturity of faith because it involves a process of dying, a death embraced in faith. One who enters into the process of the catechumenate is asked to trust other persons who have passed through this process before him or her. These others are witnesses. They are able to testify that this first death is to be one of many deaths through which the person committed to Christ must pass. The life of a Christian comes to be perceived as a dying so that one may live, a dying to the self-centered self so that one may learn to reach outward in love and service toward others.

It is in this perspective that we have spoken of the catechumenate as the path of conversion. Just as the Christian life has been trivialized, so has been the common Christian view of sin—it has been virtually trivialized out of existence. For many people, sin, if it has any content at all, is no more than certain "naughty acts." If we fail to recognize the radical nature of sin, we will inevitably fail to recognize the radical need of human beings for redemption and the radical act of God by which that redemption has been achieved. Trivialization blinds us to both the horror and the glory.

The goal of the catechumenate is the recognition of mankind's alienation from its authentic humanity. Human beings turned in on themselves, acting only out of pride, self-interest, and arrogance, are people alienated from themselves. This is where sin lies in all its destructive power, in the assertion of self above all else. Christian faith, looking at Christ on the cross, calls us to recognize the result of sin. Sin tears down, uproots, destroys. The biblical witness is that mankind is called to build up, plant, create, to be co-creators with God. To enter such a commitment to God's purposes requires the radical conversion spoken of earlier. The patient and extended structuring of the catechumenate is a method by which a person is led, step by step, to the point of rejecting the power of sin and adhering to the creative love of God. If our patterns of pastoral ministry isolate the rite of Baptism from this fundamental act of conversion, we are left with an external ritual divorced from its meaning. The meaning of the external ritual must be internalized in the life of every Christian. The catechumenate is structured to effect that internalization.

It is obvious that no single method of formation would be capable of accomplishing this internalization, given the realities of human diversity. Factors of culture, personal history, temperament, and individual personality all contribute to a profound need for a flexible and open structure through which the "Paschal Mystery" can be brought into touch with the distinctive character of the individual. Out of that diversity, we are called into an all-embracing unity, yet it is a unity that does not obliterate the rich variety of the human family. The unity of God's people lies in their common identity in Christ, not in conformity to a narrow model of theology, or spirituality, or worship. The structure of the catechumenate is thus an open structure, not a process of "formation" (as the word has often implied in the past) in which persons are pressed into a single mold. It is important to be sensitive to this contrast to the rigid concept of formation common in earlier decades, and the open pattern of formation envisaged in the catechumenate and in pastoral care as a whole. The latter is more an unfolding, an opening up of the particular and distinct ways in which the Holy Spirit is at work in the catechumen.

One of the first goals of the catechumenate is a developed awareness in the individual of their own salvation history. This involves an awakening to a sense of God's purposes in their own life, a recognition that each individual is called to a personal spiritual journey, the path of faith. It is obvious that the quality of pastoral care experienced at this preliminary stage is a matter of the highest importance to the future growth of the individual. At this point, the person is, in effect, seeking faith. The easy temptation is to respond to that search with essentially external religious answers. This is the point at which Christianity comes all too easily to be identified with a particular liturgical routine, or at which there may even be a premature rush to the font. This all-too-frequent response on the part of clergy indicates a failure at this stage to deal with the fundamental questions: What is faith? What are the implications of faith for me if I risk conversion?

If I may judge from the number of seminarians I have seen undertake theological studies without having dealt with this issue, then it seems this level of ministry is usually passed over. When it takes place, other forms of Christian education attempt to build where there is no clear foundation. The result is a body of laity (and perhaps of clergy as well) who flounder as they attempt to lead the Christian life, or else who identify that life with more or less regular performance of prescribed liturgical routines. The fact that many aspirants for Holy Orders come to seminary in this state is a sobering indication of the condition of the Church as a whole when an authentic foundation is not a primary pastoral concern for each individual, or their godparents, who asks for Baptism. Baptism is impoverished as a sign of faith if we uproot it from this wider framework of pastoral care.

Public Dimensions of Formation

Private pastoral attention to the individual, a kind of pre-catechumenate, yields in due course to a public context of preparation for baptism. It is at this point that we can speak of the catechumenate proper, the point at which those who are seeking faith in Christ stand before the assembly of baptized Christians both to acknowledge that search publicly and at the same time to enter a process of Christian socialization. This ceremony takes place at the principal Sunday liturgy of the local parish or mission. From this time onward the process of formation being engaged by the catechumens unfolds in relation to the life of the local community from whom sponsors have been chosen for each catechumen. These sponsors represent the local church with a particular intensity as they accompany the catechumen through the months of formation. The catechumens are held in the awareness of the whole community, however, as they are prayed for each Sunday in the intercession.

We see here a marvelous example of a sustaining pastoral care that is also articulated in the liturgy. This saves the intercession from being an anonymous recital of names and intentions, as is so often the case. The concern being expressed in corporate prayer is at the same time being effected tangibly in the structured ministry of the catechumenate.

Another significant aspect of this pattern is the authenticity it gives to the role of the sponsors. All too frequently, the promises made by godparents at baptism are a ritual recital of good dispositions toward the candidate, yet they are seldom reflected in serious personal attention to the spiritual nurture of the candidate. In this familiar model, the godparents' role has been reduced to a ritual and superficial routine for so long that we are no longer sensitive to its original importance. In the process of an authentic catechumenate, the sponsor is one who has stood beside the catechumen and has thus shared a potent personal and spiritual relation. By the time of the baptism itself, the voice of the sponsor is a significant witness to the readiness of the candidate to receive the sign of faith, since the sponsor has been in a position to observe at first hand the catechumen's spiritual growth and often to have experienced significant growth in his or her own life in the process.

The content of the catechumenate is multifaceted. So-called "Confirmation classes" in the Episcopal Church often focus on matters in Church history, or on external concerns about liturgical practices favored in the local parish. The sessions of the catechumenate must dig much more deeply. It is common to reflect on fundamental Christian doctrines through serious attention to the Creeds and the Catechism. This requires real skill on the part of the teachers so that these sessions do not degenerate into indoctrination but rather are the opportunity for guided reflection and sharing on the content of the Christian faith and its relevance to our daily lives.

It is also appropriate during the period of the catechumenate for the catechumens to share in the public worship of the community, to hear with them the proclamation of the Word of God and to be present when the assembly prays for them. In the ancient catechumenate, the catechumens were asked to leave after the intercession because the Eucharist was held to be appropriate only for those already baptized. Although there is much integrity in this view, it seems somewhat affected in our contemporary situation when anyone who wants to do so may come in to share in the eucharistic celebration. Further, given the predominance of infant Baptism in terms of frequency, the process of formation being described will often involve persons who have already been baptized. It is thus impossible to take over the primitive model in a rigid fashion, and pastoral flexibility is required. But perhaps in the case of unbaptized adults (including older adolescents), it might be fruitful to all if the catechumens were to leave after the Liturgy of the Word in order to take part in a catechumenal session. Their departure would also raise within the congregation an awareness of the relation of the Eucharist to their baptismal identity.

Yet another dimension of the formation process is instruction on the life of prayer. There has been an awakening in recent years to the important need for parish priests to undertake the ministry of spiritual direction. This is, quite evidently, an aspect of catechumenal formation that has been seriously lacking from our models of pastoral care. Anyone who has been involved in serious lay education in recent years can testify to the hunger among many laity for a genuine life of prayer. As it has been lacking from parish programs of lay education, it has not been part of the background of men and women who have entered seminary, with only rare exceptions. Many clergy feel intimidated when faced with this need on the part of laity because they recognize their own lack in this area. It is obviously a need that knows no laity/clergy distinction, but it is a ministry for which laity have a right to look to their pastors for guidance. Often a layperson will manifest great gifts for spiritual direction, and these gifts must be encouraged for the benefit of all. This is a vast and demanding ministry, all the more so because it has been so often neglected. A restored catechumenate offers a structure in which this ministry can be restored to its normative place in parish life, to be nurtured and developed step by step.

Finally, mature formation must involve the taking up of some specific form of ministry. For too many centuries, the ministry of the Church has been narrowly identified with the work of the ordained clergy, specifically in regard to responsibility for the celebration of the Sacraments and related areas of pastoral care. The Church is gradually awakening to the inadequacy of this clericalized view of ministry. But if the laity as a whole are to come to see ministry developing from within their own baptismal commitment, the Church must ask them to put their hands to the plow. This cannot be mere theory. Human laziness makes it all too easy to allow a narrow concept of ministry to be identified with ordination. We are formed through what we say and do, so the *doing* of ministry is a fundamental part of Christian formation.

The undertaking of some form of service through the offering of one's time and energy in an area of social justice, for example, is the means by which a faith in the Incarnation is itself made flesh in the realities of our world. One who serves receives far more than he or she gives, because through identification with the pain of others—their lack of work or of basic human necessities, or their victimization through social injustice—we find our world expanded, our humanity deepened. This is not because service of others produces warm feelings of self-justification. Rather, a true identification with others, a helpless sense of their helplessness, redeems us from the protective barriers society erects to shield us from awareness of others' pain. As Christians we are not permitted to be indifferent to that pain because, in the words of Daniel Berrigan quoted earlier, "Christ . . . takes in His gospel net all the hue and cry of existence"—and he does so through the members of his Body. Membership in the Church is our corporate identification with Christ and so also in his embracing of the whole creation. Service in the world, in all its varied forms, is our participation in the ministry of Christ according to our particular gifts. It is the action that gives honesty to our worship and builds a strong bridge between what we say in our liturgical prayer and what we do in our daily lives.

These four dimensions do not give a rigid structure to Christian formation, but they do give it a degree of substance that has not generally been characteristic of preparation for Baptism. They seem to reflect a level of commitment that in recent centuries has been an expectation for candidates for ordination, yet all four dimensions draw their meaning from the promises made in the Baptismal Covenant.[6] The words of the ritual are not an end in themselves. They are a commitment to a lifestyle for which the catechumenate is the preparation. Knowledge of the Church's faith, participation in its worship, a life of prayer, and a commitment to service are not the marks of an elite minority; they are the signs of a faithful life. The integration of these four dimensions in the lives of individual Christians will vary, sometimes to a significant degree, but the dimensions themselves are the foundations of the Christian life.

"If the Foundations Be Destroyed . . ."

The cry of the psalmist is a sobering warning to anyone who would attempt to speak of Christian foundations in such a clearly idealistic way. All through this essay there has hovered a shadow: The catechumenate, to which so much attention has been directed, is a ministry from the Church's past. Are we looking at it today through rose-colored glasses? And even if it did once enjoy the type of pastoral significance that has been ascribed to it, is it not naive in the extreme to think it can be restored to this fruitful and vital role in our time? We are living in a radically different situation, both culturally and socially, from that of the Church in the fourth and fifth centuries, and we are carrying a long history of pastoral indifference to the model that has been put forward here. Is it possible to turn all that around?

Prophetic voices remind us that the Church is always called to the reformation of its life and renewed fidelity to the Gospel. To accept defection as definitive is to replace Christian hope with an unchristian despair. Certainly our present situation is grave, but it has been grave before, and the Church's life has risen from the ashes, renewed by the gift of grace. If the signs of reform and renewal that can be seen in the Church today are to be truly effective in the transformation of the Christian life, a point of cohesion is needed. The various renewal movements often generate a type of sectarian mindset that identifies the work of the Holy Spirit with its programs. A basic point in this essay is that the Church's unity is not founded on a single spiritual model but is a unity that celebrates the marvelous diversity of God's people. If our vision takes the Incarnation as its model, we shall recognize the ultimate complementarity of our diversity.

All of this suggests a fundamental need to discover the Church, both in the light of the biblical witness and under the present guidance of the Holy Spirit in all the facets of the ecumenical movement. Christians throughout the world continue to make the creedal proclamation that the Church is "one, holy, catholic and apostolic" and yet live complacently with a practical theology of the Church that contradicts that affirmation. Here is an obvious area in which the restored catechumenate would offer an opportunity to transcend a narrow sectarianism in reflecting on the imperatives placed on us by the understanding of the Church proclaimed in the Creeds.

The rediscovery of the doctrine of the Church summons us from a sectarian mentality and from an individualized piety. The participation of Christians in corporate worship is a sign of our sense of what it means to *be* the Church. The significance of corporate worship every Sunday is complementary to the renewed doctrine of the Church spoken of above. But truly *corporate* worship is not the result merely of having a number of people attend the same liturgical celebration. The renewed liturgical principles that influenced the rites of the new *Book of Common Prayer* must be internalized in the reshaping of our attitudes toward liturgical worship. Otherwise the new rites will be only a disguise, a set of ritual adjustments without internal substance. Though we must give serious pastoral attention to formation for a life of prayer, private prayer must not be a surrogate for corporate prayer. It is in the latter—in common prayer as the people of God—that we experience the ecclesial significance of corporate worship. It is in the Sunday celebration that all the strands of ministry and pastoral care come together: The baptized servant community gathers to be nourished through word and sacrament, which are the focus of the forms of ordained service. From that assembly, that place of common memory and identity in Christ, the members of the Body go forth to serve according to all their diverse gifts.

Such a sense of being the Church has been notably lacking in most patterns of Christian education. As a result, liturgical worship has itself been skewed and has often degenerated into a routine for the cultivation of an essentially private piety. No pattern of worship is an end in itself; rather, liturgical prayer is the place of meeting between God and the community of believers. Its content is praise and thanksgiving of the God who is the Father of all, who has become incarnate in human history, and who is a continuing source of grace and power in the lives of those who believe.

It must be the goal of Christian formation to build up the community into maturity of faith. All the dimensions of pastoral care are ordered to the development and nurture of an integration of faith, worship, and a life of service. Again, in the Creeds, we profess the faith that the Church is "holy"—but to say that implies that each of its members is called to a holy life. A holy life is a whole life, an integrated life in which there is a progressive growth into an ever-deepening conformation to God's purposes. For such spiritual growth to come to fulfillment, the connections among faith, worship, and service must be nourished and matured. This growth into holiness is the goal of all Christian formation and pastoral care: the building up of the holy people of God.

6

Preaching and Pastoral Care

O. C. Edwards, Jr.

Almost sixty years ago, Henry Sloane Coffin, after dividing his time between teaching at Union Theological Seminary and being pastor of Madison Avenue Presbyterian Church and later becoming president of Union, published a set of his lectures in homiletics that had been designed to help young clergy know where to look for sermon ideas.[1] The sources of inspiration were indicated under five categories: expository, doctrinal, ethical, pastoral, and evangelistic preaching. This taxonomy, if valid, suggests that preaching related to pastoral care can be defined negatively as preaching that is neither expository nor about doctrine or ethics nor for the purpose of converting non-Christians. The mere listing of the categories, however, brings into question their adequacy as a means of classifying sermons. Ethics and doctrine relate to content, but exposition is a homiletical method and evangelism a purpose. Further, when one looks at the chapter on pastoral preaching, one discovers that it tells how one gleans sermon ideas from pastoral contacts instead of telling what distinguishes pastoral preaching from any other kind. Thus the person seeking a way of determining what demarcates the boundary between preaching related to pastoral care and other kinds of preaching will have to look further. That by itself is not gravely disappointing, because Coffin's book was published before the appearance of Harry Emerson Fosdick's essay on "problem-centered preaching," which was to give a new meaning to pastoral preaching. Nevertheless, a survey of more recent literature does not reveal any sufficiently agreed-on definition of pastoral care to make clear what preaching related to pastoral care is. Before the relation of preaching to pastoral care can be discussed, it is necessary to say what is meant by pastoral care.

What Is Pastoral Care?

One way of seeking a definition of pastoral care is to study histories of the subject. The pioneering work in this field is *A History of the Cure of Souls* by John T. McNeill. McNeill prefaces his account of the development of pastoral care in the Christian Church with brief chapters on similar phenomena in the Old Testament, among Greek philosophers, and in the "higher" non-Christian religions. According to his definition, "the cure of souls is . . . the sustaining and curative treatment of persons in those matters that reach beyond the requirements of animal life."[2] In practice, he has limited his attention largely to the treatment of sin and guilt and to spiritual direction—or, as Clebsch and Jaekle put it, he "deals mainly with pastoral discipline."[3]

A much more inclusive view of pastoral care is given by church historian William A. Clebsch and pastoral counselor Charles R. Jaekle in the essay and collection of source material they published under the title *Pastoral Care in Historical Perspective*. They classify the activities of pastoral care into four groups: healing, sustaining, guiding, and reconciling. These categories will be examined below, but first it is necessary to look at the authors' definition of pastoral care:

> The ministry of the cure of souls, or pastoral care, consists of helping acts, done by representative Christian persons, directed toward the healing, sustaining, guiding, and reconciling of troubled persons whose troubles arise in the context of ultimate meanings and concerns.[4]

The first thing to be noticed about this definition is that it limits pastoral care to ministrations to individuals, and limits it further by specifying that those individuals be in crisis. This definition, which distinguishes pastoral care from pastoral work with groups, appears repeatedly, as in the following passage:

> Frequently pastoral care seeks to introduce an individual into a group in order to place him in the way of finding relief. When that introduction is undertaken, however, *for the sake of the group, pastoral care ceases* and some other ministry, perhaps evangelism, begins.[5]

The other activities from which pastoral care is distinguished are: "preaching, conducting public worship, managing and organizing an institution, sensitizing community conscience, leading an exemplary life, etc."[6] and "institutional, liturgical, homiletical, and educational functions of the ministerial profession.[7] The authors consistently distinguish pastoral care from, on the one hand, the other work of clergy, and, on the other, that of other helping professionals. Pastoral care, they assert, is the work of (usually ordained) ministers with troubled individuals.

Clebsch and Jaekle define the four functions of pastoral care specifically. *Healing*, for instance, has normally to do with the curing of physical ailments. Though the authors use such general phrases as "restoration to wholeness" and insist that healing always involves the hope "that the troubled person will become integrated on a higher spiritual level than he has previously experienced",[8] their emphasis is on *physical* cure. It is indicated in their list of healing "instrumentalities and methods": anointing, saints and relics, charismatic healers, exorcism, and magico-medicine." Not surprisingly, they find the healing function the "most problematical" today, although they see rich possibilities for its development in combination with the other three functions.[9]

Sustaining is defined as helping persons deal with an overwhelming sense of loss. It begins with "preservation," the effort to help troubled persons cut their losses, and moves on to "consolation" for the losses that have already occurred, "consolidation" of their resources so that they can go on after the loss, and "redemption" of the loss in the appropriation of the good that comes through it.[10] *Guiding* has to do with helping persons choose between courses of action. It includes moral counsel, spiritual direction, and vocational clarification. As Clebsch and Jaekle point out, increasingly secular outlooks have undercut the authority of traditional Christian guiding and caused persons to expect greater assistance from other helping professions, especially psychotherapy.[11] (Their book, of course, appeared some time before the current revival of interest in spirituality in general and spiritual direction in particular.) *Reconciling* has to do with the restoration of relations between human beings and between them and God. The authors think that in an age like ours, in which feelings of guilt and alienation are so common, Christian pastoral care, with its ritualized authorization, has great promise for renewal in the ministry of reconciliation.

The four functions of pastoral care, which Clebsch and Jaekle derived in part from Seward Hiltner but modified to suit their needs, have greatly influenced subsequent literature on pastoral care, and their adequacy seems often to have been accepted without question. Later in this chapter the question of whether pastoral care should be restricted to ministry to individuals in crisis will be considered; the issue of whether more functions can and should be included will be prescinded. The only aspect of the list to be considered at this point is its focus, which is on ministerial activities for individuals. As a helpful analytical tool, the list is at once abstract and concerned with practice, but there is very little transcendent reference in its categories. Although it is recognized that the parties involved often thought ministers were channels of divine activity, the authors do not commit themselves to an opinion on the subject. In light of their task, their failure to do so is understandable. When such a diversity of phenomena is under consideration, it is difficult to distinguish between categories of activity and between real and unreal manifestations of that activity. Yet when Christians come to discuss pastoral care from within the community of faith and to set up norms for it, the theological perspective that analyzes it in terms of divine involvement not only *may* but *must* be present. Clebsch and Jaekle could bypass that question, but we may not. And we will not, but for the moment we shall defer it.

A recent addition to the literature has great value for the present discussion. In *A History of Pastoral Care in America*, E. Brooks Holifield has tried to look not only at the phenomena but at "popular culture, class structure, the national economy, the organization of parishes, and the patterns of theological education" as well.[12] Thus he is able to understand in their social context developments in the history of pastoral care. He has limited his study of pastoral care to the private conversations of clergy with their parishioners. The interest of the topic lies in the changing subjects of this counseling and the changing understanding of what such interviews were expected to accomplish. The basic trend of that change is indicated in Holifield's subtitle, "From Salvation to Self-Realization." Two recurrent theological themes are sin and growth, yet the self becomes the real focus of the discussion:

> The story proceeds from an ideal of self-denial to one of self-love, from self-love to self-culture, from self-culture to self-mastery, from self-mastery to self-realization within a trustworthy culture, and finally to a later form of self-realization counterposed against cultural mores and social institutions.[13]

One can speak of this as a transition from an essentially theological mode of self-understanding to an essentially psychological one. In Holifield's words, "The introspective piety in the American Protestant heritage—the preoccupation with inwardness, rebirth, conversion, revival—was easily translated into a secular psychological piety."[14] In the early sixties, when Clebsch and Jaekle wrote their book, pastoral care in American Protestantism was being limited virtually to pastoral counseling, and that counseling was wed to a Rogerian psychology of self-realization that is not coextensive with that of the gospel.

This state of affairs, Holifield saw, resulted from a combination of conditions that accrued after the Second World War:

> a theological revolt against legalism, the recovery of older Protestant doctrines, a white-collar economy, a burgeoning cultural preoccupation with psychology, postwar affluence, the constraints of seminary training, a critique of mass culture, and an ethic of self-realization.[15]

One who reflected most of these trends and blended their presuppositions into a psychotherapeutic theory that could be used by pastoral theologians was Carl Rogers, who had studied at Union Theological Seminary before transferring to Columbia University to become a psychologist. Rogers' personality theory rejected the Freudian belief that conflicts among the id, the ego, and the superego were perpetual; it asserted instead that persons become themselves through the compromise they make between their own perceptions and values and the internalized perceptions and values of other individuals and social institutions. A consequence of this theory is that society and institutions are considered oppressive.

Rogerian therapy was thus based on the assumption that individuals need a lot of acceptance in order to realize their self-potential. This "client-centered therapy" called on the therapist to resist even the attempt to clarify the feelings of the client, because doing so implied that the therapist understood them better than the client; instead, the therapist was to seek to understand the client's frame of reference. Thus Rogerian therapy was morally nonjudgmental and dedicated to the assumption that every impulse and inclination of the client was to be accepted without question.

Holifield's thesis, then, that pastoral care in America has been transformed from an effort to save souls to one directed toward enabling self-realization through psychotherapy seems to be supported. Also substantiated is his claim that this change represents broad changes in American culture. Thus Holifield's work can be understood as supporting Philip Rieff's theory that Christian culture "as a unitary system of common belief" has been replaced in our society by the concept of "psychological man."[16] This is to say that, in our very pluralistic culture, about the only remaining orthodoxy is the conviction that psychological explanation is true. This conviction is as common among those in the churches who still construct reality in a Christian way as it is among those who reject religious explanation, whether Christian or otherwise. As a result of this psychologism, it became possible for wide segments of non-Roman American Christianity to treat pastoral counseling as the major activity of parochial ministry. It is reflected even in the writings of those, such as Howard Clinebell, who reacted against the Rogerian model:

> The only relevance that really matters is relevance to the *deep needs of persons*—relevance to the places in their lives where they hurt and hope, curse, and pray, hunger for meaning and for significant relationships. Pastoral counseling is a valuable instrument by which the church stays relevant to human need.[17]

He goes on to list the various kinds of counseling (informal, marriage and family, supportive, crisis, referral, educative, group, confrontational, religious-existential, and depth) and says:

> A minister's functional self-image is derived from his picture of the types and goals of the counseling he must do in order to fulfill his ministry. With the exception of depth counseling, opportunities to do

the above types are unavoidable in a person-centered ministry. Furthermore, *the minister is in a strategic position to do them well,* provided he is adequately trained. Proficiency in all these types (excluding depth counseling) is necessary for a fully effective ministry. For these reasons they may be regarded as *normative* for *pastoral* counseling.[18]

Since it is hard to see how any cleric engaged in all these kinds of counseling in even a moderate-sized parish would have much time to do anything else, the psychologization of pastoral care seems virtually complete.

Holifield describes this shift in a paragraph worth quoting in full:

> The pastoral theologians began to distinguish pastoral counseling, therefore, as a special form of pastoral care. By *pastoral care*, they were referring to the broader range of pastoral duties; by *pastoral counseling*, they had in mind a more specific activity resting on knowledge of the psychotherapeutic traditions. They tried to avoid a one-sided preoccupation with counseling, but that was hard to do. Most pastors who followed their writings closely made it clear that counseling was their strongest interest. It might have been true, as Russell Dicks said in 1950, that 90 percent of the clergy were doing "little effective pastoral work or personal counseling of any kind," but an increasing number of ministers at least were under the impression that their parishioners were assigning them new responsibilities as counselors. A study by Samuel Blizzard at Princeton revealed that the clergy believed themselves to be devoting 175 million hours a year to pastoral counseling. That figure, which was quite unbelievable, served at least as a sketch of pastoral self-consciousness in an age of psychology. And there were indications that the public did turn with an increasing frequency to the clergy as counselors. A survey conducted during the 1950s by the National Institute of Mental Health showed that 42 percent of all people who sought help for emotional problems turned first to their ministers. "A good minister cannot now escape personal counseling," wrote Harry Emerson Fosdick in 1960. "It is in the air." Indeed it was. The ethicist Gibson Winter at the University of Chicago complained that ministers were coming to think of counseling as "*the* pastoral care of the Church," even though they might lack time to do much of it. "The atypical case," Winter charged, "is becoming the norm of the Church's pastoral function."[19]

The inadequacy of the above as an understanding of pastoral care can readily be seen when one thinks of pastoral duties. First and foremost they are liturgical. Closely related is the task of preaching. The parish and therefore the pastor needs to be involved in evangelization and missionary activity, and it must have a program of Christian education that includes (but is not limited to) catechesis. Woe to the pastor who does not recognize that administration is a ministry, not to mention a charism (1 Cor. 12:28)! Spiritual instruction, direction, and leadership are returning to favor as pastoral activities. One hopes there is no corresponding decline in Christian social action. Certainly, moral guidance of many kinds is expected from the pastor, whatever Carl Rogers may have said. New members need to be incorporated into the parochial community. All members need help in understanding the Christian construction of reality. Even though many pastors are embarrassed by its necessity, stewardship is a vital ministry. Renewal of members needs to go on constantly. Since all these tasks are more than ordained professionals can do and, more importantly, since the nature of the church requires it, the mutual and total ministry of all the body must be enabled. Beyond that there are denominational duties, ecumenical involvements, and community activities in which the pastor must be engaged. And this has not even been to mention such important pastoral tasks as visiting the sick, comforting the bereaved, and assisting families in crisis, since any of these could be claimed by an imperialistic understanding of counseling as *the* definitive pastoral duty.

All of the above is to say that the reduction of pastoral care to pastoral counseling has been a *reductio ad absurdum*. What, then, about the definitions of pastoral care given by historians: Can we limit pastoral care to care for individuals in crisis? Here, it seems, a distinction must be made between pastoral care in its narrower and its wider definitions. There is a tradition of using "pastoral" to refer to ministry to suffering persons, and a common form of linguistic usage would be ignored if this narrow sense were disallowed. At the same time, pastoral care refers to *all* the work of pastors. This wider definition can be spoken of in terms of three sets of relations. The community has a relation to God that takes the form of worship. Members of the community relate to one another in *koinonia*. They also relate to those who are not yet members by "corporal works of mercy" (to use the traditional phrase) and evangelization. Pastors furnish leadership in all these activities, and all the pastoral duties listed in the previous paragraph can be subsumed under one or another of these relations. Thus the wider sense of pastoral care includes all these duties.

What Is Preaching?

Preaching may not be as difficult to define as pastoral care. Elsewhere, the present writer has tried to define it. His first attempt was to find an adequate way of describing anything that could be recognized as a sermon. The results were as follows:

> A sermon is a speech delivered in a Christian assembly for worship by an authorized person that applies some point of doctrine, usually drawn from a biblical passage, to the lives of the members of the congregation with the purpose of moving them by the use of narrative analogy and other rhetorical devices to accept the application and to act on the basis of it.[20]

Since, however, the volume in which the present essay appears is written from an Anglican perspective, one must restrict the above definition to the specific preaching that is characteristic of liturgical churches. For that purpose we turn to the definition (given in the work just cited) of a eucharistic homily. It is a narrowing of the definition of the generic sermon:

> A homily is a sermon preached at the eucharistic assembly by a bishop, presbyter, or deacon that applies a point of doctrine drawn from that day's gospel to the lives of the members of the congregation with the purpose of moving them by the use of narrative analogy and other rhetorical devices to accept that application and to act on the basis of it both in their participation in the liturgy and as they go forth into the world.[21]

This definition, however, is sufficiently lapidary to call for some explication of the uniqueness of the liturgical homily. The first point to be made is that liturgical preaching is always related to the date in the Christian year when the sermon is preached; some topics, for instance, are more suited for Lent than for Easter. Also, the biblical passage applied to the life of the congregation is one of those appointed in the lectionary to be read at that service. There are many, including the present writer, who share the conviction that the lection on which the homily is based should be the gospel for the day. Further, the liturgical homily is not written to exist independently but rather to be part of a liturgy, and its context in the liturgy needs to be reflected in the way it is written. As William Skudlarek has said, "We need to know why we should lift up our hearts."[22] The homily's place in the liturgy, together with the rapid pace of contemporary life and the brevity of contemporary attention spans, determines the ideal length of such a homily. A sermon for a Sunday Eucharist should not normally be more than ten to fifteen minutes in length. And that length affects the scope of the homily; only certain kinds of issues can be handled adequately in the time available. Or, more accurately, only certain kinds of statements about those issues can be made successfully. Finally, good liturgical preaching takes cognizance of a point made by Urban T. Holmes III:

> The sermon or homily . . . has as its object the inscape of existence, not the landscape. Preaching is not teaching. As an act of evangelizing the deep memory, it needs to reveal to us the inner person, not describe the externals.[23]

This, like some of the other characteristics of the liturgical homily, is something more easily said than done.

Discussed has been the generic liturgical homily rather than anything distinctively Anglican. It might be asked if there is anything that characterizes Anglican preaching. Any normative answer would have to be from an individual viewpoint. The kind of preaching described in the previous paragraph and the one to follow would serve for the present writer. Any other answer would have to be descriptive and historical. It could be said that most Anglican sermons are liturgical in the sense that they are preached in the context of liturgy, based on the biblical propers for the day, fitted to the liturgical season, and applied to the life of the congregation. The liturgy has not always been the Eucharist, since until recently the main "preaching service" in the Church of England was Evening Prayer and in the Episcopal Church, Morning Prayer. But its being liturgical distinguished it from Protestant preaching, and its occurrence at all made it different from standard Roman practice. Both of these contrasts are disappearing. Post-Vatican II Roman Catholicism places great emphasis on the proclamation of the Word, and Protestants are discovering the liturgy and the lectionary, as can be seen in the book by Stratman discussed below. The liturgical homily could become the ecumenical norm.

Any other observations would have to be impressionistic. Generally Anglican preaching has been hospitable to contemporary thought and has related faith to it and expressed it in its vocabulary. It has always had a historical orientation, being very aware of the ongoing tradition of the Church. It has been very practical and down to earth and at the same time concerned with spiritual development. And, at its best, Anglican preaching has always been characterized by a kind of graceful wit. This has been a praise of God through intellectual play and joy in the beauty of language. Anyone who heard the sermon of the Archbishop of Canterbury at the wedding of Prince Charles and Lady Diana Spencer will know what I mean.

In terms of a method for sermon preparation, this definition means that one begins with a careful exegesis of the gospel. This is for the purpose of discovering the situation in the text and the attitude of the text toward that situation. Then the preacher reflects on the issues currently of concern in the congregation—whether they be pastoral in the narrow sense, spiritual, moral, theological, social, or what have you—and decides which of them reflects a situation most nearly parallel to that in the text. One tries to find a contemporary situation of concern to the congregation that has operating in it a principle in common with the situation in the text; the situation in the congregation, then, is one in which the affirmation made in the text needs to be heard. When that situation has been found (and it is discovered that it has not been preached on too often recently), it becomes the subject of the sermon. Even though the preparation has begun with the text, the order of preparation is not the order of presentation. The sermon should begin with either the situation in the congregation or with an introductory device that leads into consideration of the issues; it begins with parishioners as they are. Then it moves to the situation in the text and demonstrates the parallelism. It is the revelation of this common principle in the two situations that justifies the third step in the sermon, the transfer to the situation in the congregation of the perspective the text has on the situation in the text. Confidence in the applicability of that perspective to contemporary situations is part of what is meant when we call the Bible inspired, and it is the ground on which the whole preaching enterprise is founded[24]

The discovery of a contemporary situation that has an underlying principle in common with the situation in the text of the gospel for the day may sound more difficult than it is. For instance, a short homily was to be preached in a seminary chapel on Wednesday in Holy Week. In the gospel Jesus said it was one of the Twelve who would betray him and, incredibly, they had no idea which of their members was likely to do that. An analogy was seen between that story and the closeness of the student body with their shared hopes for future ministry. The sermon tried to prepare the students for a future time when one or more of their number would betray their vocation or leave their ministry. Or, again, on the Feast of the Ascension an interim rector used Jesus' statement to the Twelve that he had to go away so the Paraclete could come in order to say goodbye to the parish and prepare it for the first services of the new rector on the following Sunday. Other examples of this effort to discover the common principle operating between the situation in the text and that in the congregation can be seen in the sermons that make up over half the writer's book *The Living and Active Word: One Way to Preach From the Bible Today.*

What Is Pastoral Preaching?

Having discussed the thorny issue of the definition of pastoral care and the—to this writer, at any rate—less problematic one of what preaching is, we are now in a position to deal with the question that is the subject of this chapter. The topic, however, has a history, and constructive proposals should not be advanced before one has explored what previous writers have said about it.

As suggested earlier, the modern era of preaching as "personal counseling on a group scale" begins with Harry Emerson Fosdick. "It was Fosdick who persuaded a large segment of liberal Protestant clergy to refashion the sermon in the image of the counseling session."[25] Much of the interest in pastoral counseling that was subsequently to pervade pastoral care can be traced to his influence. The major statement of Fosdick's theory of preaching occurred in an article he wrote for the July 1928 issue of *Harper's Magazine* under the title "What is the Matter With Preaching?"[26] This article clearly shows three main influences on the author's thought: modern psychology, the social gospel, and John Dewey's learning theory.[27] Fosdick's method of preaching has been referred to as "life-situation" or "problem-centered" preaching, but he himself referred to it as the "project method," which seems to be derived from Dewey.

Fosdick came close to reducing his theory to one short paragraph:

> Every sermon should have for its main business the solving of some problem—a vital, important problem, puzzling minds, burdening consciences, distracting lives—and any sermon which thus does tackle a real problem, throw even a little light on it, and help some individuals practically to find their way through it cannot be altogether uninteresting.[28]

This "project method" of preaching was developed in conscious contradistinction to the two prevailing methods of the time— expository and topical. Fosdick's description of the classical expository form cannot be improved:

> First, the elucidation of a Scriptural text, in its historic occasion, its logical meaning in the context, its setting in the theology and ethic of the ancient writer; second, application to the auditors of the truth involved; third, exhortation to decide about the truth and act on it.[29]

Topical preaching, on the other hand, amounted to no more than a lecture on a subject of current interest, and it was characterized by a yearning after relevance, not to say trendiness. Fosdick saw a high correlation between those who preached topical sermons and those who lost their sense of vocation and left the ministry. And he would have argued that his method of preaching was just as biblical as that of the expository preachers; it was just that he knew folks did not "come to church desperately anxious to discover what happened to the Jebusites."[30]

Fosdick understands pastoral care and preaching in terms of ministry to indiviudals in crisis.

He says:

> I should despair, therefore, of any man's sustained enthusiasm and efficiency in the pulpit if he were not in constant, confidential relationship with individuals. Personal work and preaching are twins. As I watch some preachers swept off their feet by the demands of their own various organizations, falling under the spell of bigness, and rushing from one committee to another to put over some new scheme to enlarge the work or save the world, I do not wonder at the futility which so often besets them. They are doing everything except their chief business, for that lies inside individuals.[31]

It is not surprising that he also says: "This, I take it, is the final test of a sermon's worth: how many individuals wish to see the preacher alone?"[32]

Surprisingly enough, Fosdick never wrote a homiletical textbook that inculcated his theories, and it was some time before anyone else devoted a book-length study to the relation of pastoral care to preaching. A pioneering work was Edgar N. Jackson's *A Psychology for Preaching*, which appeared in 1961 with a preface by Fosdick.[33] It is a disappointment, however, to anyone who expects to find in it either a personality theory or much insight into how one can achieve Fosdick's goal of preaching counseling on a group scale. Instead it is the sort of book that flooded the market in the years after World War II, one that promised psychological insight to professional practitioners to help them understand their customers or clients and thus be more successful.

Jackson's first thirty pages, which constitute the longest chapter in the book, are on the "psychology" of preaching, in the sense of being helpful hints to keep sermons interesting. The next chapter deals with differing congregational responses to what is called "repressive-inspirational" preaching and "analytic" preaching. In a repressive-inspirational sermon, "the evil, the unpleasant, the injurious is denied as unreal, and the pleasant, the healthful, and the creative is given a special place in thought and meditation."[34] The following chapter tells the pastor how to achieve a sense of identity with the congregation. It is followed by another chapter on the psychological effect of the setting in which preaching (and worship) is done. Next there are two chapters that relate group dynamics to preaching. The last chapter is on the preaching of Jesus, and only the penultimate one deals with the relation of pastoral counseling to preaching, the subject that would have dominated the book if it had been written a decade later. Thus Jackson's work is, for present purposes, mainly of historical interest; it is something of a period piece.

The next important work carried with it the prestige of a distinguished series of books, Prentice-Hall's "Successful Pastoral Counseling" series, edited by Russell L. Dicks. It contains a definition ("Dynamic preaching is basically pastoral care in the context of worship") reminiscent of Fosdick's.[35] Despite every indication it would represent the first real effort to relate preaching to the high tide of the pastoral-counseling movement in the sixties, *Preaching and Pastoral Care*, by Arthur L. Teikmanis, is a real disappointment. Its first three chapters are ordinary enough: The first is a rather good defense of preaching; the second deals mainly with the importance of pastoral calling; and the third deals with various aspects of preparing to preach. The other five chapters, however, consist of nothing but outlines of sermons the author preached to meet the various pastoral needs listed at the beginning of each chapter as representing a particular category of sermon topics. "Preaching to the Crises of Life," for instance, contains sermon outlines on death and dying, grief suffering, physical sickness, emotional illness, loss of self-esteem, marital distress, handicapped living, and problems of retirement age.[36] "Ministering to the Spiritually Isolated" contains summaries of sermons preached to the overanxious, the guilty, the lonely, the discouraged, the hostile, and the bored. The next chapter synopsizes seven sermons on theological topics, and the following one shows ways in which six community problems had been dealt with. The final chapter harkens back to the difficulties felt by individuals in crisis: insecurity, temptations, unworthiness, mature relationships, and acceptance.

The first book (known to this writer) to relate preaching to the pastoral-counseling movement did not appear until 1979. In *Pastor, Preacher, Person: Developing a Pastoral Ministry in Depth*, David K. Switzer has not written an entire book about the relation of pastoral care to preaching; rather, as he says:

> The particular method which is followed in this book is that of adapting some of the insights and procedures and research data of psychotherapy to ministers' ways of thinking about themselves, their operational context within the church, and two central ministerial functions—preaching and pastoral care.[37]

Only two of the five chapters are about preaching. The first has to do with the pastor's sense of identity in his or her role, and is developed by reference to Heije Faber's famous remark about the clown as an image of the pastor, to Carkhuff's "common core of conditions conducive to facilitative human experiences" that he believes are shared by "all effective interpersonal processes," and to the traits Glasse, in his book *Profession: Ministry*, identifies as those of a professional. The second chapter explores the metaphor of the Church as the family of God, by applying to it the traits of healthy human families, as revealed in a study by the Timberlawn Psychiatric Foundation of Dallas (where the author, a professor at Perkins School of Theology, preaches on Sundays). The final chapter tells how to use the Bible in pastoral counseling and is illustrated by several excellent case histories.

Incidentally, just because Switzer illuminates pastoral work with

the findings of psychotherapeutic research, one ought not to think
he makes the common mistake of reducing pastoral activity to
psychotherapy. It is true he had not yet thought through the
justification for transferring theoretical categories from one
discipline to another, but he is well aware of the transcendental
element the Church does *not* share with the therapeutic
community. It is possible to describe him as a pastoral (or, as he
would say, practical) theologian without feeling that *theologian*
is a courtesy title.

Switzer rejects Teikmanis's opinion that "dynamic preaching
is basically pastoral care in the context of worship."[38] (It can be
questioned, however, whether the term meant to Teikmanis what
it did to Switzer.) Switzer, however, insists (quite rightly) that
statements that say "something is really something (else)" are
reductionistic and fail to do justice to either term. Still, he does
see major differences between preaching and pastoral counseling.
"Preaching in such a way as to meet person's needs does not imply
that the pulpit is to be the regular weekly source of psychological
self-help." Or, again: "We must certainly always beware the trap
of developing as our image that of the sanctuary as a large couch
and the preacher as a stand-up shrink."[39] He makes two main
points: first, that preaching should meet human needs, and
second, that

> the one way in which preaching and pastoral counseling *are* alike is that
> they are both interpersonal, primarily verbal processes engaged in by
> the minister with others, and as such there are *some* common goals and
> necessary relational ingredients if they are to be facilitative.[40]

The first of the two chapters on preaching makes the former point
and lays the ground work for the second. The second chapter is
devoted to the "necessary relational ingredients" preaching and
pastoral counseling have in common.

Switzer begins his demonstration that preaching should meet
human needs by showing that preaching can change lives, even
though, as Rodney Hunter thinks, there is "ample evidence to
the contrary."[41] He analyzes human speech from the points of
view of psychology and theology. From a psychological
perspective,

> talking is practiced by the child, first, as a necessary means of
> communicating basic survival and comfort needs, second, as a means

of winning and maintaining parental approval, and, third, as a means of holding the parents emotionally near even when the child is alone.[42]

On the basis of this understanding, he maintains that "the verbal communication of meaning, emotional and intellectual, is a necessary part of this relationship—beginning, developing, and maintaining process."[43] The theological analysis focuses on the performative character of the Word of God. This understanding, of course, when connected with the assumption that preaching is concerned with the Word of God, means that preaching can change lives:

> So with the Word of God. It is spoken, but we do not hear it. But we are not the same either. It is spoken again. We do not respond. It is spoken again. And it may finally strike a responsive chord, being the repeated stimulus which has played its role in producing a person who is now capable of both hearing and responding.[44]

By an analysis of preaching as an interpersonal process, the ground work is laid for the application to preaching of the conditions that facilitate all effective interpersonal communication. Counseling is seen to lead from one stage to another in a circular process in which there is continual feedback and reprocessing. The stages are: self-exploration, goal setting, evaluation of alternatives, decision making, and action. Since both preaching and pastoral counseling seek to effect change and the process by which change is accomplished begins with self-exploration, they have much in common—enough, in fact, to justify the application to preaching of the conditions that facilitate change without any assumption that preaching is merely one among a number of processes that effect changes in people's lives. These facilitative conditions of *all* helping relationships are applied to preaching in the second of the two chapters. Drawn from Carkhuff, they are: empathy, respect, concreteness, genuineness, self-disclosure, confrontation, and immediacy. (It is assumed that the desirability of these conditions as characteristics of preaching is self-evident and need not be argued or detailed at length here.)

In many ways Switzer has written a valuable book. This writer's major regret is that, in addition to listing insights from psychotherapy that can help pastors in their work, the author did not also analyze what is *unique* to the work of the pastor, that which is *dis*continuous with other helping relationships. The relation of preaching to pastoral counseling will only be fully understood after the differences have been explored as thoroughly as the similarities.

The next major book in our field was *Pastoral Counseling and Preaching: A Quest for an Integrated Ministry*, by Donald Capps, a professor of pastoral care and psychology at Phillips University.[45] Capps begins with questions about the relation of preaching to pastoral care and with the observation that since the heyday of the pastoral-counseling movement, it has been assumed that pastoral counseling had far more to offer to preaching than to gain from it. He discusses three theories of the relation between the two fields. The first is essentially the Fosdick approach, that preaching is counseling on a group scale. To this approach he offers the objections that (a) "one can question the view that counseling is preeminent over proclamation, exhortation, teaching, prophetic witness, and other important aspects of preaching,"[46] and (b) this view has never been linked with a clear theory of counseling (although he does concede that Switzer may have provided one at last).

The next theory Capps considers is that preaching and counseling share a common theological basis. He sees this view expressed in the work of Thomas Oden, who claims that the good news of Christian proclamation is present as the *explicit* basis of preaching and as the *implicit* basis of counseling.[47] Capps affirms the common theological basis but questions the distinction between explicit and implicit communication. He criticizes Oden for thinking of communication exclusively in verbal terms and neglecting Paul W. Pruyser and John B. Cobb, Jr.'s insight that theological language can be introduced into the counseling process. Capps also thinks Oden's implicit view of proclamation through relationship in counseling does not pay sufficient attention to the importance of relationship for preaching, especially as it is understood by Nouwen, who claims it involves a capacity for dialogue and availability.

The third understanding of the relationship, listed by Capps, is that which uses psychological theories to assess preaching methods. Here he cites Edgar Jackson as using a group-dynamics standard and James E. Dittes as drawing on the developmental theory of Erik Erikson. Though this method of relating preaching and pastoral counseling has merit, Capps writes, it "[does] not deal directly with the relation between preaching and pastoral counseling."[48] Indeed, the basic complaint against all three approaches is that they fail to show that "preaching and pastoral counseling are two foci of an integrated ministry."[49] If the pastor is to avoid schizophrenia, she or he will have to see these two activities as different manifestations of the same thing.

Capps's thesis is that preaching and pastoral care share a formal structure. In a previous book he had argued that the counseling session consists of four stages: (1) identification of the problem, (2) reconstruction of the problem, (3) diagnostic interpretation, and (4) pastoral intervention. He sees this same structure in sermons and finds it in those of preachers as diverse as John Wesley, Martin Luther King, Jr., John Henry Newman, and Austin Farrer. It should be noted that the third stage, the diagnostic, does not refer to the counselor's assignment of the counselee's problems to category of psychic illness, such as paranoia or schizophrenia; Capps follows the Rogerian view that both counselor and counselee have to eschew the "objective" stance and try to understand the problems from the counselee's internal frame of reference. Diagnosis, then, is *self*-diagnosis with the assistance of the counselor. Another major characteristic of diagnosis, as Capps sees it, is that it can incorporate theological insight and vocabulary, making it consistent with the proclamatory preaching that came to the fore at the same time as client-centered therapy.

Next Capps goes on to show, by reference to particular sermons, that there are six basic types of theological diagnosis in preaching. Each of these types is akin to a type of counseling:

1. Identifying underlying personal motivations (psychoanalysis and others, including transactional analysis).

2. Identifying the range of potential causes (various social therapies, such as social psychology and family counseling).

3. Exposing inadequate formulations of the problem (depth psychology).

4. Drawing attention to untapped personal and spiritual resources (humanistic psychology).

5. Bringing clarity to the problem (various therapies clarify various things).

6. Assessing problems in terms of the deepest intentions of shared human experience (the client-centered approach).

Capps makes some general observations about these diagnostic types. He begins by saying that "each type of theological diagnosis emphasizes a different dimension of our relationship to God."[50] Further, each type also has its characteristic way of reconstructing the problem. Finally, he sees a progression in the six types, from imposing a set of conceptual schema on the diagnosis to allowing the problem to shape the diagnosis. Yet none of these types is devoid of empathy, nor does any possess it fully. Capps does not advocate any of these methods, but he urges pastors to be consistent in the type of theological diagnosis they employ in both their counseling and their preaching. He does, however, have great faith in the value of empathy:

> We may conclude that, even as the best therapists place a high premium on empathetic understanding regardless of their chosen counseling theory, so also the best preachers place a high value on empathetic understanding, whatever their chosen form of diagnosis.[51]

Capps ends his book with a chapter on how proclamation can occur in counseling sessions. (It shares some common concerns with what Switzer had to say about the use of the Bible in counseling, but this issue is aside from our primary interest.)

In evaluating Capps's effort to find a common principle in preaching and pastoral counseling, it can be said that, though his formal structure is not necessarily significant, his recognition of the theological nature of diagnosis and of the need for proclamation in counseling points toward an overarching theological vision of the Church and its ministry, one in which pastoral counseling and preaching belong together as parts of the same work. (A type of preaching that very closely follows Capps's formal structure is discussed by Eugene L. Lowry in *The Homiletical Plot: The Sermon as Narrative Art Form.*[52]

The last book to be examined represents a turn away from the understanding of pastoral preaching as counseling on a group scale that has dominated the field since Fosdick. In *Pastoral Preaching: Timeless Truth for Changing Needs,*[53] Gary D. Stratman, a Presbyterian pastor in Nashville, Tennessee, looks for a wider definition of "pastoral" that can arise out of a study of the biblical image of the shepherd (for which, of course, the Latin word is *pastor*). He draws on David Steere's study, which sees the following as the essential elements of the biblical concept of shepherding:

I.   A positive pattern of action meeting need.

II. A negative pattern of action constituting a withdrawal of the first.

III. A sacrificial expenditure of life.

IV. Love as spontaneous, creative, and initiating.[54]

Stratman thinks the pastoral-counseling approach to preaching has been strong on the first and last of these elements, but weak on the second and third. Weakness on the second has been seen in an unwillingness to judge. Moral judgments, however, are a necessary part of pastoral leadership. Though counseling sermons have dealt with true and important matters, they have *not* treated *everything* of concern to Christians. Thus, Stratman says, "Pastoral preaching will be marked by a shepherd's compassion and concern which desires nothing less for Christ's flock than the whole counsel of God."[55]

Stratman is concerned that preaching deal not only with the truth but with the *whole* truth. This, for him, is a theological concern. The source of truth is the Bible, and preaching that presents the whole truth cannot be limited by drawing on restricted portions of the Scriptures alone; for the whole truth one needs the whole Bible. Thus, truly pastoral preaching benefits from the use of the three-year lectionary cycle.

The rest of Stratman's book is devoted to a description of the way he prepares his sermons, to three examples of the pastoral sermons he writes, and to an annotated bibliography. The only aspect of his method of preparation that was new to the present writer was the worksheet he used to make notes while he was assembling materials. The top of the page is given over to exegesis and the bottom is devoted to homiletical response, but the most distinctive feature is the left margin, which contains "in abbreviated form the names of the people for whom I am praying."[56] That should make for preaching that is pastoral indeed! His annotated bibliography refers to a far wider range of literature than can be cited here.

Though the method of preaching Stratman advocates has much in common with the recommendations of the present writer,[57] it is nevertheless regrettable that (a) he did not pursue the biblical metaphor of shepherding to specify in more detail what he meant by "pastoral," and (b) he did not say more about what the "whole" truth in the Bible is. The development of Stratman's thought was more homiletical than analytical, and, since his insights, in an area in which analysis is badly needed, seem so sound, his contributions could have been more valuable.

Constructive Proposals

This critique of the recent literature on the relation of pastoral care to preaching has centered on two needs. First, the need for an understanding of pastoral care that extends beyond ministry to individuals in crisis, even though this probably means a distinction will have to be made between a narrow and a wider definition of pastoral care. Second, the need for a theological vision of the Church and its mission and ministry that can furnish a coherent point of view by which all the activities of ministry can be related to one another.

The thesis here presented is that the list of ministerial activities presented above (at the end of the section headed "What Is Pastoral Care?") satisfies the first of these two needs and refutes Clebsch and Jaekle's effort to exclude from pastoral care the work pastors do with groups. It should be noted here that the image of the *pastor*, the shepherd, is *fundamentally* one of work with groups. The shepherd cares for the flock, and his or her attention to individuals is to keep them in and with the flock as it moves between pasture and pasture and between pasture and fold. If the metaphor of the shepherd is not dead in our technological society (a possibility worth investigating), then it should continue to shape our thought.

If, however, the definition of pastoral care is extended to embrace *all* the vocational activities of pastors, the question can well be asked: Is there any preaching that is *not* pastoral? The situation is reminiscent of the old shaggy dog story about how to catch a white elephant. The technique, prescribed in wearisome detail, is to dangle a cinnamon roll on a string from the limb of a tree in the middle of a jungle clearing, because "white elephants just love cinnamon rolls." Each time the white elephant approaches, the cinnamon roll is jerked out of its reach in such a way that the momentum of the elephant's charge causes it to fall and roll over in the dust. The process is repeated until the elephant has become dirty enough to look gray. "And then you catch it just as you would any other elephant." The moral of this chapter so far has been that you so define pastoral preaching that it becomes coextensive with all preaching, then you preach pastoral sermons just as you would any other.

Those familiar with the thought of Don Browning, for instance, may think his distinction between pastoral and practical theology leaves room for a kind of preaching that is not pastoral. A look at his distinction, however, shows that such is not the case. As he uses the terms,

> pastoral theology attempts to set forth the legitimations for specific pastoral acts—the minister's preaching, liturgical duties, pastoral care, and pastoral counseling. Practical theology goes beyond a theology of pastoral acts and sets forth a theology of practical living—a theology of work, business, sexuality, marriage, child-rearing, aging, youth, etc.[58]

Thus, to use language Browning uses elsewhere, pastoral theology is caught up in the "clerical paradigm."[59] It involves thinking of the shepherd without at the same time thinking of the sheep. But the use of "pastoral" in the present essay is concerned with the pastor only as he or she is caring for the flock. Precisely the issues, therefore, that Browning relates to practical theology would in this view be most appropriate for pastoral preaching. Pastoral preaching that assists Christians in living before God, with one another, and in the world as Christians.

This definition, of course, relates to the wider definition of pastoral care. And it obviously reflects the theological view, already advanced in the previous section on pastoral care, that the life of the Christian community is to be understood in terms of relationships to God, to one another, and to those outside the Church, in which relationships the duties are, respectively, worship, *koinonia,* corporal works of mercy, and evangelization. Yet this theological understanding of the pastoral task implies at least one additional purpose of pastoral preaching—the formation of the Christian community. One function served by the eucharistic homily week by week is to help the community realize it *is* a community. Shepherding the flock involves inculcating and reinforcing its self-understanding as a flock. The above definition of a eucharistic homily implies that its purpose is get the people of God to accept the application of the biblical principle to their lives and to act on it "both in their participation in the liturgy and as they go forth into the world." It is by this calling of the community into self-awareness as a community, by this community forming, that the community is enabled to participate in the liturgy *as* a community—being a community is a *sine qua non* for doing liturgy.

For anyone not familiar with the theological position it represents, it may be helpful to insert at this point an expansion of this rather compressed statement. The link presupposed between Eucharist, community, and preaching is not arbitrary. Those who attend Church are not regarded as isolated individuals who have exercised an option to participate in a service of worship because they find it fulfilling. Rather, they are regarded corporately as a people, the People of God. They are the community that exists to have communion with God. Though that community is expected to be consummated eternally in heaven, it is enjoyed proleptically on earth by the community as it gathers for worship. And here by worship is meant preeminently the Eucharist. Thus the link between community and Eucharist is unbreakable. But the bond with preaching is just as inseparable. Preaching illuminates the life of the People of God by focusing God's Word on it. The Bible is the adequate record of Israel's experience of God and the Church's experience of Jesus. Thus it is the normative account of the foundation of the community. It contains the templates by which the shape of the true community is discerned. It is by testing itself against these standards that the community today knows it is in continuity with the Church through the ages. This is how it knows that it is the Church. Thus Eucharist, community, and preaching are inextricably woven together.

Though it is thus affirmed that all preaching is pastoral preaching, no effort is made here to suggest that there are no criteria for pastoral preaching. Rather, pastoral preaching is seen as preaching concerned to discover and delineate analogies between the situation in the text and the situation in the congregation and to transfer to the situation in the congregation the perspective of the text. This is to say that pastoral preaching occurs when the people of God are enabled to have their situation before God, with one another, and in the world illuminated by the biblical texts appointed for each day, especially the gospel. Pastoral preaching guides the flock.

This discussion does not suggest there is no legitimate place for preaching that seeks to do pastoral care in the sense of ministering to individuals in crisis. The narrow definition is necessarily included in the wider one. Much pain can be relieved from the pulpit. In fact, in the dynamic tradition of the black Church, in which little pastoral counseling (in the technical sense) has been done, much of the pastoral care is done through preaching.[60] One could even challenge the wisdom of Fosdick and suggest that the true indication of the success of this kind of pastoral preaching is not in the number of parishioners who arrange for private counseling but in the number who no longer need to (although, admittedly, that figure can never be known).

By the same token, there is no suggestion here that psychological insight is not to be employed both in preaching and in counseling. The fact that psychology has replaced theological explanation as the only orthodoxy in our society does not mean that theology cannot be greatly assisted in its task by the use of psychological insight. This use, however, cannot be uncritical. To begin with, however much the validity of psychological explanation is presupposed in our culture, we cannot imagine there is unanimity either about what conditions are desirable for human beings or the methods for helping them achieve those conditions. The Rogerians have no dealings with the Freudians, and, as noted above, Capps has shown that various therapeutic schools align themselves with characteristic styles of theological diagnosis. Further, some schools of psychology are more consistent with Christian theology than others. This point of view is reflected in Don Browning's passionate paragraph:

> Pastoral care must never be considered as simply a matter of implementing forgiveness even though forgiveness is an essential part of all care. Pastoral care should never be understood simply as a matter of "loosening people up," helping them to become "more open" or "more spontaneous and flexible," "removing their guilt," or making them "more loving." Nor is pastoral care ever just a matter of "relativizing" another person's assumptions, character structure, cultural values, etc., although at times these emphases are important. Pastoral care must first be concerned to give a person a structure, a character, an identity, a religiocultural system out of which to live. It must first be concerned to help people discover these things and become incorporated into them. Then it should concern itself with the issues of forgiveness, guilt, and related emotional-dynamic issues connected with actually attempting to live the life that moral inquiry has found to be good.[61]

Though one would like to pursue the issue of the theological grounding of moral inquiry, it nevertheless appears that Browning is calling for the sort of community formation through individual pastoral care that has been advocated here as an important function of pastoral preaching in its wider definition. Thus, even the care of individuals seems to be related to the life of the flock, and a basic unity is seen between both definitions of pastoral preaching.

7

The Bishop as Pastor

Richard F. Grein

The Burden

The term "pastoral care" probably originated with Gregory the Great, in a treatise entitled *Book of Pastoral Rule,* which eventually came to be known simply as *Pastoral Care.* The treatise was meant to provide a rule for pastors, as Benedict had done for monks. But the immediate impetus for its writing was in response to another bishop who had chided Gregory for his reluctance to assume the office of Bishop of Rome to which he had been elected. Gregory begins the treatise:

> Most dear brother, you reprove me with kind and humble regard for having wished to escape by concealment from the burdens of pastoral care. Now, lest these burdens might appear light to some, I am explaining, by writing this book, how onerous I regard them, so that he who is free from them may not imprudently seek to have them, and he who has been so imprudent as to seek them may feel apprehension in having them.[1]

The burdens of pastoral care were not a new thing imagined

by Gregory. About two hundred years before, Augustine spoke of them in a sermon on the anniversary of his ordination:

> Ever since the day when the burden of my episcopacy was placed on my shoulders, a burden to which it is so difficult to do justice, I have been troubled by the cares that attend this honor. Today, which is the anniversary of my episcopacy, I am moved by these concerns more than ever, for this day refreshes the first memories of my duties and brings the past so vividly before my eyes that I feel as though I had just embarked today upon the duties that I took up so long ago . . . .
>
> May I be helped by your prayers so that the Lord will consent to assist me in carrying my burden. When you pray thus, you are praying for yourselves. For what is this burden of which I am speaking, if not you yourselves? Pray, just as I pray, that you will not be heavy for me.[2]

Even the leaders of God's people in biblical times were not exempt from the weight of responsibility. In the wilderness Moses said to the Lord God:

> Why hast thou dealt ill with thy servant? And why have I not found favor in thy sight, that thou dost lay the burden of all this people upon me? Did I conceive all this people? Did I bring them forth, that thou shouldst say to me, "Carry them in your bosom, as a nurse carries the suckling child, to the land which thou didst swear to give their fathers?" Where am I to get meat to give to all this people? For they weep before me and say, "Give us meat, that we may eat." I am not able to carry all this people alone, the burden is too heavy for me. (Numbers 11:11-14)

Later Paul, writing to the Corinthians about his trials as an Apostle, added this note, "And apart from other things, there is the daily pressure upon me of my anxiety for all the churches" (II Corinthians 11:28).

The question that comes immediately to mind is, why are the people of God such a burden? The cynic reading Scripture and history might conclude that it is because they are generally stubborn, easily turned from the truth, always in trouble or need, and usually helpless. But the real answer is found in the nature of the responsibility—the people belong to God. The pastor is burdened with the vocational call to care for God's people—the ones God has chosen to love in a particular way and for a particular purpose. The commission given to Peter in that wonderful appendum to the Gospel according to John demonstrates the nature of the burden. "Peter, do you love me?" "Yes,

Lord." "Feed my sheep." There in a threefold repetition of question, response, and commission, Peter is both absolved of his denial of Jesus and appointed as a shepherd of Christ's flock. As a vocational responsibility it is rooted in love—Peter's love for Christ, and Christ's love for his flock. Without Peter's love for his Lord it would not be a vocation, and without Christ's love for the flock it would not be a responsibility. Thus the burden of pastoral care is found in the vocational responsibility given to pastors with regard to God's people. One could not possibly take on such a burden, such a responsibility, unless it were a vocation, unless it were somehow founded on the summons of divine love. The paradox here is that divine love makes the task such a heavy burden, a responsibility to which the one called goes in fear and trembling, yet it is this same love that compels vocation and makes possible the task.

It is necessary then, before one speaks of the task itself, and the bishop's role in it, that something be said concerning the importance of the personal vocational attitude of those called by love. We must say some words about the relationship between the one who is called and the one who calls, and about the formation of shepherds charged with the responsibility of caring for the flock of Christ.

The Vocation of Pastors

It is significant that in his treatise on pastoral care Gregory devoted three of four sections to the personal life of the pastor—only in part three does he present the elements of pastoral care itself. In the first section he deals with the difficulties of the office and the requirements it places on those called to it. The second part describes the inner and outer life of a good pastor. And finally, in the fourth, he stresses the absolute necessity of humility. Gregory could not separate the art of pastoral care from the character of the pastor. In other words, he was not simply concerned with the doing of pastoral care but with the development of a pastor's personal life. For him, one could not be done without the other.

If the vocation originates in the question, "Do you love me?" then it is also maintained by the continuous affirmative response to that same question. For those called to pastoral service the question will not go away, because of necessity it precedes the commission to feed the sheep—without our "yes" to Christ there can be no vocation given. And because the sheep are always there to be fed, the question—"Do you love me?"—is also always there to be answered. This question is not simply a prerequisite to a vocational task but an invitation to a continuous relationship of love with the risen Lord. It is through this relationship that the vocation of the pastor is established, developed, and maintained.

Those called to minister to the flock enter into a relationship with the Shepherd in order to share his love for the sheep, to be shaped and formed by that love, and to be sustained by its grace. Without this relationship the task of pastoral care remains impossible.

In recent years the concept of professionalism has played an increasingly important role in the preparation of people for the ordained ministry and in continuing-education programs for clergy. By professionalism I mean the particular intellectual training and skill development by which one acquires expertise for specialized tasks in the area of one's profession. I suspect that this developing professional model of ministry gets much of its impetus from the clergy's need for a clearer identity, a need for credibility in a society of specialization and in a culture where religious cultic figures are disesteemed, and to find a place of significance through skill. Of course some of it stems from a healthy desire to be a more competent priest or bishop. Unfortunately for many, professionalism is becoming a substitute for vocation, and consequently skills for carrying out the task of pastoral care have taken on a greater importance than the sense of vocational calling.

By comparing the sense of vocational calling and professional competence, I am not suggesting that we have two mutually exclusive perspectives on ordained ministry. Rather, it is a matter of priority. Skill cannot be a substitute for a sense of vocation, yet competence remains a requisite for those who want to be good pastors. The priority here is vocation, the continual desire to say yes to Christ—yes to "Do you love me?" He does not say, "Can you preach?" or "Can you counsel?" or "What are your administrative skills?"; he says, "Do you love me?" It is this question and the affirmative response from the one called that precede the commission to serve the flock of Christ. From a vocational point of view, then, the relationship with the Lord must precede in every way the task of pastoring—it has the priority— it comes before our yes to feed the flock, even if we desire to do so with great skill and competence.

This vocation, then, requires that the priest conscientiously and intentionally maintain a life of prayer. This spiritual life lies at the heart of vocation because it seeks a relationship with the one who initiates vocation—the one who raises before us the question, "Do you love me?" We cannot prove our love for Jesus by acts of ministry; we can only attempt to express it in a desire for a relationship with him. To be a shepherd of Christ's flock one must seek to know the Chief Shepherd in an intimate way through the loving conversation we call prayer. No amount of pastoral skill or ability can substitute for this priority in the life of a pastor.

Having said this, we can turn to questions pertaining to competence and skill. The primary pastoral skill required of shepherds is theological. This is because all theology has the potential for becoming pastorally applicable—one could say that all theology is ultimately pastoral theology. It seems, however, that many, if not most, of the professional skills bishops and priests are interested in acquiring today come from other disciplines such as the social sciences. Administration and management techniques, planning-process methods, leadership styles, counseling skills, books on the latest interpretation of culture—all these have become increasingly important to those accepting the primacy of a professional model of ministry. The motivation here is to find something that works, that will ease the load. Unfortunately, it is not uncommon for the new professional technique, which seems to work so well, to be inconsistent with the norms of the Church's theology—such as a management model that is at odds with a Christian anthropology or ecclesiology.

The ability to make theology practical, to somehow incarnate statements of belief in pastoral methods, concepts, structures, and practice—this is the primary skill of pastors. It is a skill acquired not only by the study of scripture and the reading of theology but through a process of reflection that carries one back and forth between the current pastoral situation and the theological insights. In this process, theory can become practical and the theology in day-to-day events can be discerned. It is a process not unlike the one used by the preacher as he or she begins with scripture, seeking the insights of revelation, then brings them to bear on the human condition, or begins with the human situation, taking it to the revelation found in scripture. This hermeneutical arch unites the current situation with the revealed theology of the Church, thus applying theology in a practical way. Though many preachers seem to have the knack for doing this automatically when it comes to proclamation, they forget the method in the other areas of pastoral care. Yet even such apparently mundane occupations as parish management and administration have theological dimensions involving such things as grace, anthropology, community, and ecclesiology. A parish or diocese must be viewed as a social system that reflects and incarnates an intentional theology.

Part of our failure here is directly related to an inadequate view of what theology is—too often we simply see it as information, something to be taught or preached. We look at doctrine as something to be believed, given intellectual assent, and not something to be used, something that has practical application. To many it is the technique that appears to be useful. Yet it is revelation, arising out of the events of history, that also presents a useful theology, because it is rooted in human experience. It teaches us about human nature, relationships, vocation, and destiny. The practical application of theology in the day-to-day life of Christian communities requires a particular skill. It is competence in this area that must be the chief concern of those involved in pastoral care.

The bishop has a particular role to play with regard to vocation and competence among the clergy of a diocese. Not only must he practice what I have described, but he must also provide the environment and means for it to be realized in the clergy with whom he serves. He must practice and encourage the spiritual life, keeping alive the sense of vocation. He must provide for proper continuing education, stimulating a desire for theological learning. He must have a vision of the Church. He must be able to articulate a clear ecclesiology by which the people of the diocese, clergy and lay, have a sense of place and of participation in the communal life of the Church, are called to offer their gifts for ministry, and have a common mission. In other words, the structures of the diocese must be formed through an international theology. I will say more about this in the next sections of this chapter.

Before we leave the subject of vocation, something needs to be said about the relationship between baptism and holy orders. In the sermon by Augustine quoted above, he went on to say:

I feel fear for what I must be to you, and I am consoled by what I am with you. To you I must be a bishop and with you I am a Christian. The former I have from the office I hold and the latter I have from grace. One is a source of danger and the other is the source of salvation. I am tossed about by the storms of this office as though upon a great sea. But when we recall by whose blood we have been redeemed, we enter into a safe harbor upon the tranquility of this thought. After toiling in the performance of my duties, I find repose in our common well-being. If therefore I find more pleasure in having been redeemed with you than in having been placed over you, I shall, as the Lord commands, all the more willingly be your servant, lest I should be ungrateful for the blessing of deserving to join you as a servant of God.[3]

Like Augustine, every priest or bishop from time to time feels the tension between the office bestowed by holy orders and the baptism by which we are made members of Christ. Those in holy orders must be careful that their sense of participation in the community is not limited to the office they hold so that the relationship given in baptism becomes secondary.

Most of us can remember the days when baptisms were often private affairs—just the family and a few friends. At the same time ordinations were, and still are, quite different. Someone after careful screening and selection is sent away for three years of intensive training. After training, this person is again scrutinized and tested for knowledge and worthiness, then ordained in a glorious liturgy lasting well over an hour. It is not hard to understand the confusion many people have about the primacy between baptism and holy orders. From outward appearance ordination seems to produce a caste of superior Christians, a church within the Church.

This, of course, was not always the case. Anyone reading *The Apostolic Tradition of Hippolytus* quickly discovers a very different attitude toward the relationship between holy orders and initiation rites. New converts were carefully questioned about their reasons for wanting to become Christians and examined as to their manner of life. Then, after three years of instruction, they might be selected for baptism. From the time of their selection to the time of their baptism they underwent daily exorcisms, with fasting and prayer as the day grew near. The night before the dawn of their baptism they spent in vigil, hearing readings and instructions about salvation history. Then, in an elaborate service they renounced Satan, professed their faith, were baptized and anointed with sweet-smelling oil, joined in the prayers of God's holy people, shared the kiss of peace, received the Eucharist of the Body and Blood of Christ, and were given milk and honey, for now they were in the promised land.[4]

In contrast to this, ordination was a simple affair, perhaps five or ten minutes at the Sunday liturgy. Listen to Hippolytus:

> Let the bishop be ordained after he has been chosen by all the people. When he has been named and shall please all, let him, with the presbytery and such bishops as may be present, assemble with the people on a Sunday. While all give their consent, the bishops shall lay their hands upon him, and the presbytery shall stand by in silence. All indeed shall keep silent, praying in their heart for the descent of the Spirit. Then one of the bishops who are present shall, at the request of all, lay his hand on him who is ordained bishop.[5]

The current reemphasis on the place and importance of baptism in the life of the Church is causing a total reexamination of the relationship between holy orders and the people of God. Ordination does not create a caste of superior Christians within the community of faith; it produces a gift to the Church for the ordering of its life. And as a gift it is offered for the benefit of the people of God.

Ministry is bestowed in baptism, that is, each Christian is called to share in the life of the community and in its liturgy, to proclaim the Good News as an evangelist, to engage in works of servanthood, and to strive for social justice. This means that those who are ordained do not so much bring ministry to the Church as they bring a gift that enables a ministry already possessed by the community. In a sacramental way those in holy orders image back to the community a ministry that is theirs, as, for example, the diaconate acts as an icon of servanthood, calling forth from the people of God the servanthood they professed in baptism.

This means those clergy charged with pastoral care must constantly struggle, as did Augustine, with the tension between their baptism and their ordination. Unless this is done we will continue to act as though holy orders are of more importance than baptism, thus making the community dependent on clergy for ministry and trivializing the very nature of our newly reemphasized initiation rites. Priests and bishops need to remember that their primary relationship to the community of faith is through baptism, and that by ordination they are called to offer a particular gift to the community for its benefit.

The revitalization of the ministry of the baptized, by forcing the church to examine the relationship between the ordained and unordained, has caused a degree of anxiety among many in holy orders, particularly among priests. As the laity take on more responsibility for various ministries both within and outside the local community, the role of the priest changes. Some clergy welcome the change and are able to adapt quickly, whereas others suffer some sort of identity crisis. For many clergy, consciously or unconsciously, the question arises, "What is my role now that the ministry is shared by the whole community?"

More often than not, this identity crisis centers around questions of authority. I have noticed that in the majority of instances where there is conflict between priest and parish the issues revolve around authority. My guess is that we are shifting from a top-down, hierarchical model of authority to a collegial model. The impetus for this shift is partly cultural, some of it comes from the recent emphasis on the ministry of the laity, but much of it also comes from a recovery of the notion of the Church as servant. John Booty in writing on the servant Church summarizes nicely the dilemma:

> In order to grasp the full implications of this understanding we must realize that such an approach to a definition of the church stands in opposition to the linear view of the church and its ministry. That view presents a direct line moving from Christ through the Apostles and the ordained ministry of bishops, priests and deacons, to the faithful, the great body of laity. The emphasis in this linear view falls so heavily on the priesthood mediating between Christ and the laity that at times the church has been defined narrowly in terms of the ordained ministry of bishops, priests and deacons. Such a linear understanding has been a major reason why the movement to realize the "ministry of the laity" has been so frustrated. With the linear view predominating, the center of attention falls upon the priesthood, those through whom the divine power comes to the unordained majority. In such a view the laity is reduced to a dependent and virtually powerless entity. It should also be noted that in such a view the ordained ministers of the church have suffered, having unreasonable expectations put upon them, exercising their power reluctantly, with a sense of guilt due to their self-perceived fallibility, or tyranically because for one reason or another they choose to believe that they are indeed, "less than God but more than man," being "not men, but clergymen."[6]

If this shift in ecclesiology represents something positive for the church, and I believe it does, then the bishop as pastor of the diocese is the one responsible for seeing it is carried out with as little turmoil as possible. He must hold up the vision, articulate the basic theology, and help provide the institutional structures by which it can occur. I will at the end of this chapter offer a model of collegiality between bishop and presbyterate that provides a concrete way to begin implementing this servanthood ecclesiology. But let us briefly return to the question of authority —authority in a developing servant Church.

We usually think of those in authority, and more often than not expect to experience them, as someone in charge, who has control, and by command gives direction—someone who governs. And this, I would maintain, could, in a very general way, fit our notion of authority in the Church. We expect our leaders to lead by direction and command, to govern. And even those leaders who operate from a more collegial style, seeking consensus before making decisions, cannot escape entirely being placed in positions where they are expected to take charge, because even here the leader is conscious of voluntarily letting go of authority, an authority rooted in the power to command. It is because we understand authority in terms of "command" that it becomes a problem.

Jesus gave the Church another principle by which it was to understand authority. On the road leading to Jerusalem and the Cross, when some of the disciples got in a dispute over the places of primacy in their group, Jesus said to them:

> You know that those who are supposed to rule over the Gentiles lord it over them, and their great men exercise authority over them. But it shall not be so among you; but whoever would be great among you must be your servant, and whoever would be first among you must be slave to all. For the Son of man also came not to be served but to serve, and to give his life as a ransom for many. (Mark 10:42b-45)

Leadership in the Christian community is not based on the power to command but in a self-offering servanthood. In fact, the root meaning of the word "ministry" is "self-offering"— minus-try. When connected to the Gospel of Jesus Christ there is a power in the sacrifice of servanthood. Paul, writing about apostolic ministry, says to the Corinthians, "For while we live we are always being given up to death for Jesus' sake, so that the life of Jesus may be manifested in our mortal flesh. So death is at work in us, but life in you." Paul "dies," he suffers, that others might know life in Christ. Through Paul's self-offering Christ is revealed, and in that revelation there is power. But this power is not rooted in the authority to command but in authenticity—it is authoritative because it is authentic. Paul embodies the message of Christ in such a way that the message is believable —it appears genuine and trustworthy.

According to the definition given by Jesus, one cannot be a leader in the Church by simply proclaiming the Gospel of Christ, nor can he inaugurate a servant community by command. The message has authority because of its truth; the leader has authority because he images that truth authentically. One contemporary servant illustrates this point. Mother Teresa of Calcutta has enormous influence in the worldwide Christian community, not because she has an institutional position of leadership with the authority to command but because she has the authority of authenticity—by this alone she influences millions.

The renewal of the ministry of the baptized and the movement toward becoming a servant Church can only be accomplished if the ordained, priest and bishop, will begin to find the basis for their authority in the authenticity of being servant to the communities they serve. (I do not mention the deacons simply because I assume their role as servant is much clearer. Certainly the current recovery of the diaconate has played a major part in awakening the whole Church to servant ministry. And as the icon of servanthood one hopes their influence will touch bishops and priests as well as the laity.) If the Church is called to be servant to others, offering itself as did its Lord, for the life of the world, then those who minister to that Church are also called to be servants. In this way all ministry of the Church seeks to image the life of Christ, or as John Booty says, to reproduce the life of Christ.[7]

In the Gospel according to John, after Jesus had washed the feet of the disciples, in what must be interpreted as a ceremonial act symbolizing servanthood, he says:

> This is my commandment, that you love one another as I have loved you. Greater love has no man than this, that a man lay down his life for his friends. You are my friends if you do what I command you. No longer do I call you servants, for the servant does not know what his master is doing; but I have called you friends, for all that I have heard from my Father I have made known to you. You did not choose me, but I chose you and appointed you that you should go and bear fruit and that your fruit should abide; so that whatever you ask the

Father in my name, he may give it to you. This I command you, to
love one another. (John 15:11-27)

This is a text with many levels of meaning, but let us note only
a few that relate to our subject. It is Jesus who chooses and
appoints those who are to obey the commandment of love. The
commandment of love necessitates the work of servanthood,
which finds its highest expression in self-sacrifice. This work of
servanthood leads to a redefinition of relationship with Jesus—
they become friends because those engaged in loving acts of
servanthood know the truth about the work of Christ through
the revelation from the Father. Here we discover that Jesus' power
to command is not used at a distance but within the context of
mutual service. In other words, it is authentic, it *is* what it
commands. Further, it does not lead to a master-servant relationship, as one usually expects from those giving and receiving
commands, but to one of friendship by sharing in the activity of
love and revealed truth.

After Jesus finished washing the feet of the disciples he said:

Do you know what I have done to you? You call me Teacher and Lord;
and you are right, for so I am. If I then, your Lord and Teacher, have
washed your feet, you also ought to wash one another's feet. For I have
given you an example, that you should do as I have done to you. (John
13:12b-15)

Is not this the vocation of pastors? And is not this the only basis
of authority for the Church?

Such a change in leadership style would be revolutionary, and
it is difficult to imagine what effect it would have on the Christian
community. John McKenzie was somewhat pessimistic about such
a change when he wrote:

If one wished to be captious, one could maintain that the texts which
give *diakonia* as the function of authority and which liken persons in
authority to lackeys and children not only do not recommend command
and control, but positively forbid it. Whether this thesis could ever be
sustained or not, it is plain that the contemporary Church is not ready
for a discussion of this thesis; it is plain also that a simple adoption
of the thesis would produce instant chaos in the Church which we know.
What is to be sought is not administrative chaos, but a transformation
of the idea and the use of authority; and it would be absurd to pretend
that such a transformation can be accomplished instantly.[8]

But twenty years have passed since those words were written, and there are clear signs that the Holy Spirit is leading us in this direction. Perhaps now is the time seriously to entertain the notion of servant leadership.

In this section we have touched on a few of the vocational issues I think are important for bishops and priests in the exercise of their pastoral task, issues pertaining to spirituality, competence and skill, the relationship between baptism and holy orders, and finally authority. Now we turn to the task itself, pastoral care.

Pastoral Care: The Art of Christian Formation

Michelangelo's statue of young King David is a magnificent work of art. David stands erect—his right arm, well-muscled, hangs loosely at his side. In his left hand he holds a garment thrown casually over his shoulder. His head looks over that shoulder. He is curly-headed, youthful, handsome—with just a touch of arrogance to show that here is a confident man. The turning of the head accentuates the muscles and tendons in the neck. Even the blood vessels stand out. You're sure if you could just reach out and touch him you would feel life there. Such is the work of genius. I am told that before he laid mallet to chisel Michelangelo could see David in the block of marble; he could see his creation waiting to be called out by his art. This is, of course, a living parable about how God sees us—not simply as we are but as we can be. He sees us as an artist sees. He sees in us all those gifts and talents, all that potential for truth and virtue, waiting to be called forth. This, for me, is a way of conceiving the art of pastoral care.

But let us turn once again to the commissioning of Peter in the Gospel according to John, where the pastoral task is imaged in the feeding of sheep. In this image feeding should be understood in the sense of nurturing—that is, to foster growth and to bring into development. And further, the commissioning cannot be understood in terms of physical nurturing, as would be the case with livestock, but as the nurturing of persons in a spiritual way. We might say, then, that pastoral care is the responsibility given to the Church regarding the growth and development of God's people for their spiritual formation as a holy people. Or we might say, using the analogy from art, pastoral care is an instrument of God's art by which he creates a special people.

The analogy from art is useful because it emphasizes that pastoral care is more akin to art than to the repetition of techniques as in technology—it is not something that can be mass produced. Yet even here we want to be cautious about taking the analogy too far. For example, the word "formation" should not be understood in terms of shaping or molding, as an artist would work with clay, but in the language of living things—as nurturing for growth and development. This is also true because the object of pastoral care is not passive to the process but a participant in it.

What we speak of here is really a process of human becoming— of a growing to maturity, or, in the language of religion, becoming "holy" in the sense of wholeness or completion. "Becoming" is the operative word in describing the process, as John Macquarrie has written:

> Perhaps one should speak not of a "human being" but of a "human becoming," awkward though this usage would be. We could say that we are all *becoming* human, in the sense that we are discovering and, it may be hoped, realizing what the potentials of a human existence are. Yet, it is true that we already *are* human, because these potentialities already belong to us . . . . The point is that our humanity is not simply a natural endowment (as felinity is to a cat) but has to be discovered and realized. The first obvious complexity in the study of the human, and the major source of elusiveness, is that we have to concern ourselves with the possibilities as well as the actualities . . . . "Becoming," suggests process, transition, incompleteness, movement from non-existence into existence (or the reverse). That which is becoming is compounded of act and potency, fact and possibility.[9]

It should be noted that the process of realizing human potential and that of sanctification are the same—that is, grace perfecting nature. Pastoral care in the ideal sense bears the responsibility for human becoming, for "feeding" the flock of Christ. In this it is a gift of grace by which our heavenly Father guides and nurtures his children, that they might bear his image after the fashion of his only Son. This is why, as we noted previously, pastoral care has been such a burden throughout the history of the Church. Pastors are charged with the responsibility of being the artisans by which God in love creates and gives formation to his people.

This ideal of pastoral care, however, has not yet received

appropriate emphasis by the Church through its pastors. Today the term "pastoral care" more often than not carries with it connotations of a ministry to the troubled. What we have now is a therapeutic model rather than a growth model of parish ministry. Even our seminaries seem to put more emphasis on clinical pastoral education and crisis ministry than on training pastors in the art of nurturing people to Christian maturity. For Gregory the Great pastoring meant helping the baptized live out the implications of their baptism. It meant guidance in Christian living, teaching doctrine, exhortation for the practice of virtue, encouragement in prayer, preaching the Gospel—helping the faithful grow in Christ. Yet today, for most practitioners pastoring means caring for troubled people. And I would guess that a majority of our clergy are more comfortable, and better prepared, in dealing with a problem marriage than in giving guidance about the life of prayer. What all this means is that we have a pastoral care oriented to maintenance rather than one that forms a holy people and equips the saints for mission. I believe this situation has had a great impact on the Episcopal Church in recent years, and I believe it could account for much of our loss in communicant membership.

The most commonly proposed solution to nearly twenty years of diminishing ranks in the Episcopal Church is a vigorous and well-planned campaign of evangelism modeled after the growth churches. The main idea behind this proposal is simply that if we have lost members because of what was taken by some as an overemphasis on social concerns, coupled with the discontent over the issues surrounding *Prayer Book* changes and the ordination of women to the priesthood, the problem can be rectified by replacement of the losses through evangelism. In other words, let's accept the losses and rebuild. This is a very appealing solution because it calls the Church to action, as well as appearing to imitate success.

But apart from the fact that such a solution, to be completely successful, would necessitate a fairly radical change in ecclesiology, one modeled on the structure and style of the evangelical churches, it misses the real problem behind the losses in membership. Today 58 percent of the adult membership of the Episcopal Church come originally from other denominations. One hesitates to suggest that this indicates successful evangelization, since it is usually associated with the unchurched. It does indicate, however, that the Episcopal Church has many qualities attractive to members of other churches—and we have in fact been growing.

If over half our adult membership comes to us from other denominations, and if we have baptized and confirmed those raised in the Episcopal Church, the question, it seems to me, does not focus on getting people into the Episcopal Church so much as it does on what we do with them once they are members.

A few years ago two sociologists, Charles Glock and Rodney Stark, doing research on religion, wrote a book called *American Piety: The Nature of Religious Commitment*. Their findings on the Episcopal Church were very revealing. In a chapter entitled "The Switchers: Changes of Denomination," they state that of the denominations other than Roman Catholic, the one most able to retain its own members was the Episcopal Church. Conversely, among those best able to gain at the expense of other denominations was again the Episcopal Church. These results were based on percentage growth or decline. The authors had this to say:

> The Episcopalians excelled in both ways: they held their original flock better than did the other denominations and they proved a strong attraction to members from other bodies.[10]

This of course explains why 58 percent of our Church membership comes from other Churches. But why, then, is the Episcopal Church not growing? And what happened to all those former Episcopalians? The study showed that when Episcopalians leave the Episcopal Church most often they do not go to another Church—they simply disconnect from any Christian community. A great many continue to call themselves Episcopalians, but they are not counted in the official records. This most likely accounts for the amazing statistical indication that there are probably as many, if not more, people claiming to be Episcopalians than are actually counted on parish rolls.

All this raises some very serious questions about what occurs or does not occur within parish communities. What have we done or not done in our parishes that has effectively innoculated them against participation in a Church, any Church? Have we shown them a vision of what the Church might be, and then failed in the fulfillment of that vision? Is that why so many still claim in some nostalgic way the title Episcopalian? Even a cursory examination of the material on religious commitment presented by

Glock and Stark points to the problem. The indices for devotional life, religious knowledge, and communal participation show Episcopalians to be at or near the bottom of the scale—in other words, in the area of pastoral care.

From this evidence one could effectively argue that if the Episcopal Church is to grow, both numerically and spiritually, those charged with the feeding of the flock of Christ must take a long and serious look at the way pastoral care is being done in parishes, and begin to develop a growth model that nurtures the people of God.

At this point I would like to look at a few ingredients of pastoral ministry. Recognizing that the subject of pastoral care is both complex and broad because people are complex and come in a wonderful variety, I mention only three I think are significant: the importance of personal identity, ministry as the act of calling to remembrance, and love as expectation. I will touch on each of these ingredients in a brief way, just enough to give a flavor of how I see the art of pastoring.

Some twenty-six centuries ago a man, possibly a shepherd, stood on some Palestinian hill, gazing up into the night. His contemplation of the glorious starlit heavens made him feel small and insignificant, humbled by the greatness of God's creation, but because he was a man of faith he wrote these lines, which we have in our Psalter: "When I look at thy heavens, the work of thy fingers, the moon and the stars which thou hast established; what is man that thou art mindful of him, and the son of man that thou dost care for him?" (Psalm 8:3-4). The mystery of creation confronts our stargazer with yet more powerful mysteries: Who am I in the midst of all this? What is my purpose and destiny? Why does God give his loving care to human beings?

One of the most important issues pastoral care must address is the question of human identity. The psalmist speaks for all of us, for human beings are questions to themselves. From the beginnings of consciousness the questions come, as, for example, the child playing peek-a-boo is also asking the metaphysical question, "Do things continue to exist when I no longer look at them?" The human capacity for transcending self gives rise to self-awareness and all its attendant questions about freedom, purpose, meaning, relationship, and destiny. And because we are incomplete, in the sense of realizing our potential, we are also a mystery to ourselves—we do not know ourselves.

But the questions that surround this personal mystery are not simply interesting puzzles to be solved; they are also a source of anxiety. Self-awareness is a two-edged sword. By it we consciously make choices; acting in freedom, we create, and enter into relationships; but it also produces an awareness of ourselves in time, an awareness of death and not-being, so that in the very act of self-consciously seeking to grow and change, of becoming, we also seem to be moving toward not-being—very much like Israel in the wilderness, preferring to go back to the familiarity of slavery rather than to move forward toward the promised land, because that future was somehow confused with dying.

The difficulty with becoming is that it involves change, and change is perceived as loss and death. I remember counseling a young woman over a considerable length of time about her relationship with her mother. Mother and daughter had an extremely close relationship, sharing intimately, but they could not be together more than a few days without ending up in an argument. Then the young woman would feel guilty and seek counsel. We tried every sort of approach, but nothing seemed to work. Recently she wrote me a letter saying she had made a breakthrough in understanding her relationship with her mother. During a conversation with her mother she described a dream she had had as a young child—a dream she had thought about often but which had never made sense. In the dream the two of them were riding together in a car through the sky. Outside the car were invisible men trying to take her away. She felt safe inside the car with her mother, but then her mother let them take her away, and laughed as they did it. After hearing about the dream her mother told her she had fought against being born—even the doctor said she had resisted the birthing process. Evidently their relationship had been a continual cycle of acting out, time after time, the trauma of her birth—first a drawing close in intimacy, then a pushing away through argument. She ended her letter to me with a quote from e. e. cummings that for her explained the experience: "If most people were to be born twice they'd improbably call it dying . . . . We can never be born enough. We are human beings, for whom birth is a supremely welcome mystery, the mystery of growing."

The anxiety that interprets each new birthing of growth as death cannot be overcome except insofar as the first question—"Who am I?"—is answered. Until identity is achieved, and through that identity a sense of purpose and destiny, the realization of one's potential for becoming human will be hindered. Yet identity is not something we achieve by ourselves; it is given to us by others. Adam could name everything in creation, he could give meaning and purpose to all things, but he could not "name" himself. To know who he was, he needed the human community represented in the person of Eve. There can be no "I" without a "you." For this reason the locus of pastoral care is always some sort of community that itself has a clear identity and purpose. So that to speak of the gathered Church as the Body of Christ is both to identify the nature of the community and to state an expectation toward which it is moving.

It is clear that by identity I do not mean the isolation of individualism—in fact, true intimacy can occur only through growth in identity. The nature of identity is pointed to in the language of psychologists and philosophers when they speak of authenticity, centeredness, uniqueness, individuation, self-integration, self-actualization, and such. Erik Erikson described it well:

> By identity I mean an accrued awareness of oneself that maintains continuity with one's past meanings to others and to oneself and that integrates the images of oneself given by significant others with one's own inner feelings of who one is and of what one can do, all in such a way as to enable one to anticipate the future without undue anxiety about "losing" oneself. Identity, thought of in this way, is by no means a fully conscious matter. But when it is present it gives rise to a feeling of inner firmness or of "being together" as a self. It communicates to others a sense of personal unity or integration.[11]

Yet even the identity given us by others is not sufficient to complete the process of human becoming—ultimately only God can truly name us. It is in baptism that our real identity is given, when God claims us as his own child. For as surely as at the baptism of Jesus, God spoke the words, "You are my beloved Son," so at every other baptism God gives that identity to his beloved. This, then, answers the Psalmist's second question, "Why does God care for us?" Because without a relationship with God and the loving care he gives us, we could not achieve the destiny he has laid out for us—without grace we could not grow. And the first gift of baptismal grace is an identity in Christ.

The very heart of the pastoral task is to help those in the baptized community live out the consequences of this identity given by grace. And to do this, I have long felt, one of the chief characteristics of good pastoring is helping people remember—and in particular to remember who they are in relation to God.

In high school I had a friend named Bill, and every Friday night as we were about to leave Bill's house to go do the things kids did back then, his mother would say, "Now Bill, remember, don't forget who you are." Obviously she was not worried that Bill would forget his name or address. It was her motherly way of reminding him of his values and ideals. Bill's mother was right, because our values, goals, and ideals are all linked to our identity. And she was also right in calling identity to remembrance because human beings have a tendency to forget who they are and what the primary purpose of life is.

In a very real sense, a parish community, the locus of pastoral care, is a place of remembrance. It is a place of beginning, a place for the Font of baptism. And because we are never finished with the meaning of baptism, it is a place of return, as the natural rhythm of the Christian life is one of gathering and sending—of going out and returning. The purpose of gathering and return is for re-formation and reminding—as in that place of beginning and return Christ is "re-membered," re-lived—the community, and those in it, re-identified.

This community is also the place of the Book wherein the story is told, and in that telling remembrance becomes understanding. Each of us has a story of God to tell, out of our own lives—each of our lives is a theological story. But that story can only be comprehended in light of the story of God's people. For how would we know and understand the call of God except through the stories of Abraham, Moses, Peter, and Paul? And who among us has not experienced the joy of Exodus, freedom and the anxiety of the wilderness? The story is told and taught so that individual experiences of God are understood, so that the meaning of life is perceived, salvation known and remembered.

The local Church is also the place for a Table. Like the Font and the Book, it is a place of remembrance. As a table it is also a place of personal communion and intimacy, a place of feeding and nurture. Yet it is also a Table of the future, placed in the presence of the Father in the banquet at the end of time—in this it is the constant reminder of our destiny as God's children.

Week by week the Church gathers the flock of Christ to call to mind the saving work of God by which we achieve wholeness and sanctification. In some sense the Church is a Mother saying

to us, "Now remember, Christian, don't forget who you are."
And we lift our hands to God in prayer, "Holy and gracious
Father, in your infinite love you made us for yourself . . . ."
But a parish community also has a chair for the president of
the liturgical assembly—it is the place of pastors. Here the one
charged with the task of feeding the flock of Christ calls together
the community of the baptized, watching over the rhythm of
gathering and sending. It is this one who bears the burden of
pastors, the vocation of love, the responsibility for pastoral care.
Others may, and should, share the task, but it is the bishop or
priest who is called to see that nurturing takes place. The skills
required for this role are well known—they are those of teacher,
preacher, counselor, spiritual guide, builder of community,
practical theologian, leader of prayer, and celebrant of sacraments. But all these skills would be insufficient for the task of
pastoral care without love for the flock of Christ.

It is this love that not only inspires vocation but is the means by
which the vocation is practiced. As we saw, God extends his loving
care toward humanity as a continuation of the creating process. By
seeing us in love, God sees us not simply as we are, in incomplete-
ness, but as we can be. It is this love that sees the potential we
are and calls into becoming. Pastoral care is the gift of this love
by which we realize our humanity as grace perfects nature. For
the bishop or priest this means a love that is not only supportive,
sustaining, nurturing, and caring, but a love that *expects.*

Love that sees what is and what can be is a love rooted in
unending hope. Pastors must see with hope, that is, see what is
the possibility, the potential in each person, and in hope call forth
these gifts. I say hope because this love does not seek to control
or manipulate into becoming; rather it seeks to set free and by
expectation and solicitation call into becoming. Gabriel Marcel
puts it nicely:

> My relationship to myself is mediated by the presence of the other
> person, by what he is for me and what I am for him. To love anybody
> is to expect something from him, something which can neither be defined
> nor seen; it is at the same time in some way to make it possible for
> him to fulfill this expectation. Yes, paradoxical as it may seem, to expect
> is in some way to give; but the opposite is nonetheless true: no longer
> to expect is to strike with sterility the being from whom no more is
> expected. It is then in some way to deprive him or to take from him
> in advance what is surely a certain possibility of inventing or creating.[12]

This giving of love creates the possibility of becoming. Interestingly, however, the ones in the process of growth are not always aware of what it is they are becoming; they know only that in some way love has called. A common experience of life will illustrate this point. Most of us have had the experience of helping, or at least watching, a baby learn to walk. The process begins by standing behind the child and letting the little one take hold of a couple of fingers on each of our hands. Then, with our arms outstretched before us, and walking slowly, the baby, pulled forward, takes a few wobbling steps. Regular practice at this, and the steps become more sure. Yet the tight grip of those little fingers reminds us that the child would quickly sit down or burst into tears if our hands were withdrawn. Eventually the child will use furniture to pull itself up to a standing position, and then, by carefully reaching out from chair to table to sofa, begin to walk around the room.

But if the infant is to begin to walk alone, he or she must learn to let go of the security of supports. To help in this part of the process the parent stands across the room from the little one who clings precariously to some table or chair, and calls, "Come to Mama, come to Daddy." After some coaxing, and because the infant trusts the parent, he will let go of the support, take a few feeble steps, and then run into the outstretched arms of the parent. Notice that the child does not walk because he thinks he can, he walks because the parent thinks he can—walking is in a way called out of the child. Walking occurs because the child trusts the parent and willingly responds to the solicitation of love. Only later does the child realize he can walk. Through a process of calling, then experience itself, followed by reflection and realization, growth takes place, and at each point the expectation of love is a key factor. The good pastor, then, represents the way in which God is in the future calling us to completion through love.

In this section we have touched on only a few of the important issues for pastoral care, and we have pointed out what I consider to be several important aspects of the task—identity, remembrance, and expectant love. There are, of course, many more issues, but these few, if taken seriously, would take the Church a long way toward fulfilling the ideal—the sanctification of the people of God.

A College of Pastors

In the first sections of this chapter I have discussed pastoral care in a very general way, trying to emphasize what I consider the crucial issues for all those called to be pastors—the necessity of a sense of vocation as a continual, conscious act of personal commitment leading to competence and skill, and the importance of a growth model of pastoral care, with some suggestions concerning a few fundamental characteristics of the process. In this last section I would like to focus more specifically on the role of the bishop as pastor, recognizing that all I have previously said applies in a special way to him as chief pastor of a diocese.

One of the chief problems for bishops is that of distance from the communities in which pastoring normally occurs, that is, the parish. This distance is measured both by time and by geography, and in terms of participation in community. We must come to grips with the ambiguity of a chief pastor giving pastoral care at a distance. But for me, as one committed to a growth model of pastoral care, there is also a paradox here: As a bishop I know the opportunities I have to be a pastor to particular human situations nearly always involve a problem or a crisis. Because a bishop bears the responsibility of chief pastor he becomes the last stop for unresolved problems and is forced to be primarily a pastor to human conflicts. How, then, even at a distance, can a bishop participate in the process of pastoral care for the purpose of giving formation to the people of God?

The basic unit of the Church is the diocese. This means a diocese contains within itself that which is necessary to provide for all that is essential in the life of the Church, and it is the unit that plans and carries out mission and ministry in a given geographical region. But a diocese is also defined by its bishop—it is the jurisdiction over which he is the ordinary. In the role of apostle he is the chief evangelist for the area. As chief pastor he is responsible for the nurture of all the baptized. The bishop is also the sign of unity within a diocese, and he represents that diocese to the whole Church through its councils and in union with other bishops.

This is the ideal. There is a great gap, however, between the ideal and present practice. The problem is not so much a matter of human failure as it is of the vicissitudes of history. And because we cannot turn back the clock, we must attempt to implement

new structures, models, and styles of ministry that might draw
us closer to the ideal as it is presented in our tradition and
expressed in the ordination rites, but also one in keeping with the
current situation of the Church.

Our particular concern is for the bishop in his pastoral role.
At the examination in the ordination of a bishop the candidate
is asked:

> As a chief priest and pastor, will you encourage and support all baptized
> people in their gifts and ministries, nourish them from the riches of
> God's grace, pray for them without ceasing, and celebrate with them
> the sacraments of our redemption?

Then the candidate responds:

> I will, in the name of Christ, the Shepherd and Bishop of our souls.[13]

All that has been said is consistent with the language of this
question and response. The bishop as chief pastor is called on
to nourish the people of God, to build up the Body of Christ.
And he does so in the name of the Shepherd, who bestows the
vocation out of love for the sheep. But as we saw, given the
strictures of geography and the numbers of people involved, there
are very few opportunities for a bishop to be a pastor as described
in the service of ordination. Visits to parishes, usually once
annually, are mostly functional and of such brevity as to prohibit
any real participation in what we have presented as pastoral care.
(I must add that the suggestion that we have more and smaller
dioceses does not seem practicable to me.)

Since the locus of pastoral care is usually parish-based and left
to priests, the pattern that has developed is for the bishop to see
his primary pastoral role as the pastor to the priests. Certainly
there is some indirect pastoral care given by the bishop to the laity
through the agencies of the diocese, but generally the care and
nurture of the local community is left in the hands of the priests,
and the pastoring of priests is left to the bishop. But because the
parish priests of a diocese are not what we could call a "local,
gathered community," pastoral care is usually given to them
individually. What this does is create a model of episcopal pastoral
care that encourages separation and parochialism. It puts the
bishop in the role of an area supervisor, keeping track of a chain

of "shops" by regular visits, watching over and checking the "branch managers." Not only does this create parochial attitudes, it promotes competition and jealousy among the clergy, and it lowers the level of trust between the bishop and the clergy. All this militates against the ideal of a diocese as a basic unit, and it consequently inhibits mission. This is clear from the fact that in any given area cooperation between parishes for ministry and mission is the exception rather than the rule.

Having described what I believe to be the current situation in many, if not most, dioceses, let me present a model that would allow the bishop more direct involvement in the pastoral care of the local parishes and also foster collegiality among priests. Previously I mentioned a possible change in leadership style based on Christ's instruction to his disciples, where authority would not be based on the power to command but on an authority character-ized by the ministry of servanthood. A change in leadership style, however, cannot happen by itself; it calls for a whole new struc-ture, one compatible with that style. For example, an authority based on the power to command necessitates a structure built on a chain of command, or a hierarchical system. That is generally what we have in place now. But an authority based on the ministry of servanthood would call for a structure more horizontal than vertical—it would not so much move through hierarchical ranks as it would share collegially. In other words, a servant model of ministry would call for a rethinking of relationships and, con-sequently, a restructuring of the system. Cardinal Suenens described such a renewal:

> No aspect of renewal stands alone. For example, if we wish to see a greater exercise of collegiality on the part of the highest authority in the church, then consistency demands that the image of the bishop within the local church or of the priest within each community be also re-thought in the same perspective. It is impossible to highlight the priesthood of the faithful without reconsidering the ministerial priesthood which, while always a part of the church's life, must be lived in a different way. The creation of permanent deacons and certain new responsibilities given to lay people automatically imply a greater flexibility in our traditional structures and a pluralism of ecclesiastical functions. Thus, everything exercises a mutual influence on everything else and everyone must rethink his relationships to everyone else. But that cannot happen overnight.[14]

What I propose is that we take seriously what is implied in the ordination rites. A bishop promises to "sustain your fellow presbyters and take counsel with them,"[15] and in the address before the examination in the ordination of a priest the candidate is told:

> Now you are called to work as a pastor, priest, and teacher, together with your bishop and fellow presbyters, and to take your share in the councils of the Church.[16]

The implication here is that a bishop and the presbyters of a diocese are a collegial body. This is imaged even more clearly in the actual laying on of hands. A deacon, because he or she has a particular relationship to the bishop, is ordained alone by the bishop. And a bishop, because he stands in historical relationship to the whole Church through other bishops, is ordained collegially by those bishops. But a priest is ordained by the laying on of hands of the bishop of a diocese and its presbyters. Significant here is that a priest is ordained into a diocese and its college of presbyters presided over by its bishop.

I think one could argue that a priest should never practice priesthood apart from that diocese and its college of presbyters but always in relation to it. That means that even a priest working alone in a parish does so as a member of a diocesan college of presbyters. Some have argued that priesthood is not transportable outside the diocese of canonical residency. This is reflected to a degree in the canons requiring priests to be licensed to officiate in dioceses other than their own. But the point I want to make is that such a relationship to a diocese and its presbyterate ought to be expressed in some way other than in the ordination liturgy and a few canons. It seems to me there is an opportunity here for a real college of pastors to exist.

What if a college of presbyters actually existed in the life of a diocese? What if its members assembled regularly in meetings, presided over by the bishop, to discuss the pastoral care of the whole diocese? In a collegial way they could discuss and make decisions on pastoral matters affecting the diocese and its parishes. For example, all the questions surrounding the initiation rites might be discussed—questions concerning first communion, confirmation, times of baptism, criteria for instruction, etc. Tough issues could be discussed openly, seeking consensus in decisions. In this way the individual priest would have an ownership of the decisions by participation. It could operate after the fashion of a monastic model, where the chapter makes decisions to be carried out by the superior, but in this case it would be the bishop functioning on behalf of the college of presbyters.

Such a college would bring about a greater trust among priests, and between priests and bishop. Working on building trust would be an important item on the agenda of some meetings. There also might be opportunities for growth in pastoral skills and competence, sharing the resources and talents of the college. In this way the priests would have a sense of sharing in the responsibility for pastoral care in the whole diocese, breaking down isolation and parochialism. Further, having experienced collegiality at this level, a priest might be convinced of its value at the parish level. This would have the effect of beginning to minimize the crisis of authority experienced in so many of our parishes and enhance the ministry of the laity.

The structure of a college of presbyters would depend mainly on the size of a diocese, both geographically and in numbers of priests involved. It also might seek to provide a way for nonparochial and nonstipendiary priests to participate in the pastoral work of a diocese.

In some ways a college of presbyters presided over by the bishop would be one step toward fulfilling the vision presented by the Faith and Order Commission of the World Council of Churches in its document "Baptism, Eucharist, and Ministry." Having acknowledged the importance of a threefold, ordained ministry in a united church, it goes on to say:

> *Guilding Principles for the Exercise of the Ordained*
> *Ministry in the Church*
>
> Three considerations are important in this respect. The ordained ministry should be exercised in a personal, collegial and communal way. It should be *personal* because the presence of Christ among his people can most effectively be pointed to by the person ordained to proclaim the Gospel and to call the community to serve the Lord in unity of life and witness. It should also be *collegial,* for there is need for a college of ordained ministers sharing in the common task of representing the concerns of a community. Finally, the intimate relationship between the ordained ministry and the community should find expression in a *communal* dimension where the exercise of the ordained ministry is rooted in the life of the community and requires the community's effective participation in the discovery of God's will and the guidance of the Spirit.[17]

But most important for our discussion, it would give the bishop a clear role in the pastoral care of a diocese. It would give him a direct opportunity to be of some pastoral influence in each parish. By being the agency (the servant?) through which priests come together to discuss the role of priesthood, he would take the lead in rekindling the spirit of their vocation, inspire them for prayer, and promote their formation. By continually raising questions about the nurture of the faithful through the living out of their baptismal covenant, he would participate in a very real way in the pastoral care of the diocese and fulfill the intention of the words of the consecration prayer at the ordination of a bishop:

> To you, O Father, all hearts are open; fill, we pray, the heart of this your servant whom you have chosen to be a bishop in your Church, with such love of you and of all the people, that he may feed and tend the flock of Christ, and exercise without reproach the high priesthood to which you have called him.[18]

Suggested Readings

1. Brown, Raymond E., S.S. *Priest and Bishop: Biblical Reflections.* New York: Paulist Press, 1970.

2. Fowler, James W. *Stages of Faith: The Psychology of Human Development and the Quest for Meaning.* San Francisco: Harper and Row, 1981.

3. Holmes, Urban T., III. *Turning to Christ: A Theology of Renewal and Evangelization.* New York: Seabury Press, 1981.

4. Johann, Robert O. *Building the Human.* New York: Herder and Herder, 1968.

5. Macquarrie, John. *In Search of Humanity: A Theological and Philosophical Approach.* New York: Crossroads, 1983.

6. Mayeroff, Milton. *On Caring.* World Perspectives, edited by Ruth Nanda Anshen, vol. 43. New York: Harper and Row, 1971.

7. Moore, Peter, ed. *Bishops, But What Kind: Reflections on Episcopacy.* London: SPCK, 1982.

8. Nedoncelle, Maurice. *Love and the Person.* Translated by Sr. Ruth Adelaide, S.C. New York: Sheed and Ward, 1966.

9. Rahner, Karl. *Theology of Pastoral Action.* Studies in Pastoral Action, edited by Karl Rahner, S.J., and Daniel Morrissey, O.P., vol. 1. New York: Herder and Herder, 1968.

10. Segundo, Juan Luis, S.J., in collaboration with the staff of the Peter Faber Center in Montevideo, Uruguay. *Grace and the Human Condition.* Translated by John Drury. A Theology for Artisans of a New Humanity, vol. 2. New York: Maryknoll, 1973.

11. Stokes, Kenneth, ed. *Faith Development in the Adult Life Cycle.* New York: W. H. Sadlier, 1982.

12. Von Balthasar, Hans Urs. *Love Alone.* New York: Herder and Herder, 1969.

Notes

Chapter 1. On the Pattern and in the Power

1. John 17:21 (RSV).

2. John R. H. Moorman, *The Anglican Spiritual Tradition* (Springfield, IL: Templegate Publishers, 1983), p. 1.

3. Psalm 11:3, *BCP '79*, p. 596.

4. *The Age of Chaucer,* edited by William Frost (Englewood Cliffs, NJ: Prentice-Hall, 1961), pp. 44-45. The original text is quoted with explanatory notes by William Frost as emended and/or expanded by WHP.

5. John Donne, *Devotions Upon Emergent Occasions, Together with Death's Duel* (Ann Arbor: University of Michigan Press, 1965), pp. 108-9. It is, of course, from this passage that Hemingway took the title for his novel set in the midst of the Spanish Civil War, *For Whom the Bell Tolls.*

6. *The Showing Forth of Christ: Sermons of John Donne,* selected and edited by Edmund Fuller (New York: Harper & Row, 1964), pp. 78-80.

7. *John Donne: A Selection of His Poetry,* edited with an introduction by John Hayward (Baltimore: Penguin Books, 1960), p. 163.

8. Ibid., pp. 172-73.

9. *Hymnal 1982* (New York: Church Hymnal Corporation, 1985).

10. George Herbert, *The Country Parson, The Temple,* edited with an introduction by John N. Wall, Jr. (New York: Paulist Press, 1981), p. 54.

11. Ibid., pp. 55-115; e.g., "The Parson's Preaching, . . . Charity, . . . Library; The Parson Comforting, . . . Punishing, . . . Catechizing; The Parson in Sacraments, . . . in Circuit, . . . in Applying Remedies," and so forth.

12. Ibid., pp. 56-57.

13. Ibid., pp. 94-95.

14. Ibid., p. 316.

15. Paul A. Weslby, *Lancelot Andrewes* (London: SPCK, 1964), p. 83.

16. Pastorally speaking, Laud is a tragic figure. For no matter the quality of content, his attempts to impose a liturgical uniformity on British society in a politically and religiously turbulent era met with disaster. Similarly, Laud's related pastoral efforts to secure social justice were pursued through such authoritarian or legally coercive means as to have ultimately occasioned his trial and execution in 1645. One pastoral implication for Anglicanism is that the ghost of Laud haunted subsequent attempts to secure an episcopal ministry in England's American colonies and effectively precluded its establishment.

17. James M. Barnett, *The Diaconate: A Full and Equal Order* (New York: Seabury Press, 1981), p. 82.

18.   It is worth remarking here, as does Barnett, op. cit., that the twentieth-century poet T. S. Eliot commemorates the community of Little Gidding in the last of his *Four Quartets.*

19.   John Evelyn, *The Diary of John Evelyn, Volume III, Kalendarium 1650-1672,* edited by Edward S. de Beer (Oxford at the Clarendon Press, 1955), pp. 203-4.

20.   Daniel Neal, *The History of the Puritans,* vol. 4 (London, 1738), p. 431.

21.   Kenneth A. Thompson, *Bureaucracy and Church Reform: The Organizational Response of the Church of England to Social Change, 1800-1965* (Oxford at the Clarendon Press, 1970), p. 7.

22.   So named for Edward Hyde, Earl of Clarendon, and one of the chief architects of the Restoration of monarchy and episcopacy. This "Code" consisted of a series of parliamentary acts, passed between 1661 and 1673, intended to disable dissent and preclude Nonconformity in religion: 1661, *Corporation Act* required *inter alia* that all mayors and other civil magistrates receive Holy Communion according to the rites of the Church of England; 1662, *Act of Uniformity* required all clergy, all university teachers and students, all teachers in private houses to personally subscribe the XXXIX Articles of Religion and use only the Book of Common Prayer in worship; 1665, *Five Mile Act* forbade Nonconformist ministers to come within five miles of any town and to keep any school (two Justices of the Peace may determine offenders—penalty was commitment to gaol without bail for six months per offence); 1670, *Conventicle Act* provided that any persons assembling for dissenting religious services might be fined 5s. (first offense) or 10s. (second offense)—preachers were to be fined £20 or £40 for first and second offenses, respectively (£40 was then a significant sum); 1673, *The Test Act* effectively prevented any Roman Catholic—Recusant—from holding public office.

To this body of legislation was added in 1711 the *Occasional Conformity Act,* which laid down fines and forfeiture of position to office-holders receiving Holy Communion in the Church of England and subsequently discovered at a "conventicle"; and in 1714 the *Schism Act* aimed at supression of Dissenters' academies and schools.

The two early eighteenth-century acts were repealed in 1719, but the Clarendon Code proper was not effectively repealed until the Reform Era of 1828 to 1832. As noted, it was enforced more or less at whim when the Establishment felt threatened. All in all, this was not a glorious development in the history of Anglican pastoralia.

23.   *Vide supra,* p. 14.

24.   *Oxford Dictionary of the Christian Church,* 2nd ed. edited by F. L. Cross and E. A. Livingstone (Oxford University Press, 1974), p. 1343.

25.   H. Boone Porter, *Jeremy Taylor, Liturgist* (London: Alcuin Club/SPCK, 1979).

26.   C. FitzSimons Allison, *The Rise of Moralism: The Proclamation of the Gospel from Hooker to Baxter* (New York: Seabury Press, 1966), cf. especially chapters 3 and 4, "The Theology of Jeremy Taylor" and "Contradictions in the Theology of Jeremy Taylor."

27. Jeremy Taylor, *The Rule and Exercises of Holy Living,* abridged with a preface by Anne Lamb (New York: Harper and Row, 1970), pp. 4-5.

28. Cited in Allison, *The Rise of Moralism,* p. 89.

29. *Lesser Feasts and Fasts,* 3rd ed. (New York: Church Hymnal Corporation, 1980), p. 146.

30. *Reverend Thomas Bray: His Life and Selected Works Relating to Maryland,* edited by Bernard C. Steiner (New York: Arno Press, 1972), p. 191. [Reprinted for the *Religion in America* series from *Maryland Historical Society Fund Publication, No. 37,* Baltimore, 1901.]

31. Ibid., pp. 193-4.

32. Ibid., pp. 199-200.

33. Ibid., pp. 200-201.

34. Cf. *Oxford Dictionary of the Christian Church,* 2nd ed., p. 805. There were at least two, possibly three, nonjuring crises in the Church of England in this period. In essence, the term refers to the conscientious inability by some Church of England clergy to take the Oath of Allegience to new monarchs/rulers at times of change in English constitutional history (i.e., from James II to William III & Mary II, 1688; from the Stuarts to the Hanoverians—accession of George I in 1714, Law's crisis; or, on this side the Atlantic, from the Hanoverians to the Continental Congress, 1776 ff.). On the other point, it is at least interesting to note that the grandson of Law's aristocratic benefactor became, through his writing of *The Decline and Fall of the Roman Empire,* one of the most acidulous critics of Christianity in the Age of the Enlightenment.

35. William Law, *A Serious Call to the Devout and Holy Life,* with an introduction by Norman Sykes (London: J. M. Dent & Sons Ltd., 1961), pp. 36-37.

36. Urban T. Holmes, *A History of Christian Spirituality: An Analytical Introduction* (New York: Seabury Press, 1981), p. 123.

37. Henry Fielding, *The History of Tom Jones, A Foundling* (New York: Dodd, Mead & Company), p. 69.

38. Jane Austen, *Pride and Prejudice* (New York: Dodd, Mead & Company, 1945), p. 251.

39. *The Works of John Wesley: Volume I—Journal from October 14, 1735, to November 29, 1745* (Zondervan Publishing House, photo-offset from the authorized edition published by Wesleyan Conference office, 1872), Thursday, March 29, 1739, ff.

40. Ibid., Monday, June 11, 1739.

41. Horton Davies, *Worship and Theology in England: From Watts and Wesley to Maurice, 1690-1850* (Princeton University Press, 1961), pp. 150-51.

42. Frank Baker, *John Wesley and the Church of England* (London: Epworth Press, 1970), pp. 70 f. and p. 361. Since we have exhibited in this section the pastor

as chaplain, it will be interesting to note the manner in which Methodist ministers were at first given support and standing. Selina Hastings (1707-1791), Countess of Huntingdon, who was instrumental in introducing Methodism to the upper classes, also exercised her right as a peeress of the realm to appoint chaplains—as many priests of the Church of England with Methodist inclinations as possible! Known as Lady Huntingdon's Connexion, this development obtained until it was tested in 1779 by the ecclesiastical consistory court and disallowed. From that time Lady Huntingdon registered her chapels as dissenting places of worship under the Toleration Act (1689). In any case, and in view of her piety regarding new experiments in pastoral care, Lady Huntingdon stands in favorable contrast to the literary peeress Lady Catherine de Bourgh!

43.   The claim made here can be substantiated for most Anglicans simply by listing a number of the Charles Wesley hymns so widely known and sung: "Come, thou long expected Jesus"; "Lo! he comes with clouds descending"; "Hark! the herald angels sing"; "Jesus Christ is ris'n today"; "Hail the day that sees him rise"; "Christ whose glory fills the skies"; "O for a thousand tongues to sing"; "Let saints on earth in concert sing"; and "Love divine all loves excelling." These are but nine of the eighteen published in the *Hymnal 1940* alone.

44.   Henry Martyn is erroneously listed as a priest in *Lesser Feasts and Fasts,* 3rd ed. (New York: Church Hymnal Corporation, 1980), pp. 352-3. As his contributions were stellar, so ought the memory of his ecclesiastical dignity be accurate. A better guide is the *Dictionary of National Biography, Vol. XXXVI* (London: Smith and Elder, 1893), pp. 315-17.

45.   Such theological activity occurs on all levels (from what children perceive through catechesis, to the preacher explaining Scripture and composing a sermon, to the formal activity of the professional theologian) and in various expressions of the Church (from the parish to the seminary, which exists at the crucial nexus of *ecclesia* and *academia*).

46.   Vernon F. Storr, *The Development of English Theology in the Nineteenth Century, 1800-1860* (London: 1913), p. 63.

47.   Horton Davies, *Worship and Theology in England,* pp. 239-40.

48.   John F. Maurice, *Life of Frederick Denison Maurice, Chiefly Told in His Own Letters* (New York: Charles Scribner's Sons, 1884), vol. 1, p. 369.

49.   The closest disciple of Jeremy Bentham (himself a famous utilitarian philosopher) and the father of John Stuart Mill, James Mill (1763-1836), made this positive proposal because he could not rest content with his own negative proclamation that "the Church of England is ripe for dissolution." Cf. *Dictionary of National Biography,* Vol. XXXVII, pp. 387 ff.

50.   Owen Chadwick, *The Victorian Church,* vol. I (New York: Oxford University Press, 1966), pp. 174-76.

51.   For instance, Pusey's Tract #18: "Thoughts on the Benefits of Fasting Enjoined by Our Church." His later tracts on Baptism (#s 67-69) were full of patristic scholarship. The series itself ended abruptly with Newman's Tract #90,

"Remarks on Certain Passages in the Thirty-Nine Articles," which raised a storm of controversy by attempting to construe the Articles as not inconsistent with the decrees of the Council of Trent! Though many had found themselves able to bear the thought that after all the Church of England might be apostolical, by 1841 few were prepared to hear that its catholicity could comprehend Tridentine opinions.

52.   Chadwick, *The Mind of the Oxford Movement* (Stanford University Press, 1961), p. 49.

53.   *Oxford Dictionary of the Christian Church,* p. 1147.

54.   There is, of course, the further pastoral irony that the effective recovery of the practice of Confirmation in Anglicanism is of such relatively recent origin. Within a century and a half of the development of regular practice, the circumstances of the Church in a post-Christendom era would lead to a serious reevaluation and reunification of the Sacrament of Initiation, wherein Confirmation is now used as a pastoral office of adult commitment/reaffirmation of baptismal vows instead of a quasi-sacramental prerequisite for admission to Holy Communion.

55.   In addition to Kemper, the work of Bishops Otey and Polk in the South and Southwest, Talbot in the Great Plains and mountain territories, and Scott and Kip in the far West should be noted during the pre-Civil War period. Bishop Tuttle's career in much of the West in the later nineteenth century also demands notice. Cf. especially James Thayer Addison, *The Episcopal Church in the United States, 1789-1931* (New York: Charles Scribner's Sons, 1951), chapters 9 and 16.

56.   Chadwick, *The Victorian Church,* vol. I, p. 369.

57.   *The Church of England, 1815-1948: A Documentary History,* edited by R. P. Flindall (London: SPCK, 1972), pp. 133-34. My emphasis.

58.   Geoffrey Rowell, *Hell and the Victorians: A Study of the 19th-Century Theological Controversies Concerning Eternal Punishment and the Future Life* (Oxford at the Clarendon Press, 1974), *passim.* But cf. in particular p. 1: "Hellfire preaching was common, and not only in Evangelical circles, for much of the century, and the threat of everlasting punishment was in many instances the implicit sanction of both social morality and mission to the heathen."

59.   F. D. Maurice, *The Prayer Book* (London: James Clarke, & Co., Ltd., 1966), pp. 4-5.

60.   *Oxford Dictionary of the Christian Church,* p. 1470.

61.   John D. Gay, *The Geography of Religion in England* (London: Gerald Duckworth & Company Limited, 1971), p. 80.

62.   Owen Chadwick, *Hensley Henson: A Study in the Friction between Church and State* (Oxford at the Clarendon Press, 1983), p. 315.

63.   Chadwick, *The Victorian Church,* p. 303.

Chapter 2. Spiritual Direction and
the Struggle for Justice

1.   Martin Thornton, *English Spirituality* (London: SPCK, 1963), p. xiii.

2.   _____, *Spiritual Direction: A Practical Introduction* (London: SPCK, 1984).

3.   There are a number of studies of the Anglican tradition of social theology in the publications of the Jubilee Group (St. Clement's House, Sirdar Road, London, W11). They include John R. Orens's "Politics and the Kingdom," reprinted in *The Anglican Moral Choice,* ed. Paul Elman (Wilton, CT: Morehouse-Barlow, 1983), pp. 63-84; and the Jubilee Group symposium *Essays Catholic and Radical,* ed. Kenneth Leech and Rowan Williams (London: Bowerdean Press, 1983).

4.   T. C. Oden, cited in A. V. Campbell, *Rediscovering Pastoral Care* (London: Darton, Longman and Todd, 1981), p. 8.

5.   Douglas V. Steere in *Protestants and Catholics on the Spiritual Life,* ed. Michael Marx, OSB (Collegeville, MN: Liturgical Press, 1965), pp. 50-51.

6.   See my *Youthquake: The Growth of a Counter-Culture through Two Decades* (London: Sheldon Press, 1973).

7.   See, for example, Tilden Edwards, *Spiritual Friend* (New York: Paulist Press, 1980), and Alan Jones, *Exploring Spiritual Direction* (New York: Seabury, 1982).

8.   E. Kadloubovsky and G. E. H. Palmer, *Early Fathers from the Philokalia* (London: Faber and Faber, 1954, rev. ed. 1976), p. 263.

9.   _____, *Writings from the Philokalia* (London: Faber and Faber, 1951, rev. ed. 1975), pp. 100-103.

10.   *Macarius: Russian Letters of Direction 1834-1860,* ed. Julia de Beausobre (Crestwood, NY: St. Vladimir's Seminary Press, 1944, rev. ed. 1975), pp. 23 and 28.

11.   *The Dialogue of Divine Providence,* in *Classics of Western Spirituality* (New York: Paulist, 1980), chs. 97-105.

12.   For a more detailed study of the developments, see my *Soul Friend* (San Francisco: Harper and Row, 1980).

13.   See Edwards, *Spiritual Friend,* and Jones, *Exploring Spiritual Direction.*

14.   Thornton, *English Spirituality,* p. 237.

15.   Introduction to *Ductor Dubitantium.* See H. R. McAdoo, "Anglican Moral Theology in the 17th Century" in *The Anglican Moral Choice.*

16.   *Advice for Those Who Exercise the Ministry of Reconciliation through Confession and Absolution, Being the Abbé Gaume's Manual for Confessors . . . Abridged, Condensed and Adapted to the Use of the English Church* (Oxford: Parker, 1878), pp. clvi and clviii.

17.   Cited in Pusey, pp. clxii-clxiv.

18.   William Cunningham, *The Cure of Souls* (1908), cited in J. T. McNeill, *A History of the Cure of Souls* (London: SCM, 1952), pp. 245-46.

19.   R. A. Lambourne, "Objections to a Proposed National Pastoral Organization," *Contact* 35 (June 1971): 25-27.

20.   Thornton, *Spiritual Direction,* pp. 9-15.

21.   Campbell, *Rediscovering Pastoral Care,* p. 59.

22.   Ibid., pp. 22-23.

23.   R. D. Laing, *The Politics of Experience and the Bird of Paradise* (Harmondsworth, England: Penguin, 1967), p. 136.

24.   Viktor Frankl, *The Doctor and the Soul* (New York: A. A. Knopf, 1965).

25.   Sheldon B. Kopp, *Guru: Metaphors from a Psychotherapist* (New York: Bantam Books, 1976), and *If You Meet the Buddha on the Road, Kill Him!* (New York: Bantam Books, 1976).

26.   Theodore Roszak, *Unfinished Animal* (London: Faber and Faber, 1976), p. 240.

27.   Two questions in particular call for attention: First, since spiritual direction will often involve a confession of sins, is it reasonable to ask a person to repeat such a confession to a priest in order to be absolved? Where the director is a lay Christian, ought there not to be a provision for lay absolution? Second, where direction is separated from confession and from a priest who is bound canonically by the seal, how can the guarantee of absolute confidentiality be best maintained so that individuals feel secure in their relationships with the director?

The lack of attention to this issue in Anglican writing is striking. The late Kenneth Ross dismissed it by saying, "It is of academic interest only to inquire whether a deacon may absolve or whether a layman may. . . . These are obscure questions and of little practical relevance." K. N. Ross, *Hearing Confessions* (London: SPCK, 1974), p. 55.

28.   Max Thurian, *Confession* (London: SCM, 1958).

29.   Augustine Baker, *Holy Wisdom,* ed. J. Norbert Sweeney (London: Burns Oates, 1876), p. 85.

30.   Campbell, *Rediscovering Pastoral Care,* p. 5.

31.   Thorton, *Spiritual Direction,* p. 1.

32.   Henri Nouwen, *The Wounded Healer* (New York: Doubleday, 1972), p. 94.

33.   Gregory of Nazianzus, *Or.* 2, 71.

34.   Gail Marie Priestly, "Some Jungian Parallels to the Sayings of the Desert Fathers," *Cistercian Studies,* 11, no. 2 (1976), p. 106.

35.   Alan Jones, "Homiletics and Spiritual Direction," undated MS.

36.   David Schuller et al., *Ministry in America* (San Francisco: Harper and Row, 1980), pp. 74 and 77.

37.   Ibid., p. 244.

38.   See Widdrington's essay in *The Return of Christendom,* By a Group of Churchmen (London: G. Allen & Unwin, 1922). For a valuable account of developments since see Gresham Kirkby, "Kingdom Come" in Leech and Rowan, eds. *Essays Catholic and Radical.*

39.   Peter Selby, *Liberating God: Private Care and Public Struggle* (London: SPCK, 1983), p. 21.

40.   *City of God* 19: 5.

41.   Jim Wallis, *The Call to Conversion* (Tring: Lion Publishing, 1982), p. 132.

42.   Daniel Berrigan, *America is Hard to Find* (London: SPCK, 1973), pp. 77-78.

43.   Theodore Roszak, *Where the Wasteland Ends* (London: Faber and Faber, 1972), p. 134.

Chapter 3. Secular and Religious Models of Care

Much of the material in this chapter is taken from a paper the author read at the American Academy of Psychoanalysis in December 1981: "Psychiatry and Religion: Partners or Strangers?"

1.   Robert E. Neale, "The Healing Deception," *Union Seminary Quarterly Review* 36, nos. 2 & 3 (Winter/Spring 1981): 149-58. The quotations at the end of this chapter are also from this article.

2.   E. Mansell Pattison, "Religion and Compliance," in *Compliance,* ed. M. Rosenbaum (New York: Human Sciences Press, 1981).

3.   Andrew Abbott, "Religion, Psychiatry, and Problems of Everyday Life," *Sociological Analysis: A Journal in the Sociology of Religion* 41 (1980): 164-71.

4.   Ruth Tiffany Barnhouse, "The Theology of Pastoral Care—A Progress Report," *The Anglican Theological Review* 65, no. 4 (October 1983): 397-411. Much of the material in this chapter is taken from this article.

5.   _____, "Spiritual Direction and Psychotherapy," *The Journal of Pastoral Care* 33, no. 3 (September 1979).

6.   Ana-Maria Rizzuto, *The Birth of the Living God* (Chicago: University of Chicago Press, 1979).

7.   C. G. Jung, "Psychology and Religion," in *Psychology and Religion: West and East* (Princeton University Press, 1969, 2nd ed.), pp. 5-105 (CW Vol. 11). These lectures were given in 1937, revised and published in 1940.

8.   James B. Fowler, *Stages of Faith* (San Francisco: Harper & Row, 1981).

9.   These conclusions are based on my work as psychiatric examiner for the Episcopal Diocese of Virginia, 1978-1980, testing students at Weston School of Theology, Virginia Theological Seminary, and Perkins School of Theology, and clergy at various workshops.

10.   Ann Belford Ulanov, review of Rizzuto's *The Birth of the Living God, Union Seminary Quarterly Review* 36, nos. 2 & 3 (Winter/Spring 1981): 173-76.

11.   Ruth Tiffany Barnhouse, "The Vicissitudes of Reform," *Union Seminary Quarterly Review* 36, nos. 2 & 3 (Winter/Spring 1981): 131-40.

12.   P. Burra, letter to the editor, *American Journal of Psychiatry* 137, no. 12 (December 1980): 1623-24.

13.   Evangelos Christou, *The Logos of the Soul* (Vienna, Zurich: Dunquin Press, 1963, recently reissued by Spring Publications, Dallas).

14.   Huston Smith, *Forgotten Truth* (New York: Harper Colophon, 1977), pp. 1-13.

15.   Jerome D. Frank, "Psychotherapy: The Restoration of Morale," *Weekly Psychiatry Update Series,* no. 19, Biomedia, Inc., 1977.

16.   Robert N. Bellah, "Biblical Religion and Social Science in the Modern World," *NICM Journal* (National Institute of Campus Ministries) 6, no. 3 (Summer 1981): 7-22. Subsequent quotations are from this article.

17.   William Irwin Thompson, *At the Edge of History* (New York: Harper Colophon, 1972).

18.   Robert N. Bellah, "Response to Tidball," *NICM Journal* 6, no. 3 (Summer 1981): 48-49.

19.   Paul Ricoeur, "The Biblical Worldview and Philosophy," *NICM Journal* 6, no. 3 (Summer 1981): 91-111. Subsequent quotations are from this article.

20.   E. Mansell Pattison, "Psychoanalysis and the Concept of Evil," *The Self in Process,* eds. Marie C. Nelson & Michael Eigen (New York: The Human Sciences Press, 1981).

21.   Ruth Tiffany Barnhouse, "The Spiritual Exercises and Psychoanalytic Therapy," *The Way,* supplement 24 (Spring 1975).

22.   C. G. Jung, *The Undiscovered Self* (Boston: Little Brown, 1958. Originally published in *The Atlantic Monthly* before World War II).

23.   *"You can expel nature with a pitchfork, but she will nevertheless return."*

24.   Jean-Paul Sartre, *Existentialism and Human Emotions* (New York: Philosophical Library, 1947).

25.   Ruth Tiffany Barnhouse, *Homosexuality: A Symbolic Confusion,* "The Interpretation of Immaturity" (New York: Seabury Press, 1979), ch. 11, pp. 139-54.

26.   Robert J. Stoller, "Overview: The Impact of New Advances in Sex Research on Psychoanalytic Theory," *The American Journal of Psychiatry* 1330 (1973): 241-51.

27.   C. G. Jung, "Transformation Symbolism in the Mass," in *Psychology and Religion: West and East* (Princeton U. Press, 1969, 2nd ed., CW Vol. 11). This monograph was written before Vatican II.

28.   Urban T. Holmes, *A History of Christian Spirituality* (New York: Seabury Press, 1980).

29.   C. G. Jung, "Psychoanalysis and the Cure of Souls," in *Psychology and Religion: West and East* (Princeton U. Press, 1969, 2nd ed., pp. 348-54, CW Vol. 11). This essay was written in 1937.

30.   Francis L. K. Hsu, "Kinship is the Key," *The Center Magazine* (November/December 1973): pp. 4-14.

31.   Gregory Baum, "Theology Questions Psychiatry: An Address," *The Ecumenist* 20, no. 4 (May-June 1982): 55-59.

32.   Ann and Barry Ulanov, *Religion and the Unconscious* (Philadelphia: Westminster Press, 1975). This book lays the essential groundwork for such an exploration.

Chapter 4. Theology and Pastoral Care

1.   Henri Nouwen, *Reaching Out: The Three Movements of the Spiritual Life* (Garden City: Doubleday, 1975).

2.   In another chapter of this collection Ruth T. Barnhouse discusses the problem from her perspective as a psychiatrist and priest. William Stringfellow, in *A Simplicity of Faith: My Experience in Mourning* (Nashville: Abingdon, 1982), discusses from personal experience some of the difficulties in medical care.

3.   *Summa Theologiae* I, q. 22, a. 2 (Blackfriars' Edition).

4.   Robert M. Grant, for example, in *Early Christianity and Society* (San Francisco: Harper and Row, 1977), makes the point that those early Christians who were not called on to be martyrs displayed a great willingness to adapt to the society around them.

5.   For an interesting and informative study, see Charles Silverstein, *Man to Man: Gay Couples in America* (New York: Quill, 1982).

6.   Among the most important liberation theologians in Latin America are Gustavo Gutierrez, Juan Luis Segundo, and José Míguez Bonino. Political theologians, most of whom are European, include J-B. Metz, Jürgen Moltmann, and Dorothee Sölle. *Solidarity with Victims* (New York: Crossroad, 1982), by Matthew Lamb, is an especially important study of political theology because it is written from within the American context. In addition, there is a study by

Rosemary Radford Ruether, *Sexism and God-Talk: Toward a Feminist Theology* (Boston: Beacon Press, 1983). I found this book very helpful in relating the concerns of Latin American liberation theology to those especially important in North American liberation theology, namely, the liberation of people who have been oppressed by sexism as well as by class or poverty.

7.   Walther Eichrodt, *Ezekiel: A Commentary* (Philadelphia: Westminster, 1970), p. 478.

8.   Ibid., pp. 479, ff.

9.   In the LXX the Hebrew *hesed* is not usually translated as *charis,* but in the New Testament *charis* is used in Luke, Paul, and the other epistles attributed to Paul. For the Pauline churches it was, apparently, a technical term or even a slogan used to express the salvation brought about by Jesus Christ. See Karl Rahner, ed., *Encyclopedia of Theology: The Concise Sacramentum Mundi* (New York: Seabury, 1975), pp. 584, ff.

10.   Edward Schillebeeckx, *Jesus: An Experiment in Christology* (New York: Seabury, 1979), p. 159.

11.   In *The Trinity,* trans. Joseph Donceel (New York: Herder and Herder, 1970), p. 10, Karl Rahner refers to "the isolation of trinitarian doctrine in piety and textbook theology," and he traces briefly the origin of the problem in western theology.

12.   Ibid., pp. 23-24.

13.   *Encyclopedia of Theology,* p. 1761.

14.   Ibid., p. 1761.

15.   The Church is not, of course, the only caring community; there are many others that God, in his providence, raises up. But the Church is, we believe, an intentional community of care as well as a sacramental sign of God's care. To discuss the relationship between the Church and other such communities would, however, take us too far afield.

16.   This theme has been made more prominent in the order for Holy Baptism in the 1979 *Book of Common Prayer.*

17.   Some theological traditions, especially those deriving from the Reformation, would state the nature-grace relationship differently. (I am following that which has been common in Anglicanism since Richard Hooker.) But such differences are reconcilable—as ecumenical theology has come to recognize—when they are seen to be doctrinal formulations arising out of different ways of experiencing the Gospel of salvation, rather than as irreformable dogmas. For a brief discussion of this issue, see my *Church, Ministry and Unity* (Oxford: Blackwell, 1983), chs. 4 and 5.

18.   *Book of Common Prayer,* the Order for Holy Baptism, p. 306.

19.   Ibid., Eucharistic Prayer D, p. 375.

20. See Edward Schillebeeckx, *Christ the Sacrament of the Encounter with God,* trans. Paul Barrett (London and New York: Sheed and Ward, 1963), pp. 74-75; and *Summa Theologiae* III, q. 60, a. 3.

21. At the end of the *Summa Contra Gentiles,* IV, ch. xcvii, Thomas Aquinas writes as follows:

> Since then the corporeal creature is disposed of finally in a manner that is in keeping with man's state, and man himself will not only be delivered from corruption, but also clothed in glory . . . it follows that even the corporeal creature will acquire a certain glory of brightness befitting its capacity. Wherefore it is said (Apoc. 21:1): "I saw a new heaven and a new earth."

Apparently, from what he has said earlier in the same chapter, such a hope did not extend to "animals, plants and mixed bodies, which are entirely corruptible." However, just as Karl Barth believed that Mozart would provide the music of heaven, so we might interpret Thomas in order to believe that those corruptible things (such as animals) that have figured much in human life will be included in our glory, because God has the care of all being.

22. See Johannes C. Hoekendijik, *The Church Inside Out,* trans. Isaac C. Rottenberg (Philadelphia: Westminster, 1966).

Chapter 5. Worship and Pastoral Care

1. Daniel Berrigan, "The Face of Christ," in *A Christian's Prayer Book,* ed. Coughlan, Jasper, and Rodrigues (London: Chapman, 1972), p. 137.

2. Marcella Hazan, *The Classic Italian Cook Book* (New York City: Knopf, 1982), p. 459.

3. Cf. Ralph Keifer, "Confirmation and Christian Maturity: The Deeper Issue," *Worship,* December 1972, pp. 601-8.

4. Cf. Nathan Mitchell, "Christian Initiation: Decline and Dismemberment," *Worship,* October 1974, pp. 458-79.

5. Cf. Aidan Kavanagh, "The Norm of Baptism: The New Rite of Christian Initiation for Adults," *Worship,* March 1974, pp. 143-52, and "Christian Initiation for Adults: The Rites," *Worship,* June-July 1974, pp. 318-35.

6. Cf. *Book of Common Prayer* (1979), pp. 304-5.

Chapter 6. Preaching and Pastoral Care

1. Henry Sloane Coffin, *What to Preach* (New York: Richard R. Smith, 1930).

2. John T. McNeil, *A History of the Cure of Souls* (New York: Harper and Row, 1951), p. vii.

3. William A. Clebsch and Charles R. Jaekle, *Pastoral Care in Historical Perspective* (New York, Evanston, & London: Harper and Row, 1967), p. 14.

4. Ibid., p. 4.

5. Ibid., p. 5. Italics theirs.

6. Ibid., p. xiv.

7. Ibid., p. 68.

8. Ibid., p. 33.

9. Ibid., p. 42.

10. Ibid., p. 10.

11. Ibid., p. 56.

12. Nashville: Abingdon, 1983, p. 349.

13. Ibid., p. 12.

14. Ibid., p. 356.

15. Ibid., p. 260.

16. Philip Rieff, *The Triumph of the Therapeutic: Uses of Faith after Freud* (New York and Evanston: Harper and Row, 1966).

17. Howard Clinebell, *Basic Types of Pastoral Counseling: New Resources in Ministering to the Troubled* (Nashville: Abingdon, 1966), p. 14.

18. Ibid., p. 21.

19. Holifield, p. 274.

20. O. C. Edwards, Jr., *Elements of Homiletics* (New York: Pueblo, 1982), p. 7.

21. Ibid., p. 13.

22. William Skudlarek, OSB, *The Word in Worship: Preaching in a Liturgical Context* (Nashville: Abingdon, 1981), p. 70.

23. Urban T. Holmes, III, *Turning to Christ: A Theology of Renewal and Evangelization* (New York: Seabury, 1981), p. 216.

24. O. C. Edwards, Jr., *The Living and Active Word: One Way to Preach from the Bible Today* (New York: Seabury, 1975), pp. 1-66.

25. Holifield, p. 22.

26. Reprinted in Lionel Crocker, ed., *Harry Emerson Fosdick's Art of Preaching: An Anthology* (Springfield, IL: Charles C. Thomas, 1971), pp. 27-41.

27. For the influence of Dewey, see Halford E. Luccock, *In the Minister's Workshop* (New York and Nashville: Abingdon, 1944), p. 56. For a comparable influence on secular public speaking, see Karlyn Campbell, *The Rhetorical Act* (Belmont, CA: Wadsworth, 1982), pp. 236-38.

28. Quoted in Crocker, p. 29.

29. Ibid., p. 11.

30. Ibid., p. 30.

31. Ibid., p. 40.

32. Loc. cit.

33. San Francisco: Harper and Row, ed. 1981.

34. Ibid., p. 50.

35. Arthur L. Teikmanis, *Preaching and Pastoral Care* (Englewood Cliffs, NJ: Prentice-Hall, 1964), p. 19.

36. Ibid., p. 44.

37. Nashville: Abingdon, 1979, p. 9.

38. Ibid., p. 52.

39. Ibid., pp. 51 and 52.

40. Ibid., p. 53. Italics his.

41. Ibid., p. 54.

42. Ibid., pp. 56, ff.

43. Loc. cit.

44. Ibid., p. 62.

45. Philadelphia: Westminster, 1980.

46. Ibid., p. 17.

47. Ibid., p. 20.

48. Ibid., p. 35.

49. Loc. cit.

50. Ibid., p. 115.

51. Ibid., p. 118.

52. Atlanta: John Knox, 1980.

53. Nashville: Abingdon, 1983.

54. Ibid., p. 20.

55. Ibid., p. 37.

56. Ibid., p. 65.

57. Cited above in notes 20 and 24.

58. Don A. Browning, ed., *Practical Theology: The Emerging Field in Theology, Church, and World* (San Francisco: Harper and Row, 1983), p. 109.

59. Ibid., p. 10.

60. See Edward P. Wimberly, *Pastoral Care in the Black Church* (Nashville: Abingdon, 1979), pp. 56-64.

61. Don A. Browning, *The Moral Context of Pastoral Care* (Philadelphia: Westminster, 1976), p. 103.

Chapter 7. The Bishop as Pastor

1. St. Gregory the Great, *Pastoral Care,* trans. and ann. by Henry Davis, S.J., Catholic University of America, Ancient Christian Writers (New York: Newman Press, 1966), p. 20.

2. Quincy Howe, Jr., ed., *Selected Sermons of St. Augustine* (New York: Holt, Rinehart & Winston, 1966), n.p.

3. Howe, n.p.

4. Burton Scott Easton, trans., *The Apostolic Tradition of Hippolytus* (Cambridge: University Press, 1934), pp. 41-49.

5. Ibid., p. 3.

6. John E. Booty, *The Servant Church: Diaconal Ministry and the Episcopal Church* (Wilton, CT: Morehouse-Barlow Co., 1982), p. 55.

7. Ibid., p. 29.

8. John L. McKenzie, S.J., *Authority in the Church* (New York: Sheed and Ward, 1966), p. 93.

9. John Macquarrie, *In Search of Humanity: A Theological and Philosophical Approach* (New York: Crossroad, 1983), p. 2.

10. Rodney Stark and Charles Y. Glock, *American Piety: The Nature of Religious Commitment* (Berkeley: University of California Press, 1970), p. 187.

11. James W. Fowler, *Stages of Faith: The Psychology of Human Development and the Quest for Meaning* (San Francisco: Harper and Row, 1981), p. 77.

12. Citation lost.

13. *The Book of Common Prayer* (New York: Church Hymnal Corp., 1979), p. 518.

14. Leon-Joseph Suenens and Arthur Michael Ramsey, *The Future of the Christian Church* (London: SCM Press, 1971), p. 7.

15. *Book of Common Prayer,* p. 518.

16. *Book of Common Prayer,* p. 531.

17. World Council of Churches, *Baptism, Eucharist and Ministry,* Faith and Order Paper No. 111 (Geneva: World Council of Churches, 1982), pp. 25-26.

18. *Book of Common Prayer,* p. 521.

Contributors

RUTH TIFFANY BARNHOUSE received her M.D. from Columbia University in 1950 and her Th.M. from the Western College School of Theology (Jesuit) in 1974. She is certified by the American Board of Psychiatry and Neurology, is a Fellow of the American Psychiatric Association, and a member of the American Academy of Psychoanalysis. She has been in private practice as a psychiatrist since 1956. In 1980 she was ordained a priest in the Episcopal Church. She is Professor of Psychiatry and Pastoral Care at the Perkins School of Theology, Southern Methodist University. She is the author of numerous articles and books, the most recent of which is *Identity,* published in 1984.

O. C. EDWARDS, JR. served for nine years as President and Dean of Seabury-Western Theological Seminary in Evanston, Illinois, before returning to teaching. He is now Professor of Preaching at that institution. Before going to Evanston he taught New Testament and Patristics at Nashotah House for ten years. He is the author of several books on preaching.

RICHARD F. GREIN is a graduate of Carleton College. He attended Nashotah House, where he received the degrees of Master of Divinity and Master of Sacred Theology. Ordained to the priesthood in 1959, he has had a variety of pastoral experiences, having served over twenty years in parishes in town and country, suburban, and inner city settings. For two years he taught pastoral theology and ecclesiology at Nashotah House. Since 1981 he has been Bishop of Kansas.

JAMES E. GRIFFISS, a priest of the Episcopal Church, is William Adams Professor of Systematic Theology at Nashotah House. Prior to his appointment at Nashotah House, he taught for ten years in Puerto Rico. He is a contributor to *Theology in Anglicanism,* and his most recent book is *Church, Ministry and Unity: A Divine Commission,* published in 1983.

KENNETH LEECH, a priest of the Church of England, worked in the East End of London and in Soho in the 1960s, in particular with heroin addicts. He founded Centrepoint, an all-night center for young homeless, in 1969. From 1971 to 1974 he was chaplain and tutor at St. Augustine's College, Canterbury, and from 1974 to 1980 rector of Bethnal Green. Currently, he is Field Officer of the Board for Social Responsibility of the Church of England's General Synod. He is founder of the Jubilee Group of Anglican socialists and the author of many books, including a forthcoming study, *True God.*

WILLIAM H. PETERSEN is Dean of Bexley Hall of the Colgate-Rochester Divinity School. He was formerly Professor of Church History at Nashotah House. He is active in ecumenical affairs, currently serving as a member of the Standing Commission on Ecumenical Relations of the Episcopal Church, and he has written extensively in the area of ecclesiastical history.

LOUIS WEIL, a priest of the Episcopal Church, is Professor of Liturgics and Church Music at Nashotah House. His pastoral ministry began in Puerto Rico and included work in mountain missions as well as urban parishes. He is coauthor of *Liturgy for Living,* a contributor to *Theology in Anglicanism,* and his most recent book is *Sacraments and Liturgy: The Outward Signs.*

First Printing June, 1985   64532